THE TRIP TO ECHO SPRING

Also by Olivia Laing

To the River

OLIVIA LAING

The Trip to Echo Spring

Why Writers Drink

CANONGATE
Edinburgh · London

Published in Great Britain in 2013 by Canongate Books Ltd,
14 High Street, Edinburgh EH1 1TE

www.canongate.tv

1

For permissions acknowledgements, please see page 337
Map copyright © Norah Perkins, 2013

Supported using public funding by
ARTS COUNCIL
ENGLAND

LOTTERY FUNDED

British Library Cataloguing-in-Publication Data
A catalogue record for this book is available on
request from the British Library

ISBN 978 1 84767 794 5

Typeset in Bembo and QuadraatSans by Palimpsest Book Production Ltd,
Falkirk, Stirlingshire

Printed and bound by CPI Group (UK) Ltd, Croydon CR0 4YY

For my mother, Denise Laing,
with all my love

When alcoholics do drink, most eventually become intoxicated, and it is this recurrent intoxication that eventually brings their lives down in ruins. Friends are lost, health deteriorates, marriages are broken, children are abused, and jobs terminated. Yet despite these consequences the alcoholic continues to drink. Many undergo a 'change in personality'. Previously upstanding individuals may find themselves lying, cheating, stealing, and engaging in all manner of deceit to protect or cover up their drinking. Shame and remorse the morning after may be intense; many alcoholics progressively isolate themselves to drink undisturbed. An alcoholic may hole up in a motel for days or a week, drinking continuously. Most alcoholics become more irritable; they have a heightened sensitivity to anything vaguely critical. Many alcoholics appear quite grandiose, yet on closer inspection one sees that their self-esteem has slipped away from them.

Handbook of Medical Psychiatry, ed. David P. Moore and James W. Jefferson

Easy, easy, Mr. Bones. I is on your side

'Dream Song 36', John Berryman

CONTENTS

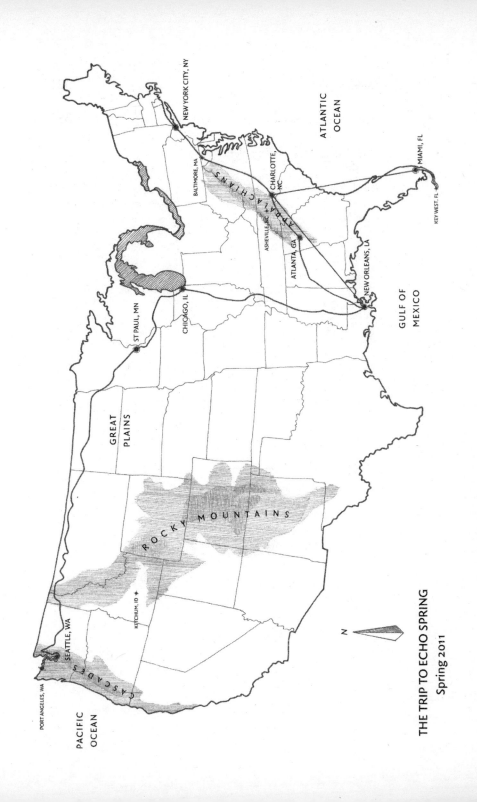

PACIFIC OCEAN

PORT ANGELES, WA

CASCADES

SEATTLE, WA

KETCHUM, ID

R O C K Y   M O U N T A I N S

GREAT PLAINS

ST PAUL, MN

CHICAGO, IL

NEW YORK CITY, NY

BALTIMORE, MA

APPALACHIANS

CHARLOTTE, NC

ASHEVILLE, NC

ATLANTA, GA

NEW ORLEANS, LA

GULF OF MEXICO

ATLANTIC OCEAN

MIAMI, FL

KEY WEST, FL

N

THE TRIP TO ECHO SPRING
Spring 2011

1

ECHO SPRING

HERE'S A THING. IOWA CITY, 1973. Two men in a car, a Ford Falcon convertible that's seen better days. It's winter, the kind of cold that hurts bones and lungs, that reddens knuckles, makes noses run. If you could, by some devoted act of seeing, crane in through the window as they rattle by, you'd see the older man, the one in the passenger seat, has forgotten to put on his socks. He's wearing penny loafers on bare feet, oblivious to the cold, like a prep school boy on a summer jaunt. In fact you could mistake him for a boy: slight, in Brooks Brothers tweeds and flannel trousers, his hair immaculately combed. Only his face betrays him, collapsed into hangdog folds.

The other man is bigger, burlier, thirty-five. Sideburns, bad teeth, a ragged sweater open at the elbow. It's not quite nine a.m. They turn off the highway and pull into the parking lot of the state liquor store. The clerk's out front, keys glinting in his hand. Seeing him, the man in the passenger seat yanks the door and lurches out, never mind the car's still moving. 'By the time I got inside the store,' the other man will write, a long time later, 'he was already at the checkout stand with half a gallon of Scotch.'

They drive away, passing the bottle back and forth. Within a few hours they'll be back at the University of Iowa, swaying eloquently in front of their respective classes. Both are, as if it isn't obvious, in deep trouble with alcohol. Both are also writers, one very well known, the other just cresting into success.

John Cheever, the older man, is the author of three novels, *The Wapshot Chronicle*, *The Wapshot Scandal* and *Bullet Park*, as well as some of the most miraculous and distinctive stories ever written. He's sixty-one. Back in May, he was rushed to hospital with dilated cardiomyopathy, testament to the almighty havoc alcohol wreaks upon the heart. After three days in the Intensive Care Unit he developed delirium tremens, becoming so violently disturbed he had to be secured with a leather straitjacket. The job at Iowa – a semester teaching at the famous Writers' Workshop – must have seemed like a passport to a better life, though it isn't quite panning out that way. For various reasons he's left his family behind, living like a bachelor in a single room at the Iowa House Hotel.

Raymond Carver, the younger man, has also just joined the faculty. His room is identical to Cheever's, and immediately beneath it. The same painting hangs on both their walls. He's come alone too, leaving his wife and teenaged children in California. All his life he's wanted to be a writer, and all his life he's felt circumstance set hard against him. The drinking's been going on for a long while, but despite its depredations he's managed to produce two volumes of poetry and to build up quite a clutch of stories, many of them published in little magazines.

At first glance, the two men seem polar opposites. Cheever looks and sounds every inch the moneyed Wasp, though closer acquaintance reveals this to be a complex kind of subterfuge. Carver, on the other hand, is a millworker's son from Clatskanie, Oregon, who spent years supporting his writing with menial jobs as a janitor, a stockboy and a cleaner.

They met on the evening of 30 August 1973. Cheever knocked on the door of room 240, holding out a glass and announcing, according to Jon Jackson, a student who was present at the time: 'Pardon me. I'm John Cheever. Could I borrow some Scotch?' Carver, elated to meet one of his heroes, stutteringly held out a vast bottle of Smirnoff. Cheever accepted a slug, though he turned his nose up at the embellishments of ice or juice.

Sensing a dual intersection of interests, the two men immediately bonded. They spent much of their time together in the Mill bar, which only served beer, talking about literature and women. Twice a week they drove out in Carver's Falcon to the liquor store for Scotch, which they drank in Cheever's room. 'He and I did nothing *but* drink,' Carver reported later, in the *Paris Review*. 'I mean, we met our classes in a manner of speaking, but the entire time we were there . . . I don't think either of us ever took the covers off our typewriters.'

What's odd about this wasteful year, not to mention all the disasters that followed on its heels, is that Cheever predicted it, in a manner of speaking. A decade earlier, he wrote a short story published in the *New Yorker* on 18 July 1964. 'The Swimmer' is about alcohol and what it can do to a man; how conclusively it can wipe out a life. It begins with a characteristically Cheeverish line: 'It was one of those midsummer Sundays when everyone sits around saying, "I drank too much last night."'

One of those people is Neddy Merrill, a slender, boyish man with an attractive air of vitality about him. Trotting out into the sunshine for a morning dip in his host's pool, he's struck by a delightful idea: that he will make his way home by way of a 'string of swimming pools, that quasi-subterranean stream that curved across the county'. He names this secret road of mixed waters *Lucinda*, in honour of his wife. But there's another liquid path he also follows: a chain of drinks taken on neighbours' terraces and yards, and it's this more perilous route that leads him downwards by degrees to the story's uncanny and tragic end.

High on his marvellous plan, Neddy swims through the gardens of the Grahams and the Hammers, the Lears, the Howlands, the Crosscups and the Bunkers. As he passes on his self-appointed way he's plied with gin by 'natives' – whose customs, he thinks to himself disingenuously, 'would have to be handled with diplomacy if he was ever going to reach his destination'. The next house he reaches is deserted, and after he's crossed the pool he slips into the gazebo and pours himself a drink: his fourth, he calculates vaguely, or perhaps his fifth. A great citadel of cumulus has been building all day, and now the storm breaks, a quick paradiddle of rain in the oaks followed by the pleasurable smell of cordite.

Neddy likes storms, but something about this downpour changes the tenor of his day. Sheltering in the gazebo, he notices a Japanese lantern that Mrs. Levy bought in Kyoto 'the year before last, or was it the year before that?' Anyone can lose their footing in time, can misstep a beat or two of chronology. But then there's another queer flicker in temporality. The rain has stripped the maple, and the red and yellow leaves lie scattered on the grass. It's midsummer, Neddy thinks robustly, and so the tree must simply be blighted, but this sign of autumn gives him an unpleasant shot of melancholy.

The sense of foreclosure deepens. At the Lindleys, the jumping ring is overgrown and the horses seem to have been sold. Worse, the Welchers' pool has been drained. The Lucinda, that magical, abundant river, has run dry. Neddy is staggered, and begins seriously to doubt his command of time. 'Was his memory failing or had he so disciplined it in the repression of unpleasant facts that he had damaged his sense of the truth?' He pulls himself together though, rallying enough to cross Route 424, a portage more effortful and exposing than he'd expected.

Next he braves the public baths, with their whistles and murkish water. No pleasure there, but he's soon up and out, clambering through the woods of the Halloran estate towards the dark, dazzled gold of their springfed pool. But here comes another offbeat, a sense that the world Neddy is travelling through is somehow strange to him, or he to it. Mrs. Halloran asks solicitously about his poor children, muttering something too about the loss of his house. Then, as he walks away, Neddy notices his shorts are hanging around his waist. Is it possible, he wonders, that he's lost weight over the course of a single afternoon? Time is slopping around like gin in a glass. It's still emphatically the same day, but now the warmth of midsummer has dissipated and the smell of wood smoke is articulate in the air.

From the Hallorans Neddy travels to their daughter's house, hoping to beg a glass of whiskey. Helen greets him warmly enough, but her house is dry and has been for three years. Bewildered, chilled to the bone, he heaves his way across the pool and cuts through the fields to the Biswangers. From the roar of voices it's evident a party is in full swing. He wanders in, still almost naked. But now, mysteriously, it's twilight, and the water on the pool has 'a wintry gleam'. Mrs.

Biswanger, who has angled for Neddy as a guest for years, has apparently suffered some change of heart. She greets him rudely, and when his back is turned can be heard saying: 'They went for broke overnight – nothing but income – and he showed up drunk one Sunday and asked us to loan him five thousand dollars.' Then the bartender rebuffs him, confirming his sneaking sense that some social loss of grace has occurred, and been remembered and recorded.

Struggling on, he passes next through the garden of a former mistress, though he can't remember precisely when or in what mood he broke it off. She isn't wholly pleased to see him either, and is likewise fretful about the possibility that he wants money. Leaving, he catches on the cooling air an autumnal smell, not quite placeable but 'strong as gas'. Marigolds? Chrysanthemums? Looking up, he sees the winter constellations have taken up their stations in the night sky. Flooded with uncertainty, he begins, for the first time in his life, to cry.

There are only two more pools to go. He flails and gasps through the final laps before walking in damp trunks up the drive to his own house. But now the hints about a downturn in his fortunes begin to clarify, for the lights are out, the doors are locked, the rooms are empty and nobody, it is clear, has lived here for a long while.

★

'The Swimmer' had come into my mind because I was plummeting through the sky above New York, where the land breaks apart in a clutter of islands and marshes. There are some subjects one can't address at home, and so at the beginning of the year I'd left England for America, a country almost entirely unknown to me. I wanted time to think, and what I wanted to think about was alcohol. I'd spent the winter upcountry, in a cottage in New Hampshire, and now it was spring and I was moving south.

Last time I'd passed over here the earth was white all the way up to the Arctic, and the Connecticut River turned through dark bars of forest frozen the metallic blue-grey of the barrel of a gun. Now the ice had melted, and the whole landscape was ablaze. It reminded me of Cheever's line – that to live 'in a world so generously supplied with water seemed like a clemency, a beneficence'.

'The Swimmer', which I would judge among the finest stories ever written, catches in its strange compressions the full arc of an alcoholic's life and it was that same dark trajectory I wanted to pursue. I wanted to know what made a person drink and what it did to them. More specifically I wanted to know why writers drink, and what effect this stew of spirits has had upon the body of literature itself.

John Cheever and Raymond Carver are hardly the only writers whose lives were made desolate by alcohol. Alongside them come Ernest Hemingway, William Faulkner, Tennessee Williams, Jean Rhys, Patricia Highsmith, Truman Capote, Dylan Thomas, Marguerite Duras, Hart Crane, John Berryman, Jack London, Elizabeth Bishop, Raymond Chandler – the list staggers on. As Lewis Hyde observes in his essay 'Alcohol and Poetry', 'four of the six Americans who have won the Nobel Prize for literature were alcoholic. About half of our alcoholic writers eventually killed themselves.'

Alcoholism is not a simple condition to define. According to the American Society of Addiction Medicine, its essential features are 'impaired control over drinking, preoccupation with the drug alcohol, use of alcohol despite adverse consequences, and distortions in thinking, most notably denial'. In 1980, *The Diagnostic and Statistical Manual of Mental Disorders* dropped the term 'alcoholism' entirely, replacing it with two interrelated disorders: alcohol abuse (defined as 'repeated use despite recurrent adverse consequences') and alcohol dependence (defined as '*alcohol abuse* combined with tolerance, withdrawal and an uncontrollable drive to drink').

As to what causes it, the jury remains out. In fact, under the heading 'Etiology', my old 1992 *Merck Manual* announces baldly: 'The cause of alcoholism is unknown.' In the intervening years there have been thousands of research programmes and academic studies, and yet the consensus remains that alcoholism is caused by some mysterious constellation of factors, among them personality traits, early life experiences, societal influences, genetic predisposition and abnormal chemistry of the brain. Listing these possible causes, the current edition of the *Merck Manual* concludes, a little dispiritedly: 'However, such generalizations should not obscure the fact that alcohol use disorders can occur in anyone, regardless of their age, sex, background, ethnicity, or social situation.'

Unsurprisingly, the theories writers tend to offer lean more towards the symbolic than the sociological or scientific. Discussing Poe, Baudelaire once commented that alcohol had become a weapon 'to kill something inside himself, a worm that would not die'. In his introduction to *Recovery*, the posthumously published novel of the poet John Berryman, Saul Bellow observed: 'Inspiration contained a death threat. He would, as he wrote the things he had waited and prayed for, fall apart. Drink was a stabiliser. It somewhat reduced the fatal intensity.'

There's something about these answers and the mixed motives they reveal that seems to catch at a deeper and more resonant aspect of alcohol addiction than the socio-genetic explanations that are in currency today. It was for this reason that I wanted to look at *writers* who drank, though God knows there's barely a section of our society that's immune to alcohol's lures. After all, it's they who, by their very nature, describe the affliction best. Often they've written about their experiences or those of their contemporaries, either transposed into fiction, or in the letters, memoirs and diaries they've used to mythologise or interrogate their lives.

As I began to read through these rafts of papers, I realised something else. These men and women were connected, both physically and by a series of repeating patterns. They were each other's friends and allies, each other's mentors, students and inspirations. In addition to Raymond Carver and John Cheever in Iowa, there were other drinking partnerships, other vexed allegiances. Hemingway and Fitzgerald tippled together in the cafés of 1920s Paris, while the poet John Berryman was the first person at Dylan Thomas's bedside when he died.

Then there were the echoes. I'd grown most interested in six male writers, whose experiences seemed to dovetail and mirror each other. (There were many women writers I could have chosen too, but for reasons that will become apparent their stories came too close to home.) Most of this six had – or saw themselves as having – that most Freudian of pairings, an overbearing mother and a weak father. All were tormented by self-hatred and a sense of inadequacy. Three were profoundly promiscuous, and almost all experienced conflict and dissatisfaction with regard to their sexuality. Most died in middle age, and the deaths that weren't suicides tended to be directly related to the years of hard and hectic living. At times, all tried in varying degrees to give up alcohol, but only two succeeded, late in life, in becoming permanently dry.

These sound like tragic lives, the lives of wastrels or dissolutes, and yet these six men – F. Scott Fitzgerald, Ernest Hemingway, Tennessee Williams, John Cheever, John Berryman and Raymond Carver – produced between them some of the most beautiful writing this world has ever seen. As Jay McInerney once commented of Cheever: 'There have been thousands of sexually conflicted alcoholics, but only one of them wrote "The Housebreaker of Shady Hill" and "The Sorrows of Gin".'

If I stopped a minute, I could picture each of them in turn. I saw Fitzgerald in a Guards tie, his blond hair slicked back, quietly certain about the merits of *The Great Gatsby*: a kind man, when he wasn't whisking you into a waltz or boiling your watch up in a pot of soup. Ernest Hemingway I always pictured at the helm of a boat, or out hunting in the clean upland air, entirely focused on the task at hand. And then later, at his desk in glasses, making up the Michigan of the Nick Adams stories, making up corridas and cities, trout streams and battlefields, a world you can almost smell.

Tennessee Williams I saw in Ray-Bans and safari shorts, sitting unobtrusively at the rehearsal of one of his own plays: *A Streetcar Named Desire*, say, or *Suddenly Last Summer*. It's not locked yet, and so he fixes sections on demand, braying his donkey's laugh at all the saddest lines. Cheever I liked to think of riding a bicycle, a habit he took up late in life, and Carver I always imagined with a cigarette, big-shouldered but walking softly. And then there was John Berryman, the donnish poet and professor, light gleaming on his glasses, his beard enormous, standing in front of a class at Princeton or the University of Minnesota, reading *Lycidas* and making the whole room see how *marvellous* it was.

There have been many books and articles that revel in describing exactly how grotesque and shameful the behaviour of alcoholic writers can be. That wasn't my intention. What I wanted was to discover how each of these men – and, along the way, some of the many others who'd suffered from the disease – experienced and thought about their addiction. If anything, it was an expression of my faith in literature, and its power to map the more difficult regions of human experience and knowledge.

As to the origins of my interest, I might as well admit I grew up in an alcoholic family myself. Between the ages of eight and eleven I lived in a house under the rule of alcohol, and the effects of that period have stayed with me ever since. Reading Tennessee Williams's play *Cat on a Hot Tin Roof* at seventeen was the first time I found the behaviour I'd grown up amid not only named and delineated but actively confronted. From that moment on I was preoccupied by what writers had to say about alcohol and its effects. If I had any hope of making sense of alcoholics – and my life as an adult seemed just as full of them – it would be by investigating the residue they'd left behind in books.

There was a line from *Cat* in particular that had stayed with me for years. Brick, the drunkard, has been summoned by his father. Big Daddy is on a talking jag and after a while Brick asks for his crutch. 'Where you goin'?' Big Daddy asks, and Brick replies: 'I'm takin' a little short trip to Echo Spring.' Physically, Echo Spring is nothing more than a nickname for a liquor cabinet, drawn from the brand of bourbon it contains. Symbolically, though, it refers to something quite different: perhaps to the attainment of silence, or to the obliteration of troubled thoughts that comes, temporarily at least, with a sufficiency of booze.

Echo Spring. What a lovely, consoling place it sounds. It set off another echo, too. By coincidence or otherwise most of these men shared a deep, enriching love for water. John Cheever and Tennessee Williams were passionate, even fanatical swimmers, while Hemingway and Fitzgerald shared an abiding fondness for the sea. In Raymond Carver's case, his relationship with water – particularly those freezing bottle-green trout streams that tumble out of the mountains above Port Angeles – would eventually come in some deep way to replace his toxic need for alcohol. In one of his late, wide-open poems, he wrote:

> I love them the way some men love horses
> or glamorous women. I have a thing
> for this cold swift water.
> Just looking at it makes my blood run
> and my skin tingle.

The word *trip* also seemed important. Many alcoholics, including the writers I was interested in, have been relentless travellers, driven like uneasy spirits across their own nations and into the other countries of this world. Like Cheever, I had a notion that it might be possible to plot the course of some of these restless lives by way of a physical journey across America. Over the next few weeks, I planned to take what is known in AA circles as a *geographical*, a footloose journey across the country, first south, through New York, New Orleans and Key West, and then north-west, via St. Paul, the site of John Berryman's ill-fated recovery, and on to the rivers and creeks of Port Angeles, where Raymond Carver spent his last, exultant years.

Looked at on a map, this itinerary seems haphazard, even a little masochistic, particularly since I'd resolved to travel largely by train. Like many things to do with the subject, though, its real meaning was encoded. Each of these locations had served as a way station or staging post in which the successive phases of alcohol addiction had been acted out. By travelling through them in sequence, I thought it might be possible to build a kind of topographical map of alcoholism, tracing its developing contours from the pleasures of intoxication through to the gruelling realities of the drying-out process. And as I worked across the country, passing back and forth between books and lives, I hoped I might come closer to understanding what alcohol addiction means, or at least to finding out what those who struggled with and were sometimes destroyed by it thought alcohol had meant for them.

The first of the cities was fast approaching. While I'd been gazing out of the window, the seatbelt sign had switched to green. I fumbled for the pin and turned again to the glass. Outside, the ground was rising swiftly through the colourless miles of air. Now I could see Long Island, and beyond the ruffled waters the runways of JFK. Silhouetted behind it were the skyscrapers of Manhattan, rising like iron filings into the pale sky. 'These stories seem at times to be stories of a long-lost world when the city of New York was still filled with a river light,' John Cheever once wrote wistfully about the city he most loved. It did indeed seem to shine, an island citadel bounded by water, the Atlantic flashing pewter as we hedged in above the waves.

2

THE COFFIN TRICK

MONTHS AGO, BACK IN ENGLAND, when I was just beginning to think down into the subject of alcohol, I became certain that whatever journey I was making would begin in a hotel room on East 54th Street, ten minutes' walk from Broadway. I don't know why this, of all possible locations, seemed the necessary place to start, but the story of what had happened there worked its way inside me, as certain stories will.

In the small hours of 25 February 1983, Tennessee Williams died in his suite at the Elysée, a small, pleasant hotel on the outskirts of the Theater District. He was seventy-one, unhappy, a little underweight, addicted to drugs and alcohol and paranoid sometimes to the point of delirium. According to the coroner's report, he'd choked on the bell-shaped plastic cap of a bottle of eyedrops, which he was in the habit of placing on or under his tongue while he administered to his vision. As a child he'd been poked in the eye with a stick, and in his twenties this damage manifested itself as a greyish cataract that covered his left pupil. Eventually it was cut away, but the sight in that eye was never good and eyedrops were among the extensive medical paraphernalia he took on all his travels.

The next day, the *New York Times* ran an obituary claiming him as 'the most important American playwright after Eugene O'Neill'. It listed his three Pulitzer Prizes, for *A Streetcar Named Desire*, *Cat on a Hot Tin Roof* and *The Night of the Iguana*, adding: 'He wrote with deep sympathy and expansive humor about outcasts in our society. Though his images were often violent, he was a poet of the human heart.'

Later, after carrying out chemical tests, the city's chief medical officer, Dr. Eliot M. Grosse, amended the autopsy report to add that the barbiturate secobarbital was in Williams's system when he died. Much later, various friends and acquaintances claimed the choking story was a cover-up to stop the press from delving into Tennessee's numerous addictions, though the official cause of death remains asphyxia.

It wasn't the death he'd hoped for, either way. In his memoir, his wandering, anti-lucid memoir, he wrote that he wanted to die on a *letto matrimoniale*, a wedding bed, surrounded by *contadini*, farmers, their faces puzzled and full of sweetness, holding out in their shaking hands little glasses of *vino* or *liquore*. He wanted it to happen in Sicily, where he'd been happiest, but if that wasn't possible he was willing to settle for the big brass bed at Dumaine Street, his house in New Orleans, where the clouds always seemed just overhead.

There should be nothing more arbitrary than the place where someone dies, on their way from one thing to the next, and yet it's telling, too, that a man who was forever on the move should finish up in a hotel room, surrounded by pills and paper, two bottles of wine open on his nightstand. We die as we live, disordered, and while the manner of his death was accidental to the point of grotesqueness, its location exposes that cast of vagrancy that was, though it sounds a funny thing to say, one of the most certain things about him.

He kept all sorts of roosts in New York, though he never stayed in them for long. For years he had an apartment around the corner on East 58th Street that he shared with his partner, Frank Merlo: Frank with his sad horse face and ready charm, Frank the protector, the aide-de-camp, who died of lung cancer in 1963, inaugurating the very worst period of Williams's Stoned Age. Later, he took an apartment in the Manhattan Plaza, the residential complex designed for performing artists. He'd been lured there by the promise of a swimming pool, but the partyish atmosphere didn't suit him and even before he'd given up the lease he generally stayed in a suite at the Elysée.

The hotel was useful because of its proximity to the theatres, but by the time he died it had been three years since he'd had a play on the Great White Way. The last was *Clothes for a Summer Hotel*, an addled rehash of the difficult marriage between Zelda and Scott Fitzgerald. 'No growth, no change, no flow of life anywhere for us to piece together,' Walter Kerr wrote in the *New York Times*, adding crossly, as if the failure were wilful: '*Clothes for a Summer Hotel* is Tennessee Williams holding his tongue.'

It was hardly the worst thing he'd heard from a critic. Back in 1969 *Life* magazine had called him a White Dwarf, continuing: 'We are still receiving his messages, but it is now obvious that they come from a cinder.' Imagine writing a play after that, let alone going on for another fourteen years, sitting down at your typewriter every morning, despite the depredations of drugs and alcohol, of loneliness and growing ill health. 'Gallant,' wrote Elia Kazan, the director who knew him as well as anyone, 'is the word to describe Tennessee at the end.'

You get a sense of that courage, that indefatigable work ethic, in a 1981 interview with the *Paris Review*, the latter half of which was conducted in his rooms at the Elysée. He talks about his plays and the people he's known, and he touches too, a little disingenuously, on the role of alcohol in his life, saying:

> O'Neill had a terrible problem with alcohol. Most writers do. American writers nearly all have problems with alcohol because there's a great deal of tension involved in writing, you know that. And it's all right up to a certain age, and then you begin to need a little nervous support that you get from drinking. Now my drinking has to be moderate. Just look at the liver spots I've got on me!

You know that. A little nervous support. My drinking has to be moderate. He was 'tired', the interviewer observes carefully, because they'd spent the preceding night in a bar called Rounds, which 'boasts a somewhat piss-elegant decor and a clientele consisting largely of male hustlers and those who employ them'. Gallant, yes: but also not an entirely reliable witness to the traffic of his own life.

The Elysée was not the kind of place I could afford but a friend at Condé Nast had wangled me a room. There was a chandelier in the lobby and someone had painted a trompe l'oeil garden on the far wall. It looked vaguely Italian: lemon trees, black and white tiles and a box-lined path that narrowed bluely towards some wooded hills. As I checked in I asked which floor Tennessee's old suite was on. I'd planned to pop up in the morning and see if a chambermaid would let me peek inside. But the Sunset Suite no longer existed. The boy at the front desk, who looked like he might play field hockey, added surprisingly: 'We divided it up to get rid of bad spirits.'

People believe strange things. Rose Williams, Tennessee's adored sister, who had a pre-frontal lobotomy at the age of twenty-eight and still outlived all her immediate family, refused to acknowledge death when it occurred. But once, or so her brother recorded in *Memoirs*, she said: 'It rained last night. The dead came down with the rain.' He asked, in the gentle tone he almost always used with her, if she meant their voices and she replied, 'Yes, of course, their voices.'

I don't believe in ghosts, but I am interested in absences, and the fact that the room had ceased to exist pleased me. I was beginning to think that drinking might be a way of disappearing from the world, or at least of slipping one's appointed place within it, though if you'd seen Tennessee blundering through the hallway, pie-eyed and legless, you might think conversely it made one all too painfully impossible to miss. It seemed appropriate, anyhow, that this place where I thought I'd start my journey should turn out to be a non-place, a gap in the map. I looked at the trompe l'oeil garden again. That was the path to follow, into the vanishing point, past the wavering blue brushstrokes with which the artist had indicated the threshold of his knowledge.

★

Time, Tennessee Williams wrote in *The Glass Menagerie*, is the longest distance between two places. I'd been trying to work out when he first came to New York. I figured from his letters that it must have been in the summer of 1928, when he was a shy, sheltered boy of seventeen – the same trip, as it happens, in which he tried alcohol for the first time. Back then he was still called Tom; still lived with his family in hateful St. Louis.

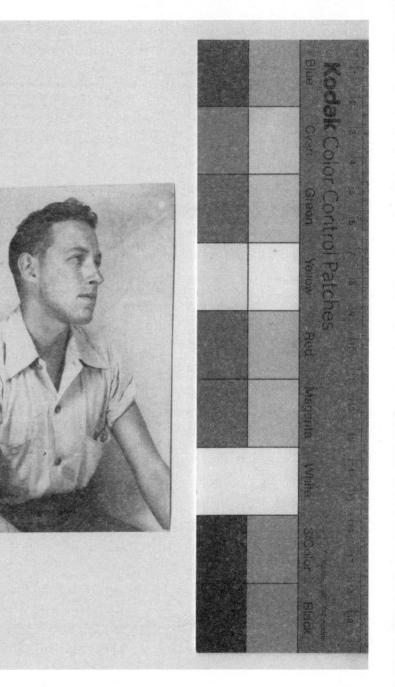

He'd been invited by his beloved grandfather, the Reverend Walter Dakin, to join a touring party made up of various adventuresome parishioners. The group would travel by way of a White Star liner from New York to Southampton, and then go on to France, Germany, Switzerland, Italy: a democratic, twentieth-century version of the aristocratic Grand Tour.

The trip began with a four-day blowout at the Biltmore, the hotel by Grand Central Terminal where Zelda and Scott Fitzgerald had spent their honeymoon eight years before. 'We have just concluded dinner with a multi-millionaire . . . in his seven room suite at the end of the hall,' the would-be sophisticate wrote home in ecstasy. 'I was sitting at the same table, in his private suite, where the Prince of Wales had sat during his stay at the Biltmore in 1921! Did that kill me!!'

Life aboard ship was even more riotous. They set sail at midnight on the ss *Homeric*, in what he recalled much later as a gala departure, with brass bands and a great deal of coloured paper ribbons tossed back and forth between the vessel and the well-wishers on Pier 54. The next day he drank his first alcoholic beverage, a green crème-de-menthe, and afterwards was violently seasick.

Not wholly convinced by this newly adult pleasure, he reported to his mother: 'Grandfather . . . keeps his tongue pretty slick with Manhattin Coctails and Rye-Ginger Ales. I have tried them all but prefer none to plain ginger-ale and Coca Cola. So I'm afraid I'm not getting all the kick out of this boat that the others are getting.' Six days on, in the Hotel Rochambeau, he changed his tune, opening a letter home with the exultant declaration:

I have just imbibed a whole glass of french champagne and am feeling consequently very elated. It is our last evening in Paris which excuses the unusual indulgence. French champagne is the only drink I like here. But it is really delicious.

He didn't add what he would later dwell on in his memoir, that in the boulevards of Paris he began abruptly to feel afraid of what he called the process of thought, and that over the weeks of travel this phobia grew so intense he came within 'a hairsbreadth of going quite mad'. Later, he described this experience as 'the most dreadful, the most nearly psychotic, crisis that occurred in my early life'.

It wasn't the first time Tom had suffered from anxiety, though it was the most serious attack he'd had so far. He'd always been an acutely sensitive boy, a condition not helped by the disruptions of his household. His parents had met in 1906 and married the next year. Edwina Williams was a pretty, popular, talkative girl who had in her youth nurtured a fantasy of going on the stage. Her husband, Cornelius Coffin Williams, was a travelling salesman who sold men's clothes and later shoes. In addition he played poker, drank heavily and generally conveyed in all his habits his congenital unsuitability to domestic life.

After their marriage the couple lived together, but when she fell pregnant with her first child in 1909 Edwina returned to her parents, moving with them through a succession of rectories in Mississippi and Tennessee. Tom came along two years later, on Palm Sunday, 26 March 1911: a concentrated, watchful baby. The south suited him. He had his sister Rose for company, and would remember this period much later as 'joyfully innocent', though his father was rarely present. As a very little boy he was active and robust, but in first grade he caught diphtheria, and was taken out of school. He spent most of the next year on his own in bed, acting out invented scenes with a pack of cards for players. By the time he returned to his classmates, he'd changed dramatically, becoming delicate and frail.

In 1918, the southern idyll came abruptly to an end. Cornelius had been promoted to a management position at the International Shoe Company and wanted to set up home in St. Louis. Living with his children for the first time, he regarded the older two with contempt, though he liked Dakin, the son born a few months after their arrival in the city. The pattern of geographic instability established in the south didn't stop once the Williamses were reunited, either. By the time Tom was fifteen, he'd lived in sixteen different houses, though it wasn't until the family's arrival in St. Louis that he realised how poor they were. The apartments they rented were tiny; the colour, he recalled later, of mustard and dried blood. In these nasty confined spaces, his parents' incompatibility was ruthlessly exposed, while Rose began her precipitous descent towards a mental breakdown.

'Life at home was terrible, just terrible,' Dakin wrote decades later in a letter to Williams's biographer Donald Spoto. 'By the late 1920s, mother and father were in open warfare, and both were good combatants. He came home drunk . . . and he'd fly into a rage . . . there'd be a vicious row and finally mother would do her famous fainting act.' The dainty, troubled Rose found these fights increasingly petrifying, while Tom harboured bitter memories of being called *Miss Nancy* for his cissyish interest in books and movies, recording as an adult that his father 'was a terrifying man'.

In his teens Williams was pathologically shy, blushing whenever another pair of eyes met his. Not surprising then that on his first trip abroad he might experience an attack of paralysing anxiety. But something else had happened on the ss *Homeric* itself, a disturbing encounter that may also have played a role. Tom spent a good deal of his time aboard ship waltzing with a dance instructor, a young woman of twenty-seven. 'I was in those days an excellent dancer and we "just swept around the floor: and swept and swept" as Zelda would put it.' Later, he overheard her friend, a man with the baroque name of Captain de Voe, making a crack about his sexuality, an incident he found singularly disturbing, though it was a good while before he figured out its meaning. What the man had said was: 'You know his future, don't you?' to which the teacher replied: 'I don't think you can be sure about that at the age of seventeen.'

As the party travelled from Paris to Venice, Milan and Montreux, Tom kept up his cheerful letters home, describing mountains, castles and the places where he swam. He never mentioned his fears, though by the time the tour reached the Rhine he was certain he was going crazy. The phobia, as he explained it later, involved the sense that 'the process of thought was a terrifyingly complex mystery of human life'. Things came to a head in a cathedral in Cologne. He knelt down and began to pray. The rest of the party left. Light was flooding in through the stained glass windows in coloured shafts. Then something miraculous occurred. He had the uncanny sense of being touched by a hand: 'and at the instant of that touch the phobia was lifted away as lightly as a snowflake though it had weighed on my head like a skull-breaking block of iron'. A religious boy, he was certain he'd experienced the hand of Christ.

For a week he was very happy, and then in Amsterdam the phobia returned. This time, he chased it away almost immediately by composing a poem on the comforts of remembering one is only an individual in a crowd of equally complex beings. The poem itself is barely more than doggerel ('I hear their laughter and their sighs, / I look into their myriad eyes'), but the experience was pivotal. In *Memoirs*, he reflected on how important this recognition of being part of a collective was, not just for his own but for any attempt to achieve balance of mind: 'that recognition of being a member of multiple humanity with its multiple needs, problems and emotions, not a unique creature but one, only one among the multitude of its fellows'.

It was a useful insight. Tom Williams, soon to become Tennessee, would suffer lifelong from moods of terror. Many of the ways he found of medicating and soothing himself were toxic, among them his relationship with alcohol. But discovering that he could dissolve anxiety by looking outward didn't just save his sanity. It also alerted him to the importance of empathy, that cardinal virtue of the playwright.

★

I lay awake most of that first night at the Elysée, dreaming in a small window of sleep of a cat with raspberries tangled in its fur. The next morning I had two unprecedented appointments. The first was to visit a psychiatrist and the second was to attend an AA meeting. My cab driver had only just arrived in the city too, and together we muddled out a route to St. Luke's-Roosevelt Hospital on 10th Avenue and 58th Street. The Addiction Institute was on the ninth floor, down a run of corridors that seemed to spiral inward like a snail's shell. By the time I was ushered into the director's office I was thoroughly disorientated.

I thought I was deep inside the building and the presence of a window startled me. The books were arranged according to colour, lavender to violet, turquoise to green; a buttress assembled in praise of order.

Back in the day, the Addiction Institute was called the Smithers Alcohol Treatment and Training Center. It's where John Cheever and Truman Capote went to dry out, though only the former was successful in his labours. At that point, in the spring of 1975, it was located in a brownstone at 56 East 93rd Street. 'The house is palatial and not at all shabby,' Cheever wrote in a letter during his voluntary incarceration. 'The tenants are forty-two drug addicts and clinical alcoholics.' He shared his room with a con man, a ballet dancer, a sailor and the owner of an unsuccessful German deli, who talked in his sleep, asking all night long: 'Haff you been taken care of? Haff you been waited on?' He was intensely miserable (hardly the place for such a distinguished Yankee as a *Cheevah*) and complained vociferously throughout his twenty-eight-day internment, but it got him sober and in all probability also saved his life.

In order to understand how an intelligent man could end up in such a place, it's necessary first to know what a shot of Smirnoff or Scotch does to the human body. Alcohol, also known as ethanol, is both an intoxicant and a central nervous depressant, with an immensely complex effect upon the brain. In simple terms, it works by interfering with the activity of neurotransmitters, the chemicals by which the nervous system relays information around the body. Its effects can be divided into two categories. Alcohol activates the pleasure-reward pathways by way of dopamine and serotonin. In psychological terms this effect is known as *positive reinforcement*, since continuing to ingest the substance leads to pleasure.

But alcohol also works by way of *negative reinforcement*. In the brain, there are two types of neurotransmitters: inhibitory and excitatory. Inhibitory neurotransmitters depress activity in the central nervous system, while excitatory neurotransmitters stimulate it. When alcohol is ingested, it interacts with the receptor sites of an inhibitory neurotransmitter called gamma-aminobutyric acid or GABA, mimicking its effects. The result is sedative, reducing activity in the brain. In addition, alcohol blocks the receptor sites of an excitatory neurotransmitter: N-methyl-D-aspartate or NMDA (a subset of glutamate, the major excitatory neurotransmitter), preventing its activity. This also causes a reduction in excitation, albeit by a different route.

These sedative effects are what makes alcohol so adept at reducing tension and anxiety. Both positive and negative reinforcement drive alcoholism, but as the addiction progresses it is negative reinforcement that tends to take the larger role. 'The click', Brick calls it in *Cat on a Hot Tin Roof*. 'This click that I get in my head that makes me peaceful. I got to drink till I get it. It's just a mechanical thing . . . I just haven't got the right level of alcohol in my bloodstream yet.'

The realisation that alcohol is capable of alleviating anxiety means that for susceptible individuals it can quickly become the preferred method of managing stress. There's more than a hint of this in a letter John Cheever wrote about an early experiment with drinking. Intimidated by a social gathering, he discovered alcohol's powerful knack for obliterating nerves. 'The next engagement that threatened to arouse my shyness,' he wrote, 'I bought a bottle of gin and drank four fingers neat. The company was brilliant, chatty and urbane and so was I.' In *Memoirs*, Tennessee Williams takes up the same refrain, noting that after a *mezzo-litro* of Frascati, 'you felt as if a new kind of blood had been transfused into your arteries, a blood that swept away all anxiety and all tension for a while, and for a while is the stuff that dreams are made of'.

For a while. The problem is that over time the brain begins to adjust to the presence of alcohol, compensating for its effects on the central nervous system. In particular, it increases the production of excitatory neurotransmitters, so that normal activity can be maintained. This neuroadaptation is what drives addiction, eventually making the drinker require alcohol in order to function at all.

In the current edition of the *Diagnostic and Statistical Manual of Mental Disorders* (known universally as *DSM-IV-TR*), alcohol dependence is categorised as a form of substance dependence, which is defined as:

> A maladaptive pattern of substance use, leading to clinically significant impairment or distress, as manifested by three (or more) of the following, occurring at any time in the same 12-month period:

> 1. Tolerance, as defined by either of the following:
>   - A need for markedly increased amounts of the substance to achieve intoxication or desired effect.
>   - Markedly diminished effect with continued use of the same amount of the substance.
> 2. Withdrawal, as manifested by either of the following:
>   - The characteristic withdrawal syndrome for the substance.
>   - The same (or a closely related) substance is taken to relieve or avoid withdrawal symptoms.

3. The substance is often taken in larger amounts or over a longer period than was intended.

4. There is a persistent desire or there are unsuccessful efforts to cut down or control substance use.

5. A great deal of time is spent in activities necessary for obtaining the substance, using the substance or recovering from its effects.

6. Important social, occupational, or recreational activities are given up or reduced because of substance use.

7. The substance use is continued despite knowledge of having a persistent or recurrent physical or psychological problem that is likely to have been caused or exacerbated by the substance (e.g., continued drinking despite recognition that an ulcer was made worse by alcohol consumption).

As it gathers momentum, alcohol addiction inevitably affects the drinker's physical and social selves, visibly damaging the architecture of their life. Jobs are lost. Relationships spoil. There may be accidents, arrests and injuries, or the drinker may simply become increasingly neglectful of their responsibilities and capacity to provide self-care. Conditions associated with long-term alcoholism include hepatitis, cirrhosis, fatty liver, gastritis, stomach ulcers, hypertension, heart disease, impotence, infertility, various types of cancer, increased susceptibility to infection, sleep disorders, loss of memory and personality changes caused by damage to the brain. As an early researcher into alcohol addiction wrote in the *American Journal of Psychiatry* back in 1935: 'The striking and inescapable impression one gets from a review of acute alcoholic intoxication is of the almost infinite diversity of symptoms that may ensue from the action of this single toxic agent.'

Not everyone who drinks alcohol, however, becomes an alcoholic. This disease, which exists in all quarters of the world, is caused by a multitude of factors, among them genetic predisposition, early life experience and social influences. In a 2011 paper entitled 'The role of early life stress as a predictor for alcohol and drug dependence', Mary-Anne Enoch, a long-term researcher in the field, wrote:

> It is well established that the hereditability of alcoholism is around 50% . . . Therefore, genetic and environmental influences on the development of addictive disorders are equally important, although the proportions of risk may vary according to societal groups.

Later, when I was transcribing my interview with Dr. Petros Levounis, the Addiction Institute's director, I realised that I'd asked the question of what causes alcoholism several times over, in varying formulations, and that each time his answer was slightly different. This isn't to say that he was imprecise. On the contrary, he was a meticulous speaker. His understanding of alcoholism involved balancing a succession of models like spinning plates. The disease was primarily genetic, but social and psychological factors were very much involved. There isn't an alcoholic personality per se, as early theorists suggested there might be, but alcohol does bring with it a constellation of behaviours (lying, stealing, cheating; the usual car crash) that will in all probability subside or disappear entirely when sobriety is attained; although – and here he laughed a little – there are plenty of jerks who become alcoholics and continue to be jerks after they're dry.

Near the beginning of the conversation he used a phrase that intrigued me. He mentioned a process called the brain switch. If someone is particularly prone to alcoholism – if the genetic and social and psychological factors are all stacked against them – then they are likely to experience a change in brain function. As Dr. Levounis put it, 'it seems that they engrave the addiction at the more primitive part of the brain, the mesolimbic system, and from that point on the addiction tends to have a life of its own, to a large extent independent of the forces that set it into motion to begin with'. He called this lively, liberated monster *the big bear*, and later *the big beast*. 'Unfortunately,' he added, 'the majority of people do not really see that and have the false hope that if they go back to the root of the problem and yank out the root cause of what happened then they will be addiction-free for the rest of their lives.'

The brain switch wasn't a concept I'd come across before. It was initially proposed about fifteen years earlier by Alan Leshner, then director of the National Institute on Drug Abuse. He suggested that neurobiological changes took place around the nucleus accumbens, the part of the mesolimbic system that deals with pleasure and reward, where addiction takes hold most strongly. These neural pathways, Dr. Levounis explained, 'don't only signify for pleasure and pain; they also signify for salience. Essentially, they tell us what is important and what is not. So instead of having all kinds of things that are pleasurable and rewarding and salient in your life, all these things start becoming less and less important and the one that remains is primarily the drug of abuse. It's alcohol.'

The permanence of this hijack is due primarily to the geography of the pleasure-reward pathways, their anatomical position within the nutshell of the human skull. He mapped it out for me with his hands, showing how the mesolimbic system is sandwiched between the hippocampus, which is the memory centre of the brain, and the limbic system, which is its emotional core. It made sense to me. Memory and emotion. How else do we make decisions, except by cognition, by the pure application of reason? But that region of the brain, the frontal lobes, is far away, anatomically speaking, and imperfectly connected, especially in the young. Little wonder that alcoholism was once characterised as a failure of will. The frontal lobes weigh right and wrong, apportion risk; the limbic system is all greed and appetite and impulse, with the hippocampus adding the siren's whisper: *how sweet it was, remember?*

I shifted in my seat. I could see *The Line of Beauty* on the shelf in front of me, filed among the blue books. There were pigeons outside. The city was hammering against the window, insistent as a drill. Dr Levounis was talking now about the long-term picture: how the pleasure-reward pathways stay hijacked even in sobriety, so that although the alcoholic might stop drinking they remain vulnerable to addiction. For how long, I asked, and he replied: 'Although a lot of people manage to beat the illness, the risk of using stays with you for a long, long time, if not for the rest of your life.'

We turned then to a discussion of treatment. Dr Levounis outlined the two basic options for recovery: the abstinence-based model and the harm-reduction model. In the abstinence-based model (the version favoured by Alcoholics Anonymous), the alcoholic stops drinking entirely, concentrating on the maintenance of sobriety. In the harm-reduction model, on the other hand, the focus is on improving the conditions of one's life and not necessarily on stopping drinking. He thought, pragmatically, that both were efficacious, depending on the individual's circumstance and needs.

There was a lot to think about in this conversation, but it was the big beast that stayed with me when I went down into the street. What would Tennessee Williams have made of it, the idea that addiction has its own momentum, its own articulated presence within the skull? I'm not sure he would have been surprised. He had a gut sense of how people are driven by irrational cravings. I thought of poor Blanche DuBois, sneaking shots of whiskey in her sister's house in New Orleans; of Brick Pollitt, hobbling back and forth to Echo Spring, saying to his dying father, 'it's hard for me to understand how anybody could care if he lived or died or was dying or cared about anything but whether or not there was liquor left in the bottle'. Williams might not have known where the frontal lobes were located (although he probably did, being a dedicated hypochondriac whose sister's lobotomy left him with a lifelong terror of psychiatric care), but he certainly understood how a human being can navigate without the use of reason. I'm not sure *Cat on a Hot Tin Roof* is about much else besides irrational compulsions – alcohol, money, sex – and how they can unshape a life.

★

The AA meeting was on the Upper West Side at 6 p.m. I slept a while at the hotel and then cut across Central Park, eating a hot dog on the way. The trees were maybe a fortnight away from coming into leaf and as I walked I saw a red cardinal in a bush beside the path. Nothing except changes in climate and language communicate so thoroughly a sense of travel as the difference in birdlife. A week later, on the way to Key West, I'd see vultures circling above Miami, ospreys in the Everglades, an ibis picking its way through a tropical graveyard. Another week on and thousands of miles north, on the outskirts of Port Angeles, I'd watch bald eagles fishing in a river and clouds of violet swallows swarming above a gorge. But the red cardinal was the first purely American bird of my trip and it heartened me. Whatever happens, happens here, in the populated earth. I was grateful for the science lesson, but I didn't want to divorce the neural drama of alcoholism from the world, the quick and grubby world in which it takes place.

No chance of that at AA. I sat at the back, with an old-timer, Andi, who'd offered to show me around. People were drifting in, clutching coffees, in baseball caps and suits. It seemed at first glance almost comically New York, right down to the couple in the front row who looked like rock stars, one in enormous sunglasses and leather shorts, the other swaddled in a floor-length fur coat.

There was a sign on the wall that displayed the Twelve Steps, next to one that read 'No spitting. No eating food on shared computers.' The combination would no doubt have amused John Cheever, who struggled for a long time with the democracy of these dingy rooms, though in his last years he softened in his loathing of AA, becoming vocally grateful for its role in his sobriety. I read through them, step by step, for the hundredth time.

1. We admitted we were powerless over alcohol – that our lives had become unmanageable.
2. Came to believe that a Power greater than ourselves could restore us to sanity.
3. Made a decision to turn our will and our lives over to the care of God as we understood Him.
4. Made a searching and fearless moral inventory of ourselves.

5. Admitted to God, to ourselves, and to another human being the exact nature of our wrongs.

6. Were entirely ready to have God remove all these defects of character.

7. Humbly asked Him to remove our shortcomings.

8. Made a list of all persons we had harmed, and became willing to make amends to them all.

9. Made direct amends to such people wherever possible, except when to do so would injure them or others.

10. Continued to take personal inventory and when we were wrong promptly admitted it.

11. Sought through prayer and meditation to improve our conscious contact with God, as we understood Him, praying only for knowledge of His will for us and the power to carry that out.

12. Having had a spiritual awakening as the result of these Steps, we tried to carry this message to alcoholics, and to practice these principles in all our affairs.

No one knows for sure how AA works. It was from the very beginning a gamble, a shot in the dark. It was established in the 1930s by a doctor and a failed stockbroker, Dr. Bob and Bill W., both of whom suffered from alcoholism themselves. Among its central tenets are the beliefs that recovery depends upon a spiritual awakening, and that alcoholics can help one another by sharing their experiences: a kind of bearing witness that proved from the outset astonishingly powerful. As a statement by AA World Services puts it: 'Together, we can do what none of us could accomplish alone. We can serve as a source of personal experience and be an ongoing support system for recovering alcoholics.'

I'd come to an open meeting. We all joined hands in the little room to singsong our way through the Serenity Prayer. *God grant me the serenity to accept the things I cannot change; courage to change the things I can; and wisdom to know the difference.* I had a flash of that tiresomely English reluctance to join in, the suspicion of group identities.

The speaker was a man in his forties, with fine dark hair and a beautiful, ravaged face. He spoke in a meandering, elegant way. Alcohol was the family disease. His father pushed him to succeed. He was gay, attempted suicide as an adolescent and at a late stage in his drinking stopped going out entirely, barricading himself in his apartment with crates of red wine. He used to suffer from blackouts and as he explained this period of vanishing from society he used another of those images that lodged itself painfully in my mind. He said: 'It was like my life was a piece of cloth that I had shredded down to lace and then I tore the connections away until there was nothing left.' Eventually he checked into a recovery programme and after that he stayed sober, even when – and here, for just a minute, he looked exhausted – his partner killed himself. No alcoholic ever dies in vain, he said then, because their story might be the one thing that catalyses someone else's recovery.

After he'd finished speaking, which might have been half an hour, the group gave their responses. Each person began by saying their first name, the nature of their addiction and the length of their sobriety, with the rest chanting back in unison, 'Hi Angela, Hi Joseph . . .' At first it seemed theatrical. There was evidently a clique at the front, and their responses were annoying a man beside me. 'Oh GROSS,' he kept saying. 'Oh fuckin' love, love, love.'

I had some sympathy for him, but the next stage made me change my mind entirely. People were asked to put up their hands if they were celebrating a sobriety birthday that month. Some hadn't touched alcohol for years; some for decades. An Indian man stood up and said: 'I can't believe my son is eighteen this week and that he's never seen me or my wife drunk.' It hadn't really dawned on me before how much of a fellowship AA is, or how powerfully it depends on people wishing to pass on the help and friendship that's been offered to them. By the time the closing prayer began I was close to tears. 'Right?' Andi said, nudging me, and I nodded back. Right.

We said goodbye at the kerb and I walked to the subway alone. I'd forgotten my coat but it didn't matter. The air was almost warm and the moon was very high in the sky, bright as a nickel, ripe as a peach. On the corner I passed a little girl of eight or so roller-skating outside an apartment building. She was hanging on to the hands of a Puerto Rican woman I assumed must be her nanny and whirling in circles, calling out in an imperious voice: 'Again! Again! I'll just do one more!' One more. It must at some time or other have been the rallying cry of every man and woman in that meeting. As I turned down towards the Elysée I could still hear her shouting 'Seven! Eight! Ten!' as she completed each triumphant, greedy circuit.

★

I'd made these two small pilgrimages as a way of immersing myself in the subject of alcoholism (an approach, now I came to think about it, not dissimilar to John Cheever's preferred method of swimming in cold water: leap in, preferably buck naked, no namby pamby fiddling about on the side). What hadn't occurred to me, foolishly, was that spending a day listening to people talk about drinking might trigger corresponding memories of my own.

My room at the hotel was very plush. The Italian influences of the lobby had given way to a French chateau (later, when I went down to breakfast, I found an English country house library, complete with hunting prints and a piano). There was a painting of smugglers huddled around a bonfire above my bed, and I slumped beneath it and tried to order my thoughts. I had ducks on the brain. I knew why, too. When my mother's partner was in treatment she sent me a card. She must have been somewhere between Step Eight, which requires one to make 'a list of all persons we had harmed, and became willing to make amends to them', and Step Nine, which is to make 'direct amends to such people wherever possible, except when to do so would injure them or others'.

What I remembered, lying on the overstuffed bed, was sitting by the bookshelves in my mother's study, reading a card with a duck on it. It wasn't a cartoon. It was a serious, sporting drawing of a mallard or pintail, its feathers marked with immaculate gradations of colour. I remembered the duck and I remembered that both sides of the card were filled with small dense writing in black ballpoint pen, but I had no idea now, beyond the vaguest sense of an apology, what it actually said.

I had only very recently become aware of these gaps in my memory. For years, I'd steered well clear of the period in which alcohol seeped its way into my childhood, beneath the doors and around the seams of windows, a slow, contaminating flood. I was aware of various exhibits tucked away in the lumber-room of my skull; the hippocampus, I suppose. Duck card, air rifle, the night with the police. I'd assumed that if I wanted to I could take them down and bring them out for scrutiny. Now, however, I was beginning to realise that they weren't dissimilar to that piece of decomposing lace the speaker had referred to in the meeting. There is a school of thought that says willed amnesia is an effective way of dealing with trauma, since neurological pathways grass over, so to speak, with disuse. I didn't buy it. You aren't fully human if you can't remember your own past. I put the duck to one side, to return to by way of daylight.

★

I woke to the sound of horns and lay in the big bed, luxuriating in the warmth. I was getting the train to New Orleans the next day, for the Tennessee Williams Centenary Festival, and so I had thirty hours or so on the loose in New York. I hadn't made any particular plans. The next few weeks were very full and I wanted a day to orientate myself before plunging south. In the end, I did what I always do: I walked. I got a subway train to East Broadway and worked my way up the flank of the island, through the havoc of Chinatown and the Lower East Side.

The city impressed itself on me by way of a repeating currency of images, a coinage of yellow cabs and fire escapes, brownstones hung with wreaths of conifer and ornamental cabbage tied up with tartan ribbon. Delis stocked with smoked pigs' legs and wheels of giant cheese. Plums and mangoes stacked in crates. Fish on ice, heaped in delicate, slippery piles of coral, silver, flint and grey. In Chinatown I passed a shop that sold lobsters in tanks brimful of greenish water, the glass murked by deposits of slime and God knows what else. I only looked for a second, enough to catch a queasy glimpse of armoured bodies lurching over one another, striped claws ticking in the insufficient space.

I got a pastrami sandwich at Katz's and went on up Second Avenue. The city was dirty and beautiful and I was entirely seduced by it. I walked almost all the way to the Queensboro Bridge, where John Cheever once saw two hookers playing hopscotch with a hotel room key. The East River was pleating in little folds of blue and gold and I leaned beside it and watched the boats chug back and forth.

After returning to St. Louis, his hated home, at the end of the European tour, Tom Williams didn't fetch up in New York again until 1939, when a play he wrote for a competition won him the attention of an agent. He'd shucked his born name by then, and loped away from his intolerable family. In a few years he'd get them down on paper for the first time with *The Glass Menagerie*, the play that made his reputation. For now, though, he was travelling: hitching and bicycling across the country, writing in the mornings and swimming and indulging himself in the afternoons, a pattern he'd stick to throughout his roaming life.

That first autumn he stayed mainly at the YMCA on West 63rd Street. 'New York is terrifying,' he wrote to an editor in Princeton. 'Even when motionless the people seem to whistle through the air like bullets.' In fact, it was he who was speeding. In his first eleven days in Manhattan alone he went through three separate addresses, and over the next year his letters from the city were interspersed with ones sent from Missouri, New Orleans, Provincetown, Key West and Acapulco, where he had an encounter with a group of unpleasant German tourists that would work its way years later into *The Night of the Iguana*.

While living at home he'd got into the habit of treating his almost-constant attacks of anxiety, insomnia and the agitated depression he called 'the blue devils' with liberal doses of membral, sodium bromide and sleeping pills. To this dangerous prescription he now added two new items. His experience of New York was 'constant suspense and nerve-wracking excitement, which I evaded with drink and with sex'. For the rest of his life, these would remain his preferred methods of escaping difficult or stress-inducing situations, from failed love affairs to problems with the production of his plays.

Drink was also his antidote to shyness, something he still suffered from to an almost pathological degree. 'I was still very shy except when drunk,' he recalled in *Memoirs*. 'Oh, I was quite the opposite when I had a couple of drinks under the belt.' His journal from the time is packed with references to evenings of applejack brandy and beer chasers or too much whiskey, one of which ended dishearteningly when he stumbled into a table and tipped all the liquor to the floor. Still, life in the city was better than those interminable, suffocating nights in St. Louis, when he'd sat up into the small hours writing stories and experiencing such waves of panic he often convinced himself he was on the verge of a heart attack. Sometimes the stillness itself had been unbearable, and he'd got up and rushed from the house, pacing the streets for hours or swimming frantic lengths in the nearest pool.

The disadvantage of alcohol as an antidote to these unpleasant states was that it interfered with his ability to work. By the summer of 1940, he was already reporting a need to curtail his behaviour, noting in a letter to his friend, the dancer Joe Hazan: 'I have started off on a rather disciplinary regime. Only one or two drinks a day, when very low, and a calm endurance of moods instead of a mad flight into intoxication and social distraction.' A few paragraphs down, warning Joe against 'trivial dissipation', he added: 'I am more likely than . . . you to be involved in these things. I have many times in the past – but always turned away in revulsion when it reached a dangerous point.'

And yet, despite all this distracting, dissipating activity, he kept on writing, producing an astonishing flood of poetry, stories and plays, a mass of material he perpetually reassembled into differing combinations. On one of his mad flights, to the resort town of Key West in 1941, he began a 'beautiful' short story that would turn by degrees into *The Glass Menagerie*, the most restrained and purely vocal of all his plays. I first read it when I was a teenager, in a pale green edition that also included *A Streetcar Named Desire*. In fact, I'd brought the book with me to America. It was in my room at the Elysée now: battered and full of mortifying marginalia in a hand long since abandoned.

All Williams's plays are claustrophobic, but this one achieves its effects most simply, without resorting to the melodramatic fireworks of rape, lynch mobs, castration or cannibalism. It's the story of a young man in an intolerable situation, and as such comes closer to home than any of his other works, never mind the fact that it's populated with doll's house versions of his own mother and sister, not to mention a Tom near-identical to the nervous, well-mannered boy he'd tried to leave behind in St. Louis. This Tom – Tom the semblance, the mirror self – is trapped in a small apartment with the two remaining players of the family quartet, Laura and Amanda Wingfield; his father having vanished some time previously. He works in a shoe factory, as did both the real Tom and Cornelius (the one a good deal longer and more diligently than the other), and spends what little free time he has at the movies, despite intense maternal opposition.

One of my favourite moments comes at the beginning of scene four. Tom blunders home late and very drunk, and drops his key on the fire escape. Williams, it should be noted, was obsessed with fire as a metaphor. Many of his plays include or end with conflagration, including the very early *Battle of Angels* and the very late *Clothes for a Summer Hotel*, both of which concern a pyrophobic who is later burned alive. In the latter play, this character is Zelda Fitzgerald, who was in many ways the archetypal Williams heroine, and who did in reality die in 1948 when a fire broke out at the mental hospital where she was incarcerated, killing all thirteen women in the locked ward on the top floor. As to the fire escape of *The Glass Menagerie*, it is, according to the stage notes, 'a structure whose name is a touch of accidental poetic truth, for all of these huge buildings are always burning with the slow and implacable fires of human desperation'.

Tom's sweet, crippled sister Laura opens the door before he wakes his mother. Swaying a little in the cold night air, he raves to her about the movies he's just seen: a Garbo picture and a Mickey Mouse and at the end a wonderful stage show by a magician who had the happy knack of turning water into wine and thence to Kentucky Straight Bourbon. 'I knew it was whisky it finally turned into,' he explains, 'because he needed somebody to come up out of the audience to help him, and I came up – both shows!' – a line that always gets a big laugh. 'But the wonderfullest trick of all,' he continues, blundering around the stage like a hooked trout, 'was the coffin trick. We nailed him into a coffin and he got out of the coffin without removing one nail. There is a trick that would come in handy for me – get me out of this 2 by 4 situation!'

As it happens, none of this tomfoolery was in the original manuscript. During the first round of rehearsals in Chicago in the winter of 1944, the director Eddie Dowling, who also played the role of Tom, improvised a much cruder drunk scene. Williams was horrified, but eventually agreed to produce his own sleeker version. Intentional or not, the coffin trick serves as an elegant figure for the play's larger concerns, its nightmare of genteel poverty and co-dependence. *Coffin* was also, it might be added, the middle name of Williams's father Cornelius, from whose oppressive influences he'd only just escaped.

The audience never actually gets to witness the mirror-Tom's version of the coffin trick. Instead, he tells them about it, in one of those lyrical asides that must have helped, along with Laurette Taylor's extraordinary performance as Amanda, to seduce the theatregoers of first Chicago and then New York. 'I didn't go to the moon,' he announces from the fire escape, as in a lighted window behind him his mother comforts his distraught sister:

> I went much further – for time is the longest distance between two places –
>
> Not long after that I was fired for writing a poem on the lid of a shoebox.
>
> I left Saint Louis. I descended the steps of this fire escape for a last time and followed, from then on, in my father's footsteps, attempting to find in motion what was lost in space – I travelled around a great deal. The cities swept about me like

dead leaves, leaves that were brightly colored but torn away from the branches.

I would have stopped but I was pursued by something. It always came upon me unawares, taking me altogether by surprise . . .

From the moment those lines first echoed around the Playhouse in New York, in April 1945, Tennessee was catapulted into a different kind of world. He became a public figure, with all the opportunity, scrutiny and pressure fame brings. It wasn't by any means a comfortable shift, though he'd longed for it since he was a sickly little boy, lying in bed in his grandfather's house in Columbus, Mississippi, acting out the fall of Troy with no audience or actors except a deck of cards, the black against the red.

Looking back decades later, in the *Paris Review* interview of 1981, he made two contradictory remarks about this sudden change in fortune. First, he described the play's success as 'terrible'. Although there were twenty-four curtain calls on the opening night and he was pulled from his seat to face wild applause, he claims that in photographs taken the next morning it's obvious he was visibly depressed. A few lines on, he contradicts himself, or seems to, saying: 'Before the success of *Menagerie* I'd reached the very, very bottom. I would have died without the money . . . So if I suddenly hadn't had this dispensation from Providence with *Menagerie*, I couldn't have made it for another year, I don't think.'

Luckily, Providence sent something else his way, or God knows how he would have borne the increasing strain of the coming years. In the summer of 1947, he spent a blissful hour in the dunes in Provincetown with a beautiful Sicilian-American called Frank Merlo. They liked one another immediately, but because Tennessee was at the time embroiled with someone else they didn't stay in touch. A year passed and then late one fall evening on Lexington Avenue, Tennessee saw the young man inside a deli. 'Accidental and marvellous,' he wrote of that re-encounter almost three decades later, when the walls had long since caved in on his own life.

Frank came back to Tennessee's apartment on East 58th Street for a midnight feast: roast beef on rye with pickles and potato salad. 'Frankie and I kept looking at one another,' he wrote in *Memoirs*, peering back wistfully at those two bright-eyed boys, their hair slicked, their hearts, I'd guess, running a little fast. The apartment belonged to a sculptor and was all white inside, with an exotic garden behind walls of frosted glass. The bedroom was decorated like a merman's cavern, with an illuminated aquarium and a tangle of sea shells, driftwood and fishing nets. 'A piece of enchantment,' he wrote, and then: 'the magical carpet of the big bed'.

As for falling in love, that took a little longer. It wasn't until Tennessee was staying in St. Louis, under his mother's roof, that he realised how much he missed Frank, who he'd nicknamed the Little Horse on account of his long face. He sent a wire, asking him to wait at the apartment, but when he arrived home it seemed deserted. 'I felt quite desolate,' the older Tennessee remembered. He went into the enchanted bedroom and there on the big bed was little Frankie, fast asleep: his companion and guardian for the next fourteen years.

★

It was getting late. I walked back to the hotel through Sutton Place, took a bath, put on a dress and heels and went out again into the twilight. It was the cocktail hour, that lovely moment which in cinema is called magic time, the hour of the wolf. On its way to darkness the sky had turned an astonishing, deepening blue, flooding with colour as abruptly as if someone had opened a sluice. In that instant the city resembled a huge aquarium, the skyscrapers rising in the wavering light like underwater plants, the cabs flashing through the streets like shoals of fish, darting north at changeover as the lights tripped green all the way to Central Park.

I walked by way of 55th Street to the King Cole bar at the St. Regis, where among ten thousand other illustrious events the opening night party for *Cat on a Hot Tin Roof* was held. If you want old-style glamour in New York you come here, or else go to the Plaza, or to Bemelman's at the Carlyle, where the walls are painted with debonair rabbits getting up to mischief in a fantastical version of the park.

The room was low-lit and subtly burnished. I ordered a King's Passion and sat on a banquette by the door, catty-corners from a Russian woman in a slippery white blouse. I'd entered Cheever territory, no doubt about it. John Cheever: the small, immaculately dishevelled Chekhov of the Suburbs, who despite his long association with the wealthy upstate town of Ossining lived in Manhattan from the age of twenty-two until the morning after his thirty-ninth birthday.

His last residence was just around the corner, on East 59th Street, and the St. Regis was among his favourite haunts. He liked anything that smacked of old money. In 1968, long after he'd left the city, his publishers put him up at the hotel for a two-day press junket, during which time he impressed one reporter by ordering two *bottles* of

Scotch and gin. ('Guess what the bill is?' he said gleefully when they arrived. 'Twenty-nine dollars! Wait until Alfred Knopf sees that!') 1968: five years before he went careering around Iowa City with Raymond Carver, and seven years before he found himself at Smithers, sharing a room with a failed delicatessen owner and learning how to live without either the sorrows or the consolations of gin.

Cheever fascinated me because he was, in common with many alcoholics, a helpless mix of fraudulence and honesty. Though he feigned patrician origins, his upbringing in Quincy, Massachusetts was both financially and emotionally insecure, and while he eventually attained all the trappings of the landed Wasp he never managed to shake a painful sense of shame and self-disgust. He was an almost exact contemporary of Tennessee's, and though they weren't friends, their worlds in the New York of the 1930s and 40s often overlapped. In fact, Mary Cheever first realised her husband wasn't entirely hetero-sexual while they were at the first Broadway production of *A Streetcar Named Desire*.

According to Blake Bailey's beautiful biography, *Cheever*, there was a leitmotif associated with Blanche's dead homosexual husband and this tune lodged in Mary's head and led to some kind of underwater realisation that her husband's sexuality was not as she'd assumed. She never mentioned it to him. 'Oh Lord, no,' she told Bailey. 'Oh Lord, no. He was terrified of it himself.' As for her husband, he noted in his diary, 'as decadent, I think, as anything I've ever seen on the stage'. He loved the play, adding rapturously:

There is much else; the wonderful sense of captivity in a squalid apartment and the beauty of the evening, although most of

the chords struck seem to lie close to insanity. Anxiety, that is
– confinement and so forth. Also, he avoids not only the
common clichés but the uncommon cliché, over which I trip,
and also works in a form that has few inhibitions and has
written its own laws.

The entry concludes with a prescription to himself 'to be less inhib-
ited, to be warmer . . . to write, to love': the same arenas in which
he'd struggle for the next three decades of his life.

John Cheever was conceived after a sales banquet in Boston and
born in Quincy, Massachusetts on 27 May 1912. Like Tennessee
Williams, he was the second child of a profoundly ill-suited couple,
and though he adored his brother Fred he was aware that he wasn't
his father's favourite child. Indeed, on learning of his wife's pregnancy,
Frederick Senior's first recorded act was to invite the local abortionist
to dinner. He already had one much-loved son; why did he need
another? Cheever never felt like he secured much of Frederick's affec-
tion, and some of this mood of neglect and longing wells up in his
short story 'The National Pastime', in which a small boy tries to
persuade his father to teach him to play baseball, that needful hand-
me-down of American masculinity. Frederick was a shoe salesman, and
when this business failed in the Depression he withdrew into eccen-
tricity and depression. He drank heavily, and it seems that his father
was also an alcoholic, who died of delirium tremens.

Luckily, Cheever's mother, Mary Liley, was an immensely capable
woman, though she was profoundly unaffectionate and suffered from
a neurotic and overbearing temperament. She was claustrophobic, and
as an adult Cheever remembered with intense irritation her behaviour

at the theatre. Often she'd have to grab her bag and gloves and push her way out, overwhelmed by the confinement of the stalls. Financially, though, it was she who kept the family afloat during the black years of the mid-twenties. Before her husband's downfall she'd channelled her chilly and remarkable energies into various good works. Now she established and ran a gift shop in Quincy, the existence of which filled her snobbish son with shame.

As for Cheever, he was a skimpy, lonely boy, a little effeminate and dismally untalented at sports. His real gift was for telling stories, marvels of fabrication and ebullience. Apart from a brief spell at Quincy High, he was educated largely at private schools, where he failed to shine academically despite an evident flair for English. His academic career ended for good when he left his last school, Thayer Academy, voluntarily at the age of seventeen. Showing a flash of his mother's enterprising spirit, he wrote a story about what he cannily reframed as his expulsion and sent it off to the *New Republic*.

The editor who bought it, Malcolm Cowley, was an old friend of F. Scott Fitzgerald. He took a shine to Cheever, and as well as inaugurating his literary career was responsible for providing him with what was probably his first experience of New York-style intoxication. He threw an afternoon party and invited his protégé, who fifty years later would queasily recall:

> I was offered two kinds of drinks. One was greenish. The other was brown. They were both, I believe, made in a bathtub. I was told that one was a Manhattan and the other Pernod. My only intent was to appear terribly sophisticated and I ordered a Manhattan. Malcolm very kindly introduced me to his guests.

I went on drinking Manhattans lest anyone think I came from a small town like Quincy, Massachusetts. Presently, after four or five Manhattans, I realized that I was going to vomit. I rushed to Mrs. Cowley, thanked her for the party, and reached the apartment-house hallway, where I vomited all over the wallpaper. Malcolm never mentioned the damages.

Perhaps realising he was in need of some city polish, Cheever moved to Manhattan in the summer of 1934, renting a fourth-floor walk-up on 633 Hudson Street for the princely sum of three dollars a week. His neighbours were longshoremen and sea cooks, and his room so epitomised the poverty of the period that it was photographed by Walker Evans (with whom Cheever had a brief liaison) as part of a series documenting the Great Depression. The image crops up periodically in reportage of the period: a claustrophobic low-ceilinged cell, furnished with a single bed that smelled powerfully of lice-preventive, the walls lumpily plastered, a pair of too-short curtains dragged shut against the night.

That first winter was intolerably cold. Cheever lived off milk, stale bread and raisins, spending his days with the drifters and down-and-outs in Washington Square, bundled up against the chill and talking obsessively about food. He worked at odd writing jobs, publishing occasional stories and précising novels for MGM, but none of these endeavours added up to anything like a steady income. Rescue came, once again, in the form of Malcolm Cowley. He suggested over dinner that his young friend might stop banging away at his hopeless novel and instead attempt much shorter stories, adding that if four were turned out over the next four days, he'd take a stab at placing them.

The challenge paid off. A few weeks later Cheever received his first cheque from the *New Yorker* for 'Buffalo', initiating one of the most constant associations of his life.

Despite his growing reputation as a writer, for a long while Cheever's life in the city remained fundamentally unmoored. Then, on a rainy afternoon in November 1939 he went to visit his literary agent and encountered a pretty, well-bred, dark-haired girl in the elevator. 'That's more or less what I would like,' he thought, and married Mary Winternitz just before the start of the Second World War. Over the next decade they moved from Greenwich Village to Chelsea and then on to the bourgeois splendours of Sutton Place, renting a ninth-floor apartment with a sunken lounge and views out across the East River.

It was during the Sutton Place period that Cheever began to write some of his greatest short stories, among them 'The Enormous Radio', 'The Day the Pig Fell into the Well', 'The Common Day' and 'Goodbye, My Brother'. These stories possess two kinds of magic. The first is a superficial conjuring of light and weather, of uptown cocktail parties and islands off the coast of Massachusetts. 'The darkness would come as thickly into the soft air as silt.' 'The sea that morning was a solid colour, like verd stone.' 'There were a hundred clouds in the west – clouds of gold, clouds of silver, clouds like bone and tinder and filth under the bed.' There then follows a deeper, more disquieting thrill, which arises from the way these radiant surfaces are undermined. In his best work there exists an almost perpetual ambiguity, a movement between irony and sheer enchantment that only Scott Fitzgerald has ever seriously rivalled. Listen, for example, to this:

That late in the season, the light went quickly. It was sunny one minute and dark the next. Macabit and its mountain range were canted against the afterglow, and for a while it seemed unimaginable that anything could lie beyond the mountains, that this was not the end of the world. The wall of pure and brassy light seemed to beat up from infinity. Then the stars came out, the earth rumbled downward, the illusion of an abyss was lost. Mrs. Nudd looked around her, and the time and the place seemed strangely important. This is not an imitation, she thought, this is not the product of a custom, this is the unique place, the unique air, where my children have spent the best of themselves. The realization that none of them had done very well made her sink back in her chair. She squinted the tears out of her eyes. What had made the summer always an island, she thought; what had made it such a small island. What mistakes had they made? What had they done wrong? They had loved their neighbours, respected the force of modesty, held honor above gain. Then where had they lost their competence, their freedom, their greatness? Why should these good and gentle people who surrounded her seem like the figures in a tragedy?

'Remember the day the pig fell into the well?' she asked.

Although he's often described as a realistic writer, Cheever is stranger and more subversive than his increasingly Waspy scenery suggests. Sometimes an unexplained 'I' will assume control of the narrative, or else an eerie, collusive 'we'. Stories blast forward in time, or contain false endings, false beginnings, midway swerves and points at which the thread of narrative is abruptly severed. He seems to take his greatest pleasure in abandoning responsibility for his characters, only to lean in, split-seconds from collision, and whirl them back into motion again.

In 'The Pot of Gold', a story from 1950, there's a line of description I thought of often while I was in Manhattan. Two women meet regularly to talk in Central Park. 'They sat together with their children through the sooty twilights, when the city to the south burns like a Bessemer furnace, and the air smells of coal, and the wet boulders shine like slag, and the Park itself seems like a strip of woods at the edge of a coal town.' I found it pleasurable to say out loud. *When the city to the south burns like a Bessemer furnace.* There's no writer I can think of so effortlessly capable of reconditioning the world.

The problem, as anyone who has read Cheever's journals will know, is that the same gulf between appearance and interior that makes his stories so beguiling was also at work in his own life, though here it produced less pleasurable effects. Despite an increasingly command performance as an upstanding member of the bourgeoisie, Cheever couldn't shake the sense of being essentially an impostor among the middle classes. Partly, this was a matter of money. Even when he was packing his daughter into the cab that took her each morning to private school, he was painfully aware that he remained too poor to tip the doorman or pay his bills on time. 'The rent is not paid,' he noted despairingly in his journal of 1948, 'we have very little to eat, relatively little to eat: canned tongue and eggs.'

An oft-repeated anecdote from the Sutton Place years has Cheever taking the elevator each morning: a dapper little figure in suit and tie, indistinguishable from the other hard-working, well-scrubbed men who crowd in on every floor. But while they stream out of the lobby, rushing off to workplaces across the city, he descends to the basement, strips to his underwear, and settles at his typewriter, emerging, suited once more, in time for pre-lunch drinks. The sense of himself as both forger and forgery could be thrilling, but in his journal Cheever added dolefully: 'It is a tonic to my self-respect to leave the basement room.'

Writers, even the most socially gifted and established, must be outsiders of some sort, if only because their job is that of scrutiniser and witness. All the same, Cheever's sense of double-dealing seems to have run unusually deep. After a New Year spent upstate with some wealthy friends, he wrote in baffled fury a thought that had occurred to him while folding, of all things, a monogrammed towel:

> It was my decision, early in life, to insinuate myself into the
> middle class, like a spy, so that I would have an advantageous
> position of attack, but I seem now and then to have forgotten
> my mission and to have taken my disguises too seriously.

This burden of fraudulence, of needing to keep some lumbering secret self forever under wraps, was not just a matter of class anxiety. Cheever lived in the painful knowledge that his erotic desires included men, that these desires were antagonistic and even fatal to the social security he also craved, and that as such 'every comely man, every bank clerk and delivery boy was aimed at my life like a loaded pistol'. During this period, his sense of failure and self-disgust could reach such agonising heights that he sometimes raised in his journals the possibility of suicide.

Who wouldn't drink in a situation like that, to ease the pressure of maintaining such intricately folded double lives? He'd been hitting it hard since his late teens: initially, like Tennessee Williams, out of a desire to quell his acute social anxiety. In the bohemian Village of the 1930s and 40s, alcohol was still the omnipresent lubricant of social exchange, and even in the depths of poverty, he'd managed to find the funds for nights that might, head-splittingly, take in a dozen manhattans or a quart apiece of whiskey. He drank at home and in friends' apartments, at Treetops (his wealthy wife's family estate in New Hampshire), in the Breevort Hotel, the back room at the Plaza or in the Menemsha Bar on 57th Street, where he'd pop in after collecting his daughter from school and let her eat maraschino cherries while he attended to his needs.

Though not all these scenes were exactly civilised, alcohol was an essential ingredient of Cheever's ideal of a cultured life, one of those rites whose correct assumption could protect him from the persistent shadows of inferiority and shame. In a journal entry written the summer before he married Mary, he recorded the following fantasy:

> I found myself driving up the road to Treetops in a large car, creaming the Whitneys at tennis, a game I've never learnt to play, giving the head-waiter at Charles' five dollars and instructing him to get some flowers and ice a monopole of Bollinger, deciding whether to have the Pot au Feu or the trout merinere [sic], I can see myself waiting at the bar in a blue cheviot suit, tasting a martini, decanting a bottle of Vouvray into a thermos bottle to take out to Jones' Beach, coming back from the beach, burned and salty . . . moving among my charming guests, greeting the late-comers at the door.

In this pleasant daydream, drinking is not about anything so vulgar as gratifying an appetite, but rather part of an elaborate social code, in which the right thing done at the right time conveys a near-magical sense of belonging. The monopole is ordered and iced, not drunk; the martini only tasted; while the Vouvray is merely transferred from one container to another, more appropriate to the demands of the season and the hour.

The same note sounds again from another, later diary entry, written in September 1941, when Cheever was on a ten-day furlough from the army. 'Mary was waiting,' he writes happily, 'all shined up and dressed up, the apartment was clean and shining, there were bottles of scotch, brandy, French wine, gin and vermouth in the pantry, and clean sheets on the bed. Also joints, shell-fish, salad-greens, etc., filled the ice-box.' What's interesting about this memory, which recalls Ratty's gleeful iteration of his picnic in *Wind in the Willows*, is the emphasis on cleanliness as well as largesse. *Shined, clean, shining, clean*: an antidote to the grubby privations of camp life, perhaps. But in its obsessive repetitions, it also resembles an incantation, a spell for safety and good health (clean, after all, is a hospital word, particularly clean sheets, while the preserving ice-box also has a hospital, even a morgueish, chill about it). As such, it's hard not to read those ranked bottles as a kind of medicine, a prophylactic against the sense of dirtiness and disorder that would continue to dog Cheever from house to house, from year to year.

I was jolted out of this line of thought by a man in the bar saying distinctly *Ossining*. How strange. Ossining is a small town in Westchester County, forty miles up the Hudson River from Manhattan. It's still best known, years after his death, as Cheever's adopted hometown (after he died the flags of the public buildings were lowered for ten days). Coincidentally, it's also where Tennessee Williams's mentally ill sister Rose spent most of her adult life, in an institution he both chose and paid for. It's one of those places that exist in the limbo of the reader's mind, inexorably associated with the melancholy, suburban stories Cheever used to write for the *New Yorker*.

I looked up. The Ossining man was sitting with the woman whose blouse I'd coveted. He was balding and wore one of those jaunty navy blazers with gleaming buttons that are supposed to lend one a nautical air. They were evidently cornering into a spectacular row.

'So,' she said. 'What is your marriage? Are you happily married? What is your home situation?'

'Happily? Happily would be the right word. I guess I'm happily married. But I'm attracted to you. I can't control that.'

'I'm just wondering what you've been doing since this morning.'

'As a matter of fact I went home around noon. I told work I had a very important client to entertain. Don't be hurt or confused if I say I have a happy marriage. Really, if I was truly happy I wouldn't be here with you.'

Jeez. I wondered for a minute if they could be actors, rehearsing for some rotten soap, though perhaps I'd just seen *Tootsie* one too many times. The man got up and moved around the table, sliding in beside her on the banquette. 'I think most men would think they'd have sex with a Russian woman with their wallet in their hand,' he said. 'Russian women are crazy about money.' She looked at him blankly and he added: 'Oh come on, you've heard that before.' I began to gather my things, and as I did I heard him say: 'It was the most important moment of my life. I remember every second of it. And now you've ruined it for me.'

If this was a Tennessee Williams play she'd lose the plot and start screaming, or else she'd crush him like Alexandra del Lago in *Sweet Bird of Youth*, who can't be made into a victim by anyone, even though her looks are fading and she is terrified of death. And if, on the other hand, it was a John Cheever story, he'd have sex with her and then go home to his wife and children in Ossining, where no doubt someone would be playing a piano. He'd mix a martini and go out on to the porch and look over the orchard to the lake, where the family skate in the winter months. Gazing dreamily into the blue light of evening, he'd see a dog, a dog named Jupiter, who'd come prancing through the tomato vines, 'holding in his generous mouth the remains of an evening slipper. Then it is dark; it is a night where kings in golden suits ride elephants over the mountains.'

I'd stolen, of course, the closing scene of 'The Country Husband', with its swerve up and away, out of the trenches, the animal earth, as if gravity were just a joke and the yaw and pitch of flight was somehow in our repertoire. Recently, I'd begun to become suspicious of this weightless element in Cheever's work, to see it as another manifestation of the escapist urge that fuelled his drinking. Now, however, the line seemed very lovely, an antidote to the harshness that is all too present in the world. I folded a few dollars on the table and left the King Cole then, spinning through the revolving door and escaping, a little tipsy myself, into the cold, illuminated air.

3

FISHING IN THE DARK

WHEN I TOLD AN AMERICAN friend I was travelling by train from
New York to New Orleans she looked at me incredulously. 'It's not
like *Some Like It Hot* any more,' she said, but I didn't listen. I love
trains. I love gazing out of the window as the cities slide by, and I
couldn't think of anything more pleasurable than taking a sleeper,
crossing in darkness through the Blue Ridge Mountains and waking
with the dawn in Atlanta or Tuscaloosa.

In the interests of thriftiness I'd decided that since the journey
only took thirty hours I'd do without a cabin, sleeping instead in
what was promisingly described as a 'wide, comfortable reserved
coach seat'. Before I left the Elysée for Penn Station I looked again
at the route map. New York, New Jersey, Pennsylvania, Delaware,
Maryland, Virginia, North Carolina, South Carolina, Georgia, Alabama,
Mississippi and Louisiana: twelve states. Still, I guessed it would be
less arduous than Tennessee Williams's first trip to New Orleans. In
December 1938 he travelled by bus from Chicago, stopping off to
see his family in St. Louis and arriving in the south just in time to
ring in the New Year. It was the Depression and he had no job and

hardly any money, but all the same he felt at home immediately, writing in his journal three hours after arrival: 'Here surely is the place that I was *made* for if any place in this funny old world.'

At the station there were people charging in every possible direction, and yet as soon as I worked out which check-in desk I needed, it all proceeded with beautiful efficiency. A uniformed porter took my bags down to the train and advised me against the seats above the wheels. It seemed like a return to a more civilised age and I felt for a moment, if not like Sugar Cane, then at least equal to Jack Lemmon's Daphne, sashaying along the platform in his ill-fitting heels.

The first stop was Philadelphia. I took a window seat, stowed my bags and arranged all my little bits and bobs in easy reach: that strange homemaking impulse that overcomes travellers on overnight trips. iPod, notebook, water, a bag of sticky grapes I'd bought after hearing yet another horror story about Amtrak food. I spread my plaid blanket over my knees and as I did a great wave of claustrophobia overtook me. I was at the time at the tail end of a period of chronic insomnia. I could barely sleep in my own bed, with earplugs and an eye mask. My flat had been broken into ages back, and ever since my reticular activation system had locked on red alert.

Only those who are persistently deprived of sleep can understand the panic that wells up when the conditions it requires are likely to go unmet. Sleeplessness, as Keats put it, breeds many woes. That maggoty word *breeds* is exactly right, for who lying awake at three or four or five in the morning hasn't felt their thoughts take on an insectile life, or experienced a minute crawling of the skin? Sleep is magically efficacious at smoothing out the tangles of the day, and a shortage makes one agitated to the point of lunacy.

As anyone who's ever drunk too much will also know, alcohol has a complicated relationship to sleep. Its initial effect is sedative: the slumpy somnolence most of us are familiar with. But alcohol also disrupts sleep patterns and reduces sleep quality, limiting and postponing the amount of time spent in the restorative waters of REM, where the body both physically and psychologically replenishes itself. This explains why sleep after a wild night is so often shallow and broken into pieces.

Chronic drinking causes more permanent disturbances in what's known prettily as the *sleep circuitry*: damage that can persist long after sobriety has been attained. According to a paper by Kirk Brower entitled 'Alcohol's Effects on Sleep in Alcoholics', sleep problems are more common among alcoholics than the population at large. What's more, 'sleep problems may predispose some people to developing alcohol problems', and are in addition often implicated in relapse.

Both F. Scott Fitzgerald and Ernest Hemingway suffered from insomnia, and their writing on the subject is full of submerged clues about their drinking. The two men first met in May 1925 in the Dingo American Bar on the Rue Delambre in Paris, when Fitzgerald was twenty-eight and Hemingway was twenty-five. At the time, Fitzgerald was one of America's best known and best paid short story writers. He was the author of three novels, *This Side of Paradise*, *The Beautiful and the Damned* and *The Great Gatsby*, which had been published a few weeks before. A pretty man, with neat little teeth and unmistakably Irish features, he'd been careering around Europe with his wife Zelda and their small daughter Scottie. 'Zelda painting, me drinking,' he recorded in his *Ledger* for the month of April, adding in June: '1000 parties and no work.'

In a way, the bingeing shouldn't have mattered. He'd just finished *Gatsby*, after all; that perfectly weighted novel. Its great strength is its indelibility: the way it enters into you, leaving a trail of images like things seen from a moving car. Jordan's hand, lightly powdered over her tan. Gatsby flinging out armfuls of shirts for Daisy to look at: a mounting pile of apple green and coral and pale orange, monogrammed in blue. People drifting in and out of parties, or riding away on horseback, leaving behind some lingering suggestion of a snub. A little dog sneezing in a smoky room and a woman bleeding fluently on to a tapestried couch. The owl-eyed man in the library, and Gatsby's list of self-improvements, and Daisy being too hot and saying in her lovely throaty voice that she hopes her daughter will be a beautiful little fool. The green light winking, and Gatsby calling Nick *old sport*, and Nick thinking of catching the train back to St. Paul and seeing the shadows of holly wreaths cast on to the snow.

A different man could have survived a blowout after building something as lovely and as durable as that. But Fitzgerald was too unanchored to be able to tolerate his chosen pace of life. For years, he and Zelda had been reeling hectically around the globe, ricocheting from New York to St. Paul, to Great Neck, to Antibes and Juan-les-Pins, trailing wreckage in their wake. Just before he'd arrived in Paris there'd been a particularly troublesome spell. Zelda had an affair with a French aviator and was becoming very strange, while Fitzgerald was drinking heavily and getting into fights, at one point ending up in a Roman jail, a scene he'd later use to mark Dick Diver's definitive loss of control in *Tender is the Night*, the novel he'd just begun.

As for Hemingway, he was knee-deep in what he'd later remember as the happiest period of his life. He was married to Hadley Richardson, his first wife, and had a small son he nicknamed Mr. Bumby. There's a photograph of him taken around that time, in a thick sweater, shirt and tie, looking a little chubby. He has a new moustache, but it doesn't quite disguise the boyish softness of his face. Three years back, in 1922, Hadley had accidentally lost a suitcase containing all his manuscripts, and so the book of stories he'd just published, *In Our Time*, represented entirely new material, or at the least new versions of lost originals.

The two men liked one another immediately. You can tell from even the most casual glance through their letters, which are stuffed with good-natured insults and statements as frankly loving as: 'I can't tell you how much your friendship has meant to me' and 'My god I'd like to see you'. As well as being good company, Fitzgerald was also of professional assistance to Hemingway that year. Before they'd even met, he recommended him to his own editor at Scribner, Max Perkins, suggesting Max sign up this promising young man. In a letter to Perkins written a few weeks after their first meeting in the Dingo, Hemingway noted that he was seeing a lot of Scott, adding enthusiastically: 'We had a great trip together driving his car up from Lyon.'

The next summer Fitzgerald helped out again, this time by casting a critical eye over Hemingway's new novel, *The Sun Also Rises*. In a characteristically insightful and badly spelled letter, he suggested that the first twenty-nine pages (full of 'sneers, superiorities and nose-thumbings-at-nothing . . . elephantine facetiousness') be cut, though in the end Hemingway could only bring himself to dispense with fifteen. 'You were the first American I wanted to meet in Europe,' he adds, to soften the blow, before confessing a few lines on: 'I go crazy when people aren't always at their best.'

At the time this letter was written, Hemingway had got himself into a fix. He'd fallen in love with a wealthy, boyishly attractive American, Pauline Pfeiffer. Over the course of the summer (in which he, Hadley and Pauline holidayed together in Fitzgerald's old villa in Juan-les-Pins), it became increasingly clear that his marriage was finished. 'Our life is all gone to hell,' he wrote to Scott on 7 September. He spent a suicidal autumn alone in Paris, was divorced from Hadley on 27 January 1927 and by spring had resolved to marry Pauline.

During the course of the break-up he suffered punishing insomnia. In the same 7 September letter, he used the word *hell* a second time to describe his condition ever since meeting Pauline, adding:

> . . . with plenty of insomnia to light the way around so I could study the terrain I get sort of used to it and fond of it and probably would take pleasure in showing people around it. As we make our hell we certainly should like it.

Insomnia as a light to view a hellish terrain. The idea evidently appealed to him, because it reoccurs as the foundation of a story he wrote soon after. A long time back, before he'd met even Hadley, Hemingway had served as a Red Cross ambulance driver in Italy in the First World War. While bringing chocolate to the soldiers on the front, he'd been blown up by mortar fire and had spent a long time in hospital with a badly damaged leg. In November 1926, he wrote a story inspired by this experience, though it ranged out much further than that.

'Now I Lay Me' begins with Nick Adams (not Hemingway exactly, but rather a kind of stand-in self or avatar, who shares various items of his childhood and wartime record) lying on the floor of a room at night, trying not to sleep. As he lies there, he listens to silkworms feeding on mulberry leaves. 'I myself did not want to sleep,' he explains, 'because I had been living for a long time with the knowledge that if I ever shut my eyes in the dark and let myself go, my soul would go out of my body. I had been that way for a long time, ever since I had been blown up at night and felt it go out of me and go off and then come back.'

To ward off this terrifying eventuality, he carries out a nightly ritual. Lying in the dark, listening to the small noises of feeding from above, he fishes very carefully in his mind the rivers he knew as a boy: the trout rivers of Michigan, with their deep pools and swift, shallow stretches. Sometimes he finds grasshoppers in the open meadows, and uses them for bait, and at other times he collects wood ticks or beetles or white grubs with brown heads, and once a salamander, though that's not an experiment he repeats. Sometimes, too, the rivers are imaginary, and these can be very exciting, and easily carry him through to dawn. These fishing adventures are so detailed it's often hard to remember that they aren't real; that they're fictional even inside the fiction: a story a man is telling himself in secret, a manufactured substitute for the sort of wayward, nocturnal journeys he might otherwise be making.

On this particular night – the night of the silkworms in the mulberry leaves – there's only one other person in the room, and he too is incapable of sleep. Both are soldiers, in Italy in the First World War. Nick is American, and the other man has lived in Chicago, though he's Italian by birth. Lying there in the dark they get to talking, and John asks Nick why he never sleeps (though actually he can manage just fine when there's a light on, or after the sun has risen). 'I got in pretty bad shape along early last spring, and at night it bothers me,' he says casually and that's all the explanation he offers, except for the mention of being blown up at night at the very beginning of the story. Instead, the weight of his injury is carried by those dream rivers, its severity only really gaugeable by the enormous efforts he makes to circumvent it. He's certainly not going to tell the reader directly how bad it feels to lie there, thinking you might die at any minute.

Fitzgerald's own take on the hells of sleeplessness came seven years later, with an essay called 'Sleeping and Waking'. It ran in *Esquire* in December 1934, when he was careering into the breakdown he'd confess to eighteen months later in 'The Crack-up', a much more famous trio of essays for the same magazine. At the time of writing, Fitzgerald was living in Baltimore with his daughter. His wife was in a mental institution, he was drinking heavily, and the days of being carefree in Paris and the Riviera had vanished as conclusively as they did for poor Dick Diver in *Tender is the Night* – though you could argue that they'd only been carefree in the sense that a man on a tightrope is carefree, soft-shoeing along without the slightest sign of strain or effort.

Writing in praise of Fitzgerald years later, John Cheever observed that his genius lies in the provision of details. Clothes, dialogue, drinks, hotels, incidental music: all are precisely rendered, plunging the reader into the lost world of the Riviera or West Egg or Hollywood or wherever it is we are. The same is true in this essay, though it's by no means the most glamorous of his stage sets. Aside from one brief visit to a New York hotel room, the drama is confined to the bedroom of the author's own house in Baltimore, with small forays out into the study and the porch.

In this room he suffers what might be described as a rupture in the fabric of sleep, a widening interval of wakefulness between the first easy plunge into unconsciousness and the deep rest that comes after the sky has begun to lighten. This is the moment, he declares in grand and untranslated Latin, that's referred to in the Psalms as 'Scuto circumdabit te veritas eius: non timebis a timore nocturno, a sagitta volante in die, a negotio perambulante in tenebris', which means: 'His truth shall compass thee with a shield: thou shalt not be afraid of the terror of the night, of the arrow that flieth in the day, of the business that walketh about in the dark.'

Things that flieth are certainly part of the problem. If Nick Adams's difficulties with sleep are, as we're asked to assume, the result of shellshock – a manly, even heroic reason for developing such a childish ailment as fear of the dark – Fitzgerald by contrast emphasises the absurd smallness of his inciting incident. His insomnia, according at any rate to this deposition, began in a New York hotel room two years previously, when he was attacked by a mosquito. The ridiculousness of this assailant, its comic insignificance, is emphasised by a preceding anecdote, about a friend whose own chronic case of sleeplessness began after being bitten by a mouse. Perhaps both are simply true stories, but I can't help feeling they represent an odd kind of minimisation that Fitzgerald seems compelled to repeat.

If the mosquito incident took place in 1932, then it occurred during a profound downturn in the Fitzgeralds' fortunes. In February Zelda had her second breakdown (the first took place in 1930) and was hospitalised in Baltimore at the Henry Phipps Clinic at Johns Hopkins University. There she produced a novel, *Save Me the Waltz*, which used so much of the same material as *Tender is the Night*, the book Fitzgerald had been working on increasingly frantically for the past seven years, that he wrote to her psychiatrist in a fury, demanding extensive deletions and revisions.

Later that spring he rented La Paix, a big rambling house a little out of town, with a garden full of dogwoods and black gums. Zelda came home in the summer, at first on day release, but they argued increasingly bitterly and in June 1933 she accidentally set the house on fire while burning some clothes or papers in an unused fireplace (an incident, funnily enough, that Tennessee Williams didn't use in *Clothes for a Summer Hotel*, his portent-obsessed, fire-obsessed play about the Fitzgeralds). 'THE FIRE,' Fitzgerald wrote in his *Ledger*, adding '1st borrowing from Mother. Other borrowings.'

They had to move, though Scott insisted they stay on in the smoke-stained house for another few months until he had at long last finished his novel. In the beginning, it was called *The Boy Who Killed His Mother* and was about a man called Francis who falls in with a glittering group of expats and ends up going to pieces and murdering his mother. For some reason Fitzgerald couldn't make this alluring idea fly, and his gruelling failures were at least partially responsible for the insufferable badness of his behaviour at the time.

Later, he realised the story he really wanted to tell was much less fantastical. He turned the novel inside out and made it instead about Dick and Nicole Diver, and how Dick saved his wife from madness and in so doing destroyed himself. It's structured like a see-saw, Nicole rising up with her white crook's eyes, and Dick sinking down into alcoholism and nervous exhaustion, though he once boasted that he was the only living American who possessed repose.

The worst of it comes in Rome, where he goes on a bender after burying his father. He falls in with Rosemary, the young film star he thought he loved, and somehow they get up too close and disappoint each other. Bitter and confused, he goes out to get drunk, whirling

in an immaculate progression of scenes through dances and conversations into arguments, fist-fights and at last to prison. *Tender* isn't by any means as coherent or as streamlined as *Gatsby*, but I can think of very few books that choreograph a downward spiral with such elegant and terrifying precision.

When it was finished, Fitzgerald went with his thirteen-year-old daughter Scottie to a townhouse at 1307 Park Avenue, while Zelda was institutionalised again, this time in the Shepherd Pratt Hospital, where she tried to kill herself at least twice. Little wonder that he described the period in his *Ledger* as 'a strange year of work and drink. Increasingly unhappy', adding in pencil on a separate draft sheet: 'Last of real self-confidence.' The long-awaited publication of *Tender* in April 1934 didn't exactly help matters. It sold better than tends now to be thought, but tenth on the *Publisher's Weekly* bestseller list can hardly be described as the summation of long-cherished dreams.

By November 1934, at around the time 'Sleeping and Waking' was written, he made the seemingly frank admission to his editor, the eternally loyal Max Perkins: 'I have drunk too much and that is certainly slowing me up. On the other hand, without drink I do not know whether I could have survived this time.' This ambivalence, which could be interpreted as a refusal to see alcohol as a cause rather than a symptom of his troubles, is echoed several times in the essay itself. At first he announces his insomnia to be the result of 'a time of utter exhaustion – too much work undertaken, interlocking circumstances that made the work twice as arduous, illness within and around – the old story of troubles never coming singly'. A paragraph or two later, drink is dropped casually into the equation with the throwaway phrase, 'I was drinking, intermittently but generously.'

Intermittently implies that one can stop; *generously* that there is pleasure, perhaps even largesse in the act. Neither was exactly true. For a start, Scott didn't at the time count beer as alcohol. Not drinking might mean avoiding gin, but consuming instead perhaps twenty bottles of beer a day. ('I'm on the wagon,' he says in Tony Buttitta's not wholly reliable memoir of the summer of 1935. 'No hard liquor. Only beer. When I swell up I switch to cokes.') As to liquor, the Baltimore novelist H.L. Mencken, a friend at the time, recalled it made Scott wild, capable of knocking over dinner tables or smashing his car into town buildings.

A few sentences on there's another, more deeply buried clue as to how problematic his drinking had become. He notes that alcohol has the capacity to stop his nightmarish insomnia ('on the nights when I took no liquor the problem of whether or not sleep was specified began to haunt me long before bedtime'), which begs the question of why he doesn't just use it, since the lack of sleep is evidently agonising. The answer comes a couple of paragraphs down: because having a drink means feeling 'bad' the next day. *Bad* is a strangely flat word to use in such a lavishly detailed setting. Just as in Hemingway's story one gauges the intensity of the suffering by the efforts made to avoid it, so this opaque little word must outweigh the considerable, meticulously described horror of insomnia, since if it didn't the equation would surely be reversed.

Instead, when Fitzgerald wakes in the grim midsection of the night he takes a minute pill of Luminal from the tube on his bedside table. While he waits for it to work he walks around the house, or reads, or looks out over Baltimore, which is for the moment hidden by greyish mist. After a time, when the pill has begun to take effect, he climbs back into bed, props the pillow against his neck and tries, like Hemingway, to build himself a counterfeit dream, a runway into sleep.

In the first – God how this made me cringe in sympathy – he imagines something he has been imagining since he was an unpopular boy at boarding school, too small to be much good at sports and too imaginative not to cook up a countervailing fantasy. The team is down a quarterback. He's tossing passes on the sidelines when the coach spots him. It's the Yale game. He only weighs 135 pounds, but in the third quarter, when the score is –

It's no good. The dream's been overused and no longer possesses its consolatory magic. Instead he turns to a war fantasy, but this too sours, ending with the extraordinary line 'in the dead of the night I am only one of the dark millions riding forward in black buses toward the unknown'. What does this even mean? Is he still talking about soldiers, or is it a vision of death itself, as sinister and democratic as those fleets of black buses? It's one of the most nihilistic images he ever set down, though he was always a writer with a real eye for horror.

Both fantasies had their roots in the actual failures of Fitzgerald's youth, when he didn't play quarterback or distinguish himself in the army, or fight in France, or grow tall and dark like the boys he admired, or finish his degree, or even play the lead in the musical comedy he wrote for the Triangle Club, which was his main reason for going to Princeton in the first place. Now, in this never-ending night, the failure of wish-fulfilment topples inexorably into a contemplation of failure itself.

A sense of accumulating terror begins to pour unstoppably on to the page. Walking madly about the house, he hears the cruel and stupid things he has said in the past repeated, magnified in the echo chamber of the night.

> I see the real horror develop over the roof-tops, and in the strident horns of night-owl taxis and the shrill monody of revelers' arrival over the way. Horror and waste –
>
> – Waste and horror – what I might have been and done that is lost, spent, gone, dissipated, unrecapturable. I could have acted thus, refrained from this, been bold where I was timid, cautious where I was rash.
>
> I need not have hurt her like that.
>
> Nor said this to him.
>
> Nor broken myself trying to break what was unbreakable.
>
> The horror has come now like a storm – what if this night prefigured the night after death – what if all thereafter was an eternal quivering on the edge of an abyss, with everything base and vicious in oneself urging one forward and the base-ness and viciousness of the world just ahead. No choice, no road, no hope – only the endless repetition of the sordid and the semi-tragic. Or to stand forever, perhaps, on the threshold of life unable to pass it and return to it. I am a ghost now as the clock strikes four.

And on this horrifying, annihilating thought – the thought of a lapsed Catholic who never quite lost his acute sense that bad deeds were being totted up for punishment – he falls abruptly asleep. He falls asleep and dreams of girls like dolls: sexless, pretty girls with real yellow hair and wide brown eyes. He hears a song, a song that might have drifted in from the dances of his early twenties, when he was newly rich and newly married and all of a sudden golden, riding on the hood of a taxicab along Fifth Avenue at dawn like a man who, in the words of Dorothy Parker, had just stepped out of the sun. He's asleep, deeply asleep, and when he wakes it is to one of those stray lines of dialogue that Chekhov also loved: an interpolation from the inconsequential outer world that Fitzgerald always knew was more powerful than any individual, however rich or charming.

'. . . Yes, Essie, yes. – Oh, My God, all right, I'll take the call myself.'

★

We were coming into Philly. A goods train passed in the opposite direction, the trucks deep brown and rusty brown and iron red, each printed with the legend HERZOG. The woman next to me was eating a hot dog. 'I don't know what'll you'll call him,' she said into her phone. I was listening to Patti Smith singing 'Break It Up', a song I'd last heard while shooting beer bottles in the snow outside a friend's cottage in New Hampshire.

Next time I looked up we were travelling through a wood in which a single species of tree was flowering. Redbud, I figured. The blossom was pink and pinkish red, an absurdly frothy foretaste of spring. We passed a lake with wooden jetties and white wooden houses far out around it. There were three people in a green boat, fishing. Someone was barbecuing on a farm. 'It was cold, I was like oh my goodness,' the woman said. Another wood, set back behind a verge of tawny grass and sedge, the same pink and red tipped trees lit gold by the setting sun. A hawk drifted in circles. Red-tail? I couldn't see it properly against the light, just a silhouette of long-tipped wings.

By the time we reached Baltimore the sun was very low in the sky. There were mountains of shale and aggregate and corrugated iron warehouses with burned and smoke-stained panels. We shuddered by a line of derelict row houses, the bricks caved in like teeth. The shops were boarded up. I saw torn curtains in the windows and between the buildings cherry trees just coming into bloom.

The house where Fitzgerald had written 'Sleeping and Waking', 1307 Park Avenue, was only two blocks from the station, while his last address in the city, a seventh-floor apartment at what's now a hall of residence at Johns Hopkins university, was maybe a mile further north. In December 1935, Hemingway wrote Fitzgerald two letters at this latter address. In the decade since their first meeting, their relationship had undergone a profound transformation. While Fitzgerald had been putting out fires and trying to finish *Tender*, Hemingway had published a bestselling novel, *A Farewell to Arms*, two collections of short stories, *Men Without Women* and *Winner Takes Nothing*, and two non-fiction books, *Death in the Afternoon* and *Green Hills of Africa*. He'd also divorced his first wife, married his second, moved to Key West and had two more sons.

Richer, more successful, more productive and more happily established in his domestic life, Hemingway was less inclined to play nursemaid than bully. In the first of the December letters, he harangued Scott for the way he seemed to be compelled to 'get stinking drunk and do every possible thing to humiliate yourself and your friend' – though it was by no means clear any more that he could be so counted ('I miss seeing you and haveing a chance to talk,' he adds, softening a little).

He was probably referring to a meal in New York two years previously with Edmund Wilson, when Fitzgerald had got so wretchedly drunk he lay on the floor of the restaurant, pretending to be asleep but occasionally emitting needling little remarks or struggling off to the bathroom to be sick. Later, Wilson escorted him back to his room at the Plaza, where he put himself to bed and lay in silence watching his old Princeton friend with 'expressionless birdlike eyes'. The Plaza, which in the looking-glass world he'd created for it was where Gatsby and Daisy and Nick and Tom took a suite one broiling summer's afternoon, to drink mint juleps and edge up on the quarrel that would pull the whole rich tapestry of the novel apart.

In Hemingway's second letter, written a few days later, he takes up the subject of his own insomnia, presumably (Scott's letter is lost) in answer to some similar complaint or plea:

> Non sleeping is a hell of a damned thing too. Have been haveing a big dose of it now lately too. No matter what time I go to sleep wake and hear the clock strike either one or two then lie wide awake and hear three, four, five. But since I have stopped giving a good goddamn about anything in the past it doesn't bother much and I just lie there and keep perfectly still and rest through it and you seem to get about as much repose as though you slept. This may be of no use to you but it works for me.

The stance is characteristic: first the gruff acknowledgement of pain (*hell of a damned thing*), and then the stoic refusal to be touched by it (*it doesn't bother me much*). Of course Hemingway would know exactly how to treat insomnia, just as he knew the correct technique for any number of physical activities, from boxing to fishing to shooting a gun. Of course he wouldn't whimper about it. What was he, some kind of yellow-bellied dog? Fitzgerald, on the contrary, was more than happy to abase himself. After all, he'd opened 'Sleeping and Waking' with the craven line: 'When some years ago I read a piece by Ernest Hemingway called Now I Lay Me, I thought there was nothing further to be said about insomnia,' which is pretty much as low to the floor as you can get without actually rolling under someone's boot. Mind you, it could also be read as an undercut, a quick little feint to the jaw, since what he's actually saying is Hemingway hasn't had the last word, not by any means at all.

I sat back in my seat, turning these different testimonies over in my mind as the train shuttled from day into night. Story, essay, letter: all of them covering the same rough ground. None of them were straightforward. None of them were reliable, at least not in the way that we commonly use that word. Later in the second letter Hemingway invites Scott to come out on his boat and get himself killed. He's kidding, of course. But jokes are resistant to outsiders' eyes. It's entirely possible that you could read it and think you were dealing with a psychopath ('we can take your liver out and give it to the Princeton Museum, your heart to the Plaza Hotel').

Part of the problem was the common or garden issue of literary biography: that while a writer may draw very deeply on events they've experienced or felt, what they make of them is never straightforwardly factual and can't be treated as such. Even an essay – even Scott's confessional 'Sleeping and Waking' – is produced for a fee, and subject to the usual shaping, the usual scissoring and moulding by which real life is converted into art. As for letters, they're written for an even more specific audience, and only rarely give a neutral sense of the whole person. In his *Paris Review* interview, Tennessee Williams touched a little embarrassedly on this, explaining that his letters to Donald Windham, which had recently been published, 'had a great deal of malicious humor in them. I knew he liked that. And since I was writing to a person who enjoyed that sort of thing I tried to amuse him with those things.'

When the writer is also an alcoholic, however, this migration of lived experience becomes entangled with another slippery process: the habit of denial. According to *DSM-IV*, the standard guide for all psychiatric disorders: 'Denial is ubiquitous in alcoholism. Almost all alcoholics deny they have a problem with drinking or rationalize it one way or another. They are often quick to lay blame for their drinking on situations or other people . . . The main impediments to the diagnosis of alcoholism are the denial seen in alcoholics and the low index of suspicion held by most physicians.'

The desire to drink, and the repercussions it has on the drinker's physical, emotional and social selves, are buried beneath excuses, elisions and flat-out lies. An alcoholic might be understood in fact to live two lives, one concealed beneath the other as a subterranean river snakes beneath a road. There is the life of the surface – the cover story, so to speak – and then there is the life of the addict, in which the priority is always to secure another drink. It's not for nothing that the first step of the Twelve Step Programme is simply 'to admit we were powerless over alcohol – that our lives had become unmanageable'. This single step can take a lifetime to face up to, or never be achieved.

In the particular case of the writer who drinks, the ways in which autobiographical material is used requires more than ordinary scrutiny, since what denial means in practice is an inconsistent mass of material that moves bewilderingly between honest accounting, self-mythologising and delusion. *Intermittently. It doesn't bother me much. Generously. Bad.* None of these words could be taken at face value. They were carrying out a secret function, sometimes directly at odds with what was apparently being said. Perhaps this is what made 'Now I Lay Me' so compelling: the sense that one's hook is snagging on something far beneath the bright waters of the surface.

I once came across a statement that captured this tendency towards concealment so precisely it made me reel. I was reading *The Impossible Profession*, Janet Malcolm's short, incisive book on psychoanalysis. During a discussion of the profession's founding principles, she quoted Sigmund Freud on the apparently universal disinclination of humans to be transparent on the subject of sexuality.

> Instead of willingly presenting us with information about their sexual life, they try to conceal it by every means in their power. People are in general not candid over sexual matters. They do not show their sexuality freely, but to conceal it they wear a heavy overcoat woven of a tissue of lies, as though the weather were bad in the world of sexuality.

The weather, it seems, is also bad in the world of alcoholism, and those heavy overcoats are favoured by almost all its inhabitants. And yet, without falling too far into the honey-trap of romanticism, I was also aware of a corresponding desire in all these writers to expose and scrutinise themselves in ways that seemed almost abnormally courageous. Imagine writing that quarterback fantasy down, let alone sending it out for publication. It must have been like undressing in public – though this, it must be admitted, is something else Fitzgerald was prone to do. Once, in the 1920s, he stripped to his underclothes in the audience of a play. Another time, according again to Mencken, he shocked a Baltimore dinner party 'by arising at the dinner table and taking down his pantaloons, exposing his gospel pipe'. But even undressing is an act of concealment sometimes. You can yank down your pants and show off your gospel pipe and still be a man in mortal terror of revealing who you are.

★

We reached DC at 6 p.m. The tannoy sang out, 'This is a smoking stop. This is a rest stop,' and people began to get up and shift their bags. I was starving. I waited till we pulled out again and then went to the dining car. So much for the urban myths. The food was wonderful: steak and jacket potato with sour cream and a chocolate peanut butter pie. After dinner I napped a while and was woken at half past ten by my phone. The woman beside me was still talking. 'Freak it, am I on speakerphone? No, no, hell no. She asked about cutting it and I said no, hell no.' She was massive and dressed all in black, with a hooded leather jacket pulled up over her head. Despite her bulk her voice was very soft and girlish and even after I put my iPod on I could still hear her saying periodically *uh huh, uh huh, uh huh.*

For a long time I stayed just beneath the surface of sleep, and then all of a sudden I dropped into a nightmare, as if I had fallen into one of those deep trout pools in Hemingway's imaginary rivers. An ex-boyfriend – for what it's worth also an alcoholic – was about to hang himself. I woke abruptly, my heart thumping. It was very late. I looked out of the window. We were travelling through hill country. The Blue Ridge Mountains? I guessed from the time that we must be nearing Clemson, the home, according to the itinerary I'd practically memorised, of one of the two men who'd resigned the office of vice president. Christ, I was tired. My skin felt like it'd been put on wrong: back to front or inside out.

Eventually I got up to use the bathroom. The carriage was full of sleeping bodies curled up under coats and blankets. Couples huddled together, their faces almost touching, and I saw a woman feeding a tiny baby, the only other person awake in the whole coach. It's not often, in the privileged West at least, that one finds oneself in a room full of sleepers. Hospitals, boarding schools, homeless shelters: none of them places I much frequented. There was something almost eerie about it, like those Henry Moore drawings of people sheltering in the stations of the London Underground during the Blitz. They lie in rows and could be sleeping, though their boneless immobility makes one wonder if the platform hasn't been turned into an impromptu mortuary.

I went back to my seat and looked out into the dark again. The train was following the trajectory of Fitzgerald's fall through time. After Baltimore he went to Asheville, North Carolina in 1935 to recover from what he was told was an attack of tuberculosis. He stayed in the Grove Park Inn, a vast, rambling resort hotel. It must have been somewhere in that bulk of hills, in the clean thin air that was supposed to be good for damaged lungs. That summer he made friends with Laura Guthrie, a palmist at the hotel who he employed as something between a companion and a secretary. She kept a diary of the season and much of it ended up, by way of an essay in *Esquire*, in *Scott Fitzgerald*, Andrew Turnbull's soft-hearted, thoughtful biography.

Turnbull was the son of Fitzgerald's landlord at La Paix. He was about Scottie's age, and had the advantage over other biographers in not only having known Fitzgerald, but also in having seen what a sweet man he could be, how compassionate and honourable, how exceptionally gifted and hard-working. People used to speak of someone being refined by suffering, and that's the sense one carries away from Turnbull's account. Unlike his subject, he also seems a notably reliable witness, acknowledging the failings without ever seeming to smack his lips.

He describes Fitzgerald in his room at the Grove Park Inn making endless lists 'of cavalry officers, athletes, cities, popular tunes. Later, he realised that he had been witnessing the disintegration of his own personality and likened the sensation to that of a man standing at twilight on a deserted range with an empty rifle in his hands and the targets down.' The images are drawn from Fitzgerald's own account in 'The Crack-up', but somehow have more impact here. At the same time he was trying to write stories to keep his family afloat, though the old easy facility had long since gone. Not cheap, having a wife in hospital, and a daughter in private school. He was also trying to stop drinking, for the sake of his lungs if nothing else, though what that meant in practice was the usual heroic consumption of beer.

After a while he lapsed, returning to hard liquor. One day Laura found him working in his room swaddled in a thick wool sweater over pyjamas, his eyes very red and his legs shaking. He was trying to sweat out the gin, he told her, though since he was still drinking it at the time his method seemed doomed to failure. When he said he'd been spitting blood she called a doctor and he was taken to the local hospital to dry out, something that had already happened several times back home in Baltimore. He stayed five days, and – here's a classic Turnbull detail – finished off the story from the sanctuary of his bed.

At some point that summer he told Laura: 'Drink heightens feeling. When I drink, it heightens my emotions and I put it in a story. But then it becomes hard to keep reason and emotion balanced. My stories written when sober are stupid – like the fortune-telling one. It was all reasoned out, not felt.' It's hard not to read this as justification, particularly since he was already bitterly regretting the necessity of writing so much of *Tender* drunk. Later, walking in the hills above Asheville together, on the way down from Chimney Rock, he changed his mind, saying instead: 'Drink is an escape. That is why so many people do it now. There is Weltschmerz – the uncertainty of the world today. All sensitive minds feel it. There is a passing away of the old order and we wonder what there will be for us in the new – if anything.'

I drink because it improves my work. I drink because I am too sensitive to live in the world without it. There are hundreds more of these excuse notes, but the one that stuck in my mind wasn't by Fitzgerald at all. It came from a letter Hemingway wrote in 1950, almost a decade after Scott had died of a heart attack in Hollywood, midway – how death exposes us – through eating a chocolate bar and reading the Princeton newsletter. Hemingway was writing to Arthur Mizener, the first of Fitzgerald's biographers, and in his self-serving way he said something at once dissembling and true. He was trying to get to the bottom of his old friend's difficulties with life and, almost as an afterthought, jotted down: 'Also alcohol, that we use as the Giant Killer, and that I could not have lived without many times; or at least would have cared to live without; was a straight poison to Scott instead of a food.'

What a bizarre, entangling sentence this is. A food that kills giants; a poison you can't live without. It strikes the same ambiguous, riddling note as the porter's speech in *Macbeth*, which ends, 'much drink may be said to be an equivocator with lechery: it makes him, and it mars him; it sets him on, and it takes him off; it persuades him, and disheartens him; makes him stand to, and not stand to; in conclusion, equivocates him in a sleep, and, giving him the lie, leaves him'.

★

I must have dropped off again, lulled by the rocking motion of the train. Next time I woke the sky was pinkening. There were buildings in the distance, one of them crowned with the ubiquitous Wells Fargo logo. Atlanta. Sure enough, the tannoy crackled into life, announcing: 'Atlanta, Georgia is the station stop. If you'd like to leave the train and get a breath of fresh air please do so. However, please do not leave the platform. Atlanta, Georgia is the station stop.' The clock on the platform said 7:50, though I had a feeling we might have crossed a time zone in the night. I was stiff and hungry and I walked up and down sniffing the air, which seemed already softer, balmier than it had in New York.

When we pulled out again an hour later the pink had given way to gold, and all the trees we passed were green. Green! I'd vaulted winter in the night and landed altogether in the spring. Pigeons were flying in sixes and sevens, their wings splayed back in some sort of joyous display. Beneath them, the outskirts of the city looked abandoned. I took a photograph of a broken-down brick factory. Its roof was gone and the lower windows were boarded up, the upper open to the sky. Next to it was a glasshouse that had been systematically smashed to pieces. In places there was no glass at all: only iron girders covered in kudzu, that insidious vine that despite its foreign origins has become one of the surest visual indicators of the south. Later, I'd see whole hillsides covered in it: dead hay-brown kudzu; nothing else but a few half-strangled pines.

The girl behind me was joking with the conductor. 'We didn't pass DC yet?' she asked. 'Cause we fell asleep a while here,' and he replied: 'You got me there. You got me.' A few minutes later he spotted a boy in a Yankees shirt. 'Yankees! Down in the south? Oh sir, what are you thinking? Switch in quiet for Rebels or something, then you might blend in.' I went to the dining car and got a cobbled-together breakfast: coffee and orange juice, Special K and a slab of cornbread. There was a red carnation on my table, and through the window I could see forests and farmland, white houses with porches and American flags, main streets running parallel to the tracks. We whipped through a pine forest full of little streams muddied sky blue, and those same red-tipped trees I'd seen in Washington.

I was still thinking about what Hemingway had said. *Alcohol was a straight poison to Scott instead of a food*. He'd been spinning the food line for a long time. In a letter written in Key West in August 1935, a few months before that dig at Scott for being *stinking*, he set out what amounts to a credo on the benefits of alcohol.

I have drunk since I was fifteen and few things have given me more pleasure. When you work hard all day with your head and know you must work again the next day what else can change your ideas and make them run on a different plane like whisky? . . . The only time it isn't good for you is when you write or when you fight. You have to do that cold. But it always helps my shooting. Modern life, too, is often a mechanical oppression and liquor is the only mechanical relief.

Right to the end of his life, when he was keeling under the combined weight of depression and alcoholism and a string of head injuries, the complex inheritance of a life lived at full tilt, he maintained an unshakeable belief in alcohol's essential beneficence, its ability to nourish and uplift. All his writing runs brimful, but it's especially noticeable in two of his last books, *Across the River and Into the Trees* and *A Moveable Feast*. The first is a novella published in 1950 about an American colonel in Italy (that tune again), who comes to Venice just after the war to shoot ducks and see the woman he loves, a nineteen-year-old contessa he calls 'Daughter', as Hemingway did all women he liked or desired. It's so gluttonous, so richly populated with people eating and drinking, that one feels a little liverish by the time it's finished. Grappa. Valpolicella. Martinis that are 'icy cold and true Montgomery' and that 'glow happily' all through one's upper body. The Colonel is obsessed with things being true, which is to say deeply anxious that they might be false or fake, and afraid even to voice the thought. His compulsion to apply it to the most unlikely of objects seems to stem from a deep sense of breakage that is ascribed to the war, though it ripples uneasily likewise through Hemingway's letters of the time.

A Moveable Feast, which was published posthumously in 1964 and edited by his widow, is lighter on the palate, even if it shares the same desire to settle scores that marks all Hemingway's late work. It's a memoir of his years in Paris, when he was newly married and had a small son, and spent his days writing in cafés, and eating roast chestnuts and mandarins, or sausages, or watching bicycle races, or skiing in the mountains of the Voralberg in Austria, where things were very simple and very good. There's a line in it somewhere about visiting Gertrude Stein's apartment. She served 'natural distilled liqueurs made from purple plums, yellow plums or wild raspberries. These were fragrant, colorless alcohols served from cut-glass carafes in small glasses.' How delicious these drinks sound: how edible and nourishing.

Not for Scott, that's for sure. He staggers through the book, every bit the card-carrying alcoholic. This toxic version of events begins once again in the Dingo Bar. Scott is drunk and gives an embarrassing speech on Hemingway's writing, while Hemingway sits there wincing and making a silent, spiteful assessment of his appearance: the long, perfect Irish upper lip, spotted lightly with sweat; the Brooks Brothers clothes and phoney Guards tie, the presence of which Scott later furiously denies. He even comments on how short Scott's legs are (two more inches and they'd be *normal*, an unpleasant word that underlines Hemingway's persistent, increasingly crude attempts to make himself the yardstick).

They drink a bottle or two of champagne, and after a while something strange happens. The skin on Scott's face, which has been a little puffy, begins to tighten. Then his eyes sink and he becomes abruptly 'the colour of used candle wax. This was not my imagination. His face became a true death's head, or death mask, in front of my eyes.' Hemingway wants to call an ambulance, but another man in the bar, who knows Fitzgerald, is unconcerned. That's just the way it takes him, he reports, and so they put him in a taxi, though Hemingway remains perturbed.

A few days later they meet again on a terrace at dusk, and sit together watching the people passing by. This time Scott is charming and self-deprecating and good-humoured, and though he drinks two whiskey and sodas there is no sign of the 'chemical change' that overtook him in the Dingo. During their conversation, he proposes a more substantial adventure. He's left a car in Lyon. Would Hemingway like to join him to pick it up and drive it back? It is, of course, the 'great trip' Hemingway described in his letter to Perkins in June 1925.

In this new, retrospective version, the trip is an unmitigated disaster. Scott misses the train, the car has no roof, they while away a morning wasting money on foolishly extravagant food, and inch towards Paris waiting out rainstorms under trees while sharing bottle after bottle of Mâcon. After a few hours, Scott decides he's got pneumonia, and insists they go to a hotel, where he pulls off an excellent impression of Baby Jane, demanding a thermometer be brought and that Hemingway take care of his wife and daughter after he's dead. A few whiskey sours put a stop to this nonsense and soon he's well enough to go out for another delicious dinner, accompanied by a bottle of Montagny, 'a light, pleasant white wine of the neighborhood'.

It's pretty funny, this story, but it leaves a bad taste in the mouth (reading it, John Cheever commented that it was like encountering 'some marble-shooting chum of adolescence who has not changed'). Fitzgerald's inability to tolerate alcohol evidently both puzzled and disgusted Hemingway. Musing in the knowledgeable, faintly medical tones of the doctor's son from Oak Park, Illinois, he wrote:

> It was hard to accept him as a drunkard, since he was affected by such small quantities of alcohol. In Europe then we thought of wine as something healthy and normal as food and also as a great giver of happiness and well-being and delight . . . I would not have thought of eating a meal without drinking wine or cider or beer . . . and it had never occurred to me that sharing a few bottles of fairly light, dry, white Macon could cause chemical changes in Scott that would turn him into a fool. There had been the whisky and Perrier in the morning but, in my ignorance of alcoholics then, I could not imagine whisky harming anyone who was driving in an open car in the rain. The alcohol should have been oxidized in a very short time.

Normal as food. A few lines on, he added crossly: 'Anything he drank seemed to stimulate him too much and then to poison him.'

Very little of this analysis is accurate. For a start, alcohol *is* a poison. One unit contains 7.9 grams of ethanol, a depressant of the central nervous system that has considerable short- and long-term effects on the human body. Large amounts consumed rapidly can cause respiratory depression, coma and death, while a chronic consumption damages the liver and many other organs, among them the peripheral nervous system, heart, pancreas and brain.

He was also mistaken in that pseudo-scientific statement about oxidisation (properly oxidation). Alcohol tends to accumulate in the blood because absorption is more rapid than oxidation and elimination, which occurs largely by way of the liver. His most telling statement, however, concerns Fitzgerald's sensitivity to alcohol. What Fitzgerald was probably experiencing was the abrupt and often profound loss of tolerance that can occur in some cases of late-stage alcoholism. It was, as Hemingway figured, a sinister sign. But what it didn't mean – and what he evidently assumed it did – was that high tolerance was somehow either healthy or desirable.

Hemingway's tolerance to liquor was legendary. In a letter written a few weeks after the Lyon trip he boasted about being able to 'drink hells any amount of whiskey without getting drunk'. What he didn't know, at least back then, is that tolerance is one of the defining symptoms of alcoholism, and that high tolerance tends to be accompanied by profound physical dependence. What's more, recent research suggests low sensitivity and high natural tolerance to alcohol may be contributory factors in the development of the disease.

As the *Merck Manual* puts it: 'There is evidence of genetic or biochemical predisposition, including data that suggest some people who become alcoholics are less easily intoxicated; ie, they have a higher threshold for CNS effects.' Or take John Cheever on the same subject, boasting of his prowess against even the notably hard-drinking Russian writers, the spelling of whose names he never quite mastered: 'I can drink Yevtushenke to the floor and in south-west Russia when the *tamadan* orders *bruddershaft* I can drain my glass again and again without any trouble, while my companions sometimes fall down.'

Looked at through these uncompromising lenses, it's evident that Hemingway, who'd been drunk since he was fifteen and put more

faith in rum than conversation, was engaged in as dangerous a relationship with alcohol as Fitzgerald, even before one takes into account
the staggering volumes he regularly consumed. If you want an example
of someone flat-out denying their own disease, there are worse places
to start than with this sour, comical story, particularly when one
considers the circumstances in which it was written.

As legend has it, *A Moveable Feast* was inspired by a chance discovery.
In November 1956, Hemingway and his fourth wife Mary stayed at
the Ritz in Paris, where he was presented by the management with
two mouldy suitcases, which he'd stored for safekeeping back in 1927
and had completely forgotten to reclaim. According to one of several
accounts written by Mary after Hemingway's death, he was given 'two
small, fabric-covered, rectangular boxes, both opening at the seams . . .
The baggage men easily pried open the rusted locks, and Ernest was
confronted with the blue-and-yellow-covered penciled notebooks and
sheaves of typed papers, ancient newspaper cuttings, bad water colors
done by old friends, a few cracked and faded books, some musty sweat
shirts and withered sandals.'

There are subtle variations to this account. Hemingway's friend A.E.
Hotchner, who also claimed to have been in attendance when the
locks were cracked, only counted one trunk, which 'was filled with a
ragtag collection of clothes, menus, receipts, memos, hunting and fishing
paraphernalia, skiing equipment, racing forms, correspondence and, on
the bottom, something that elicited a joyful reaction from Ernest: "The
notebooks! So that's where they were! Enfin!"' Carlos Baker,
Hemingway's legendarily meticulous biographer, corrects the date of
storage to 1928, the year Ernest and his then wife Pauline Pfeiffer left
Paris for Florida. But despite these minor quibbles, the consensus tends

to be that the discovery of the notebooks inspired the creation of *A Moveable Feast*.

Not everyone agrees, though. In an essay by the alluring title of 'The Mystery of the Ritz-Hotel Papers', the academic Jacqueline Tavernier-Courbin picks away at the suitcase story's discrepancies. It seems from her account that Hemingway, that prodigious letter writer, left no record whatsoever of his momentous discovery, either at the time or after the event. Her suspicion is that the find was a fabrication, designed to give Hemingway a cast-iron excuse for writing about his former friends. Her essay closes with a sidelong quote from his papers:

> It is not unnatural that the best writers are liars. A major part of their trade is to lie or invent and they will lie when they are drunk, or to themselves, or to strangers. They often lie unconsciously and then remember their lies with deep remorse. If they knew all other writers were liars too it would cheer them.

I don't know whether the rusting, rotting suitcases existed or not, but what I'd begun to realise is that the legend concealed a different story about the conditions out of which *A Moveable Feast* arose. In her original essay on the discovery in the *New York Times*, Mary Hemingway mentioned that at the time her husband was 'valiantly following a severely restricted diet which would reduce the cholesterol content of his blood'. Dig a little deeper, though, and it becomes apparent that the writing of the book also took place at a time when Hemingway was coming as close as he ever would to confronting the deleterious effects of alcohol on his own body.

A few weeks before he arrived in Paris in 1956, he'd been diagnosed by a doctor in Madrid, Juan Madinaveitia, with inflammation of the liver as well as raised blood pressure and cholesterol levels. He was put on a low-alcohol diet (five ounces of whiskey and one glass of wine a day, a letter reports), but this failed to achieve the desired effects. A few months later, back at his finca in Cuba, his own doctor prescribed an even stricter regime. From the evidence of his correspondence, it wasn't an easy process. In a letter to his friend Archie MacLeish dated 28 June 1957, he wrote:

> On the corporal front the last examinations didn't turn out as well as hoped . . . So am now cut to one wine glass with the evening meal. Must cut it out entirely it seems but they do not want to treat the nervous system too violently. After all been drinking wine with meals since I was 17 or before. Anyway let's not talk about it. Makes you plenty nervous and very difficult to be with people you don't know . . . The good thing is that if I go through with it (haven't had a real drink for four months when we reach July 4th) and use no wine at all for three more then I will be able to drink wine again and test along to see how much I can drink without damage . . .
>
> Trouble was all my life when things were really bad I could always take a drink and right away they were much better. When you can't take the drink is different. Wine I never thought anyone could take away from you. But they can. Anyway in about ten hours now I am going to have a nice good lovely glass of Marques de Riscal with supper.

By the end of the summer his remarkable constitution had begun to recover and he was drinking again, albeit more moderately than before. Still, I wondered how much the experience of confronting his own dependence informed the attack on Fitzgerald, the bulk of which (three hundred triple-spaced pages, according to Mary, who'd typed it up) was written in that dry year. After all, it's infinitely more comfortable to play doctor than patient. As Fitzgerald had put it years earlier in a rueful letter to Max Perkins: 'I am *his* alcoholic, just like Ring is mine.'

Something else was bothering me, though. What was the line again? 'Also alcohol, that we use as the Giant Killer, and that I could not have lived without many times; or at least would have cared to live without; was a straight poison to Scott instead of a food.' What did he mean by the Giant Killer? I'd read an essay by Alfred Kazin, a critic I admired, which said the giant was America, and the bitch goddess success and that drinking was a way of being better than everybody else. I didn't buy that though; not when I thought of Scott in his room at the Grove Park Inn, a jumper over his pyjamas, sweating out the alcohol almost as fast as he sucked it in. In the *Merck Manual*, the entry on alcoholism observes:

> The maladaptive pattern of drinking that constitutes alcohol abuse may begin with a desire to reach a state of feeling high. Some drinkers who find the feeling rewarding then focus on repeatedly reaching that state. Many who abuse alcohol chronically have certain personality traits: feelings of isolation, loneliness, shyness, depression, dependency, hostile and self-destructive impulsivity, and sexual immaturity.

I thought the giant was all those things, and most of all I thought it was fear. In his sore and tender memoir of his father, *Papa*, Gregory Hemingway recalls lying in bed in the house in Havana in the summer of 1942 with what the doctors thought was polio, at the time a life-threatening disease. At night his father lay beside him on the cot and told him stories about fishing in the trout rivers of Michigan, and about the times he'd been scared as a boy. He recounted a recurring nightmare he'd had in those days, about a furry monster that would get taller every night, 'and then, just as it was about to eat him, would jump over the fence. He said fear was perfectly natural, and nothing to be ashamed of. The trick to mastering it was controlling your imagination.'

Funny, that deep association with trout rivers as an antidote to fear, a thought to console a child who might be frightened in the night. Controlling the imagination is one thing, but what if as well as telling yourself soothing stories you found a substance, a magical substance, that could do it for you, providing what you might call *mechanical relief* from the *mechanical oppressions* of modern life? This is the practice Petros Levounis termed self-medication: the use of alcohol to blot out feelings that are otherwise unbearable.

Here's the rub. As we have seen, a drink, whether it's a nice good lovely glass of wine or whiskey or one of those little yellow plum liqueurs taken in Gertrude Stein's sitting room in Paris, affects the central nervous system, creating that euphoric surge of what Hemingway described as *well-being and happiness and delight*, followed by a diminishment in fear and agitation. But then, as one becomes dependent on it, the brain begins to compensate for alcohol's inhibitory effects by producing an increase in excitatory neurotransmitters. What this means is that when one stops drinking, even for a day or two, the increased activity manifests itself by way of an eruption of anxiety, more severe than anything that came before. As an ADAM report on the subject elegantly explains:

> When a person who is dependent on alcohol stops drinking, chemical responses create an overexcited nervous system and agitation by changing the level of chemicals that inhibit impulsivity or stress and excitation. High norepinephrine levels, a chemical the brain produces more of when drinking is stopped, may trigger withdrawal symptoms, such as increasing blood pressure and heart rate. This hyperactivity in the brain produces an intense need to calm down and to use more alcohol.

What a mess. What a bloody mess. I thought of Hemingway in Paris then, right back in the autumn of 1926. Lying rigid in his bed, listening to the sound of rain. Making up a man who makes up rivers and sits beside them with a rod, fishing for trout and sometimes losing them, until the sun comes up and it is safe to close his eyes.

*

In Alabama the earth was red and there was wisteria in the trees. Somewhere deep in the country the train stopped in a pine forest. It was very quiet. A needle dropped lazily through the warm air. The woman beside me was on the phone again. 'We're stopping at Tuscaloosa. We should be there by one-fifteen I think. I'll see you at three. Okay, baby.' Another goods train came rumbling past, the cars painted once again in those muddy browns and reds.

Between Tuscaloosa and Meridian we ran through uninterrupted miles of forest. The hills were covered in bone-grey timber, split and weatherworn into fantastic shapes. Then open country with cows grazing, or a clearing in the woods filled with corrugated iron houses painted white or mint green or left zinc-grey, with spreading spots of rust the size of dinner plates.

I got talking to the waitress. She was from New York, and had blonde streaks in her hair. 'When we get into New Orleans,' she said, 'we all go out for chicken in a box.' More goods trains came clattering by. There were sand-coloured cows asleep on sand-coloured grass. The other waiter, Michael, stopped by my table and whispered meaningfully: 'Look out for bears.' I kept seeing houses I coveted: houses swagged in wisteria with swings on the porch, or fishing shacks on stilts like the one in *Walk the Line*. There was a graveyard in a field under a big live oak; bunches of dirty silk flowers scattered beneath the headstones.

I looked away, looked back. A clearfell, melancholy as a whale graveyard. It ran on almost as far as the eye could see, with a line of Christmas trees beyond. Next time I turned there was a run of wooden houses beside the tracks. Each had a porch out front, and they were painted in seaside colours – white and cream, tangerine, sky blue. One had green carpet tacked to the steps, another a wreath of artificial pink flowers hung on the front door.

At 18:30 Central Time we pulled into Picayune, Mississippi. The sun was backlighting water towers and gas stations, a train stopped on the opposite track. After that, the land began to change. We were heading into bayou country. The trees grew up out of pools and stagnant streams, casting dark reflections on a surface coloured in a dazzle of silver, blue and pale gold, so that it seemed there were splashes of light all through the forest floor.

The girls behind me were chattering, animated now the journey was coming to an end. 'I know a lot of men who prefer girls' deodorant,' one said. Later they got talking to a little dark-haired boy. 'Do you like to fish? What do you catch, little sir? What was the biggest one? Seven pounds, wow!' All of a sudden there was water outside the windows. We were crossing what I thought at first was the Gulf of Mexico, though days later I realised it must have been Lake Pontchartrain, which breached its banks so cataclysmically in the days after Katrina.

The bridge was very long. The sun was setting now, and because I was on the right I had a ringside seat. Two men in shades were fishing with rods under the tracks. I could see smoke in the distance and then what I thought was an oilrig far out to sea, a grey smudge on the rosy skyline. Or perhaps it was the far coast, because when I looked again there were three or four of them: pleasure domes or palaces. How lovely they looked from here, like the outposts of some floating city. It took a good ten minutes before I realised I was looking at New Orleans, which is after all nearly marine, rising up from the Mississippi Delta, in the swampland between the lake, the river and the Gulf.

By the time we reached the shore the sky was putting on a real show. The clouds were mauve on their upper parts and a mottled orange underneath. There was a violet cast to the shadows and the palms were printed very sharply against the rose-coloured sky. An odd thing happened then. A single starling had appeared, and as it stuttered and weaved through the air I saw a boy standing on the tracks holding a cardboard box in one arm and gesticulating with the other. His mouth was moving, but there wasn't a soul else in sight.

We passed Metairie cemetery. 'How come they don't sink?' the girl behind me asked, and her friend replied, 'They put pilings in. There's like water two feet down there.' Then we were unmistakably on the outskirts of a big city. The freeways were up on piers, and I caught a confused glimpse of red taillights and stop signs. Everyone got up out of their seats and began bustling about in the gangway, reaching down bags and pulling on jackets. The Mexican boy in front still had his Yankees shirt on. I felt a swift uprush of excitement. The air coming in through the open door was warm and damp as taffy. 'If I can be said to have a home,' Tennessee Williams once wrote, 'it is in New Orleans, which has provided me with more material than any other part of the country,' adding to this ambivalent praise Stella's line in *Streetcar*: 'New Orleans isn't like other cities.'

4

A HOUSE ON FIRE

FROM THE MOMENT I STEPPED off the train into the humid air, I found it almost impossible to piece New Orleans together. It wasn't like any place I'd ever visited, though at times it reminded me in its rich confusion of Addis Ababa, especially at night. Up in the Garden District, where the rich people lived in their gingerbread houses, the streets were deserted except for an occasional van, circling at walking pace and branded discreetly with the logo of a private security firm. The air up there smelled bewitchingly of jasmine, but a streetcar ride away, in the French Quarter, it reeked of mule piss and rotting refuse, that clinging, contaminating stench that Blanche DuBois was thinking of when she cried out at the end of *Streetcar*: 'Those cathedral bells – they're the only clean thing in the Quarter.'

I'd never been anywhere so abandoned, so profligate in its desire to pander to the basest impulses of its visitors. On Bourbon Street, I passed beneath a barrage of gleaming signs offering BIG ASS BEERS, FISH BOWLS and CHERRY BOMBS. Everywhere I looked there were photographs of life-sized half-naked women, crouching in their underwear or riding two on a tandem, their hair in schoolgirl plaits.

THE BARELY LEGAL CLUB. BABE'S CABARET. LARRY FLYNT'S HUSTLER. BOURBON STREET BLUES. A girl came pelting past me, screaming, and on the street outside Walgreens a scratch jazz band started knocking out some swing.

I wanted to find the magical city Williams had inhabited in the 1940s. The fall of 1946, say, when he lived in one of the loveliest apartments he'd ever find. It was on St. Peter Street, in a building owned by an antiques dealer, who'd filled it with beautiful furniture, including a long refectory table set up under a skylight. The falling light made the room ideal for morning writing, a habit Tennessee stuck to in even the most dissipated phases of his life. He'd get up just after dawn and come to the table with a cup of black coffee, sitting at his typewriter beside a picture of Hart Crane. Years later, he wrote musingly:

> You know, New Orleans is slightly below sea level and maybe that's why the clouds and the sky seem so close . . . I suppose they are really vapor off the Mississippi more than genuine clouds and through that skylight they seemed so close that if the skylight were not glass you could touch them. They were fleecy and in continual motion . . .

He'd started the play he was working on that winter the previous year, just before the New York premiere of *The Glass Menagerie*. In a letter to his agent Audrey Wood sent in March 1945, he'd mentioned that he was fifty-five or sixty pages into a first draft of a new work about two sisters, 'the remains of a fallen southern family. The younger, Stella, has accepted the situation, married beneath her socially and moved to a southern city with her coarsely attractive, plebeian mate. But Blanche has remained at Belle Reve, the home place in ruins, and struggles for five years to maintain the old order.' Then he reeled through a list of possible titles – *The Moth, Blanche's Chair in the Moon, The Primary Colors* and *The Poker Night* – for what would become, of course, *A Streetcar Named Desire*, the most famous of all his plays.

Under the St. Peter Street skylight he took it out again. He'd been feeling a little dismal all summer: a little ragged and run down. He kept getting spells of abdominal pain, which he'd begun to suspect were the first signs of pancreatic cancer. By December he'd convinced himself he was dying, and so he set about the play with renewed fury, hammering away from early in the morning until two or three in the afternoon, when he'd go out and soothe himself in a bar or at the pool.

His afternoons generally began around the corner in Victor's bar, where he'd order a Brandy Alexander – 'a marvellous drink' – and set the Ink Spots crooning 'If I Didn't Care' on the jukebox. After a sandwich he'd stroll on to the all-male Athletic Club on New Rampart Street, with its spring-fed pool beneath an elegantly balustraded gallery, where one could watch the swimmers or, conversely, enjoy the sensation of being observed.

This amiable, cosmopolitan, unashamedly erotic city worked its way deep into the bones of *A Streetcar Named Desire*. Indeed, it's the first character to be introduced. On the opening page, there's one of those long, lyrical set notes Williams loved to write. He describes a New Orleans of raffish charm and ornamented gables, where the races mingle happily, blues piano pours from all the windows and the sky in May turns 'a peculiarly tender blue, almost turquoise, which invests the scene with a kind of lyricism and gracefully attenuates the atmosphere of decay. You can almost feel the warm breath of the brown river beyond the river warehouses with their faint redolences of bananas and coffee.'

I couldn't smell any bananas, but by evening I'd started to see what he was getting at. Even the curving four-storey frontage of the CVS looked beautiful with its glowing red lines of neon. The streetcar tracks ran between palm trees and the sky got very pale before it went dark. I went into Royal House on Royal Street and had a beer and a plate of grilled oysters. At six o'clock the room was empty. 'It's game night,' the bartender said. 'We'll see how it goes.' When I emerged a jazz wedding was parading past, twirling handkerchiefs and white umbrellas. A second line! The bride had stopped to be embraced by a man in a Mardi Gras costume, purple and green with a jester's hat. His face was painted gold and though I figured he was mostly out to bilk tourists, he still seemed to represent some private essence of the city: a particoloured spirit of misrule.

Blanche came into my mind then. Perhaps it was the white handkerchiefs, or the bride's lace dress. There's something mothlike about her, something feathery and antipathetic to the light. She likes illusions and pretty shadows, and she likes drinking too and for the same reason: to protect her from the harsh glare, the horror of reality, a thing she's too delicate to stand. Practically the first thing she does when she arrives at her sister Stella's apartment on Elysian Fields is toss down half a tumbler of whiskey, to soften what will become an unbearable flare of anxiety. All through the play she keeps sneaking little glasses. 'Open your pretty mouth and talk while I look for some liquor! I know you must have some liquor on the place!' *The music is in her*

mind; she is drinking to escape it and the sense of disaster closing in on her.'
'Well, honey, a shot never does a coke any harm!' 'Why, it's a *liqueur*,
I believe,' to which her one-time beau Mitch replies: 'You ought to
lay off his liquor. He says you been lapping it up all summer like a
wild-cat!' *He* being, of course, Stanley, her nerveless, macho brother-
in-law, who exposes all her secrets, wrecks her romance and then rapes
her on her sister's bed, precipitating her final journey to the lunatic
asylum, dressed in a Della Robbia blue jacket with a seahorse pin on
the lapel.

★

The next morning I'd booked on to what was advertised as the Tennessee
Williams walking tour. It started at 10 a.m., but by then I'd become
suspicious of the vagaries of streetcars and so had risen very early and
come into the Quarter when it was almost empty. On Bourbon Street
men were sluicing down the sidewalks with buckets of soapy water,
swilling away a debris of Mardi Gras beads and cigarette ends and
adding a piercing note of bleach to the omnipresent smell.

The Royal Sonesta was quiet too, the neon sign that spells out
DESIRE a little melancholy in the daylight. I took a seat in the lobby,
a marble box decorated with urns of flowers like the beaks of tropical
birds. There was a bank of telephone booths at the far end of the
room, and this obsolete apparatus added to the sense, familiar to the
over-punctual, of having wandered on to a stage set before the actors
have received their final call.

A man was waiting on a chair beside me, at the centre of an
enormous pile of luggage. He was a little overweight, in an orange

tracksuit and luminous white trainers. After a while a woman with puffy sugar-coloured hair came clicking towards him, snapping contemptuously from thirty feet: 'We're not ready yet. You'll have to wait.' 'Well, why did you make me get my stuff?' he asked, reasonably enough, and she spat back, 'I didn't tell you to get it,' and then turned on her heel and walked away. He fidgeted miserably in the red chair, his big sorrowful face reminding me irresistibly of the weeping baby Alice rescues from the Duchess during her adventures underground.

I wanted to make some consoling remark, but by then the tour had begun to gather in an antechamber by the front desk. The guide, Nora, was a freckled woman with a straw hat toggled emphatically beneath her chin. I was by a good three decades younger than anyone else in the room and as we stepped out on to the street, following her like ducklings, a rangy sixty-something man slid up beside me and said, 'I'm guessing by your accent you're not from these parts.' He had a daughter, he told me quickly, at university in Scotland who was studying the cello. She was predicted a 2:1 and hoped afterwards to go on and train to be a lawyer.

For the next two hours he pottered along beside me down the narrow streets, chatting amiably of this and that – how dirty the Quarter used to be, how it was nearly knocked down in the 1960s, the meaning of the word *graft* and then a long story about Andrew Jackson and his battle against the English, which took place in a meadow edged with live oaks on the outskirts of the city. All the while, Nora was whisking us through the stations of Tennessee's life. We whipped by two of his favourite restaurants: Galatoire's, where Blanche and Stella have dinner while Stanley hosts his poker game, and Arnaud's on Bienville Street. 'Tennessee hated so much to eat alone,' she told us cheerfully, 'that he'd join groups of strangers at their table!'

I had an image of him then in his last decade, when he was very lonely and desperate for companionship: an unsteady figure in shorts and thick glasses, with a laugh you could hear from the other end of the street. Next, she pointed out the site of the old American Hotel on Exchange Place, where he used to come for casual sex. I expected some ripple of disapproval from the group at this, but they were evidently entirely unphased by the notion of picking up a cool hustle and seeing whether the nightingales could be persuaded to sing or not.

On we went, past the apartments he'd once rented, some shuttered and some with those beautifully ornate balconies that are so prevalent in the Quarter. Outside the brick-pink walls of 632½ St. Peter Street we stopped to admire the brass plaque about *Streetcar*. Nora quoted the line about clouds and we all looked up into the clean air, where swifts were sky-writing their unreadable letters against the wisps of cirrus.

Around the corner we stopped again and with the pleased air of a conjurer she produced the keys to 1014 Dumaine Street, the only house Williams owned in the city and the one in which he hoped he'd die. We filed in, past a Great Dane who sniffed warily at my hand before letting me pat her silky head. In the garden there was the spreading banana tree described in *Memoirs*, and a tiny, kidney-shaped pool, a few leaves circling at the bottom.

After that there didn't seem to be anything left to see, and so we drifted in a loose group back to the Sonesta. On the way my companion asked me what I did. When I mentioned I'd written a book about

Virginia Woolf, he thought I was talking about the Albee play and became all of a sudden very animated. His wife had directed it in college and he told me that of the four actors in that long-ago production three had died: one of suicide, one of liver disease and one of what he described as 'a slow suicide of alcohol and drugs'. He looked me in the eye to tell me how very beautiful this woman was, adding with a sculptural gesture of his wrist, 'but large'.

We shook hands twice, but minutes later, when I stopped to write up my notes on the steps of the Supreme Court, I found I had no clear sense of what he looked like. In fact, each time he'd turned to me in the crowd he'd seemed unfamiliar, as if his image had failed to develop in whatever darkroom it is the skull conceals. I was disconcerted by this experience until it occurred to me that it chimed with one of Williams's most passionately held beliefs about people: that they remain resistant to knowing, no matter how long or short the acquaintance.

Before I'd set off on my journey, I'd been reading *Notebooks*, the published version of Williams's diaries, which exist in the form of thirty cheap, undistinguished drugstore pads, kept more or less regularly from 1936 to 1958 and then again from 1979 to 1981. It had been unsettling. On Thursday 30 May 1940, Tennessee wrote in the spiral-bound stenographer's notebook he was using that year: 'Holocaust in Germany – it really does sicken me, I am glad to say,' adding in the next breath: 'Of course my reactions are primarily selfish. I fear that it may kill the theatre.' He continues in this self-interested vein for another paragraph, before breaking off with a thought that evidently pleased him so much he gave it a fresh line: '"*Me*" – that should be an adequate one-word-two-letter entry for every day!'

Experiences of this kind kept recurring. Unlike any other writer's diary that I've encountered, Williams used it only rarely to reflect on the mechanics of his work. Instead, his grand theme (and the published version of *Notebooks* runs, with extensive, meticulous footnotes, at an almighty 868 pages) is the unremitting drama of his physical self, which is to say sex, illness, anxiety and self-medication in the form of alcohol, Seconal and the sedatives he called *pinkies*, though from the 1960s onwards speed injections also take a role.

The difference between this voice and the voice of the plays and essays is so profound that at times it's hard to believe they belong to the same person. One is large-hearted and attentive to human pain; the other self-interested, his attention directed not out into the world but inward, illuminating as if by torchlight the smallest shifts in his own person, from the condition of his stools to the disgust he experiences after ejaculation.

It's discomfiting to encounter this other Williams, just as it's discomfiting to come across the punch-drunk, bullying Hemingway of the later letters, or to glimpse the welter of misery that floods John Cheever's diaries. Because it's so evidently raw, one tends instinctively to believe this sort of material represents a writer's truest, most secret self: the kernel of their being. I'm not sure, though, that it's anything like such a simple matter. 'So I turn to my journals. I always do when things look bad. That's partly why I seem such a morbid guy in these journals,' Williams wrote on 16 March 1947: a statement that ought to stand as a warning that with any of this type of material one has entered no more than a single room in what might be called the mansion of the self.

A version of this thought crops up as a stage direction in *Cat on a Hot Tin Roof*, the greatest of all Williams's plays and the one he turned to after *Streetcar*. *Cat* is, like a classical tragedy, set in a single location over the course of a unified stretch of time: a bed-sitting room in a plantation home in the Mississippi Delta on the night of Big Daddy's sixty-fifth birthday. Big Daddy is a cotton millionaire, the owner of 'twenty-eight thousand acres of the richest land this side of the valley Nile'. He believes he's just been given the all-clear from cancer, but in fact he's riddled with it ('it's spread all through him and it's attacking all his vital organs including the kidneys and right now he is sinking into uraemia'). Over the course of the evening, the truth leaks out, both about his illness and about the causes of his son's drinking.

Brick is a former pro-football player and has, as his wife Maggie puts it, 'fallen in love with Echo Spring'. His ankle's in a cast, after jumping hurdles drunk on the Glorious Hill High School track the night before. When the curtain rises on the first act, he's in the shower. Maggie rushes in, rattling out a torrent of anxiety about his drinking and their estrangement and Big Daddy's will and the manipulative presence of Brick's brother Gooper and his wife Mae. As for Brick, he's off some place in his head alone, almost entirely oblivious to the drama gathering in the big house.

In the second act, the family members who have crowded into Brick's room disperse, and he and Big Daddy are left alone together. During their fraught conversation, Big Daddy suggests, tentatively and with some trepidation, that his son's relationship with his best friend Skipper might not have been entirely *normal*. Brick responds with a swift disavowal but his detachment has been broken for the first time in the play. At this pivotal moment, the playwright himself bursts on to the page with the longest of the many italicised stage directions that exist between the lines of dialogue.

The thing they're discussing, timidly and painfully on the side of Big Daddy, fiercely, violently on Brick's side, is the inadmissible thing that Skipper died to disavow between them. The fact that if it existed it had to be disavowed to 'keep face' in the world they lived in, may be at the heart of the 'mendacity' that Brick drinks to kill his disgust with. It may be the root of his collapse. Or maybe it is only a single manifestation of it, not even the most important. I'm trying to catch the true quality of experience in a group of people, that cloudy, flickering — fiercely charged! — interplay of live human beings in a thundercloud of common crisis. Some mystery should be left in the revelation of character, just as a great deal of mystery is left in the revelation of character in life, even one's own character to himself.

He sounds, particularly in that last emphatic sentence, as if he's trying to convince someone of something. In fact, this printed declaration represents an overspill from a more private argument. From the moment he read the first draft, Williams's director and long-term collaborator Elia Kazan loved *Cat on a Hot Tin Roof*, but he was unconvinced by the character of Brick, the married alcoholic who, as another stage direction has it, possesses the 'charm of that cool air of detachment that people have who have given up the struggle'. In Williams's original version, Brick doesn't change in his disinclination to love his wife or show more than the most grudging attention to his family, even when he learns his father's dying of cancer. His energy is directed exclusively towards his own personal mission, which is to drink enough Echo Spring to bring on the *click*: the moment when all the agitating noise in his head goes blessedly to silence.

On 29 November 1954, Williams wrote miserably in his diary: 'Got a 5 page letter from Gadg elucidating, not too lucidly, his remaining objection to the play. I do get his point but I'm afraid he doesn't quite get mine. Things are not always explained. Situations are not always resolved. Characters don't always "progress".' Two days later, in his suite at the Beverly Hills Hotel, he elaborated this gut instinct into an impassioned letter, in which he sets out in detail his thoughts about both Brick and the alcoholic character in general:

> I 'buy' a lot of your letter but of course not all . . . To be brief: the part I buy is that there has to be a reason for Brick's impasse (his drinking is only an expression of it) that will 'hold water'.
>
> Why does a man drink: in quotes 'Drink'. There's two reasons, separate or together. 1. He's scared shitless of something. 2. He can't face the truth about something. – Then of course there's the natural degenerates that just fall into any weak, indulgent habit that comes along, but we are not dealing with that sad but unimportant category in Brick. – Here's the conclusion I've come to. Brick *did* love Skipper, 'the one great good thing in his life which was true.' He identified Skipper with sports, the romantic world of adolescence that he couldn't go past. Further: to reverse my original (somewhat tentative) premise, I now believe that, in the deeper sense, not the literal sense, Brick *is* homosexual with a heterosexual adjustment: a thing I've suspected of several others, such as Brando, for instance . . . he's the nearest thing to Brick that we both know. Their innocence, their blindness, makes them very, very touching, very beautiful and sad. Often they make fine

artists, having to sublimate so much of their love, and believe me, homosexual love is something that also requires more than a physical expression. But if a mask is ripped off, suddenly, roughly, that's quite enough to blast the whole Mechanism, the whole adjustment, knock the world out from under their feet, and leave them with no alternative but – owning up to the truth or retreat into something like liquor . . .

You know, paralysis in a character can be just as significant and just as dramatic as progress, and is also less shop-worn. How about Chekhov?

The letter ends: 'This play is too important to me, too much a synthesis of all my life, to leave it in hands that aren't mine.' It's possible that this last comment is meant as a debater's flourish, a way of winning Kazan's sympathy. I don't think so, though, since it's also reiterated in the published version of the play, which opens with a note entitled 'PERSON – TO – PERSON' that begins: 'Of course it is a pity that so much of all creative work is so closely related to the personality of the one who does it. It is sad and embarrassing and unattractive that those emotions that stir him deeply enough to demand expression . . . are nearly all rooted, however changed their surface, in the particular and sometimes peculiar concerns of the artist himself.'

★

Even when a writer makes a statement as frank and unequivocal as this, there are those who will resist it. The interrelation of life and art makes certain sensibilities deeply uneasy, perhaps out of embarrassment and perhaps from a desire to see art as separate from the contaminating muck of personal concerns. Inevitably, this uncomfortable subject came up at the Tennessee Williams Scholars' Conference, which took place a few days after I arrived in the city. The conference ran in tandem with the Tennessee Williams Festival, which had been in existence a quarter century and was that year celebrating the centenary of Williams's birth.

All week the real city, whose material is crumbling green and pink plaster, was infiltrated by the more plastic city of the plays. Almost every hotel and theatre in town was hosting some sort of event. There were performances and lectures, and a competition in the street in which 'contestants vie to rival Stanley Kowalski's shout for "STELLAAAAA!!!" in the unforgettable scene from *A Streetcar Named Desire*'.

One afternoon, as I walked past the open windows of the Sonesta, I saw Carroll Baker eating her lunch. Decades earlier she'd played the nubile, thumb-sucking lead in the film *Baby Doll*. Now her hair was white-blonde, not gold, and her perfect face a little swollen. The night before I'd heard her speak in Le Petit Theatre about her long friendship with Tennessee. In the course of the evening she described an apartment he kept in Manhattan, which was preposterously tiny even by the standards of that hive-like city. 'Why don't you move?' she asked, and he pointed out a little vine of night-blooming jasmine that had worked its way up to the window. She said other things too, but that was the one I wrote down in the dim light of the upper circle, because it seemed so touching that a man who felt almost perpetually lonely and out of place, who believed he could maintain his meteoric rise only by vast and unremitting effort, might stay in an apartment so claustrophobically tiny that the elevator gave him panic attacks, just because he felt kinship with a plant.

The Scholars' Conference took place at the Williams Research Center on Chartres Street. I got there early too, and found myself among a chattering crowd of men in sand-coloured blazers, their hair subject to the sort of damp-combing that made me nostalgic for England. Papers were being presented on a diversity of topics, from 'The Whoredom of a Loveless Marriage in Williams' Plays' to the role of Italian culture in *The Rose Tattoo*.

The speaker I'd come to hear was Dr. Zeynel Karcioglu, a Turkish-American ophthalmologist who had in the years of his retirement become preoccupied by the role of illness in Williams's work. His paper 'Diagnosing Tennessee: Williams and his Diseases' began by discussing the litany of health problems he'd suffered from since child-hood. Some were the delusions of a hypochondriac, but among the verifiable conditions were diphtheria, a sclerotic heart valve, gastritis, dyspepsia, the old injury to the left eye, genital warts and a benign fatty lump in his nipple, which, predictably enough, he told the press was breast cancer.

'Williams,' the doctor said, 'was very knowledgeable about illness, though it was hard to tell if he was really experiencing symptoms or imagining them,' adding that his interest in the afflictions of the body informed much of his work. His next statement was more controver-sial. He raised the possibility that the chaotic structure of the late plays in particular might be due to brain damage caused by alcohol addic-tion: that Tennessee's habit of using broken sentences and incomplete dialogue could suggest a form of aphasia, an acquired language disorder that is seen in chronic alcoholics and which manifests itself as a difficulty with word retrieval and sentence creation.

The conference began to buzz. After Dr. Karcioglu had finished a man raised his hand and when called upon announced firmly: 'Aphasia is *the* disease that was discovered by the early twentieth-century avant garde – the Dadaists, Samuel Beckett.' Another added: 'The focus on pathology devalues his artistry. The use of aphasia is a factor in Southern speech that he was trying to replicate. He was a very conscious artist.' Dr. Karcioglu accepted these possibilities, conceding that it wasn't implausible that Williams was aware he was suffering from aphasia and purposely exposed it in his work, forcing readers to see 'his own inner world of confusion'. He added that his hypothesis needed checking, perhaps by quantifying incomplete sentences in the plays of the 1940s and 1950s with those written more recently.

As it happens, the idea that alcohol might be affecting his ability to write had occurred to Williams. Waking in a Madrid hotel room early one October morning in 1953, he wrote in his black-backed notebook:

> Looked through the new play script and was so disheartened that I closed it and prepared to descend to the bar. What most troubles me is not just the lifeless quality of the writing, its lack of distinction, but a real confusion that seems to exist, nothing carried through to completion but written over and over, as if a panicky hen running in circles.
>
> Some structural change in my brain? An inability to think clearly and consecutively? Or simply too much alcohol?

The prospect of returning to America with this defeat in
my heart which only drink can assuage is a mighty dark
one.

If I'd seen this quote in isolation I would have assumed it referred to
one of the very late works – *In the Bar of a Tokyo Hotel*, say, or *Clothes
for a Summer Hotel*. Both possess a panicked, indistinct quality, as if the
writer is no longer capable of producing a consecutive sequence of
thoughts. Instead, the play he's describing is *Cat*, which despite its
structural near-perfection was from the moment of its conception
deeply entangled with Tennessee's drinking.

Like *The Glass Menagerie*, *Cat* had its origins in a short story: 'Three
Players of a Summer Game', which was published in the *New Yorker*
in November 1952. It anticipates the later play in the identity of two
characters: Brick Pollitt, a Mississippi planter with a drinking problem,
and his wife Margaret – though all she can be said to share with
Maggie the Cat is her exceptional vitality.

The story has about it a wistful, distanced quality that makes one
think of Fitzgerald. Brick throws raucous, liquored parties that resemble
in their confusion the night in *The Great Gatsby* when Tom gets drunk
and breaks his mistress's nose. Brick himself is a drinker in the gentle,
self-deceiving mould of Dick Diver, and as in *Tender is the Night* his
demise is associated with a corresponding gain in potency for his wife.
He lectures the workmen repairing his house on his strategies for
getting sober. After a while, he drifts back indoors and stays there half
an hour. 'When he came back out, it was rather shyly with a sad and
uncertain creaking of the screen door pushed by the hand not holding
the tall glass.'

The play that grew out of this melancholy material seems from the uncertain evidence of the journals to have been started at some point in 1953, at a time when the casual observer might have been forgiven for thinking Tennessee among the luckiest men alive. In 1948, he'd won a Pulitzer Prize for *A Streetcar Named Desire* and a few months later had re-encountered Frank Merlo. In those early years, Williams and the Little Horse spent a good deal of their time in Europe, drifting around Mediterranean cities and resorts. Dinner with Noel Coward, Gore Vidal or Peggy Guggenheim, followed by white or half-white nights with the beautiful street boys of Madrid, Amalfi, Rome. Happy days, one might think; but the Williams who sat up late drinking Scotch and scribbling in his journal, sometimes in the first person and sometimes in an admonitory second, was not by any means awash with the pleasures of la dolce vita.

The first reference to *Cat* in the notebooks is the disheartened one from October 1953 that describes the lifeless quality of the writing. (The following year, in a letter to his agent, he pinpoints its origins as 'the play that threw me into such a terrible state of depression last summer in Europe, I couldn't seem to get a grip on it'.) Still, he kept slogging away, juggling the script with edits to *Baby Doll*. With the advance of winter, he moved from Venice to Rome and then to Granada and on over the sea to Tangier, where he wrote in pencil in his looping hand:

> The sun shines over the straits of Gibraltar as I sit impotently before the portable Royal and my glass of Scotch, and a blank white wall.

By November he'd had enough of this fugitive existence. He flew back to America, arriving in New York in time to attend Dylan Thomas's funeral (an event John Berryman also attended). A month later disaster struck. On the night of 27 December he woke with a frighteningly painful rectal swelling, and within two days was installed in a shabby little hospital on the outskirts of New Orleans. 'All hell is descended on me,' he wrote in the small hours of the first morning, 'retribution for all my misdoings and the things undone.' Within an hour he'd called the nurse and had a hypodermic injection of morphine 'on top of 3 Seconals and several whiskies. Perhaps a mistake but I'm beginning to feel like Miss Alma's water lily on that chinese lagoon' – a reference to the intoxicated heroine of his recent play, *Summer and Smoke*.

The next day he was transferred to another hospital, where he waited miserably for Frank to visit. The operation initially offered was twice postponed, and the next few nights were purgatorial. 'If I could just give myself to the steady peace of the rain,' he wrote hopelessly in his notebook. 'Now I am doing that, giving myself to the steady peace of the rain,' adding as an afterthought: 'I guess fear must be the most interesting of all our emotions. We engage in it so much.'

This terror, which was intensified by the suspicion yet again that he was suffering from cancer, spread through *Cat on a Hot Tin Roof* like smoke from a fire. There'd been no Big Daddy in 'Three Players of a Summer Game', though there was a doctor who succumbed to a brain tumour (described, horribly enough, as a 'fierce geranium that shattered its pot'). Still: no pain like fox teeth in the gut; no terror of extinction, or that compulsion to truth-telling that comes when death is very close.

The promised operation never took place. After a few days the symptoms faded and Williams was allowed to return home to Key West. For a couple of months he was bothered only by what he called his 'cardiac neurosis', but then in March he developed a troubling numbness in his feet. He described this condition as dropsy, though his physician informed him uncompromisingly that he was suffering from early peripheral neuritis 'induced partly by liquor' – a condition caused by the adverse effects of alcohol on vitamin B12 absorption. His reaction to this diagnosis was once again weighted towards denial. 'Of course I would love to believe the good doctor but I don't quite believe him,' he wrote: a statement that indicates how hard it is to realise agency or accept the deleterious consequences of one's own behaviour.

Still, he kept on moving. In New Orleans he experienced yet more palpitations while finishing a first act of *Cat* that seemed disappointing and somehow low voltage. He suffered from claustrophobia and sleeplessness, which he medicated sometimes with glasses of milk as well as those old faithfuls, Seconal and Scotch. On a visit to New York, his dear smelly dog Mr. Moon died in the night, giving a single heartbreaking cry, like the goose in Chekhov's story. In Spain he read *Sons and Lovers* and watched the bullfights he'd later discuss with Hemingway, whose book *Death in the Afternoon* he read admiringly that summer. In Rome it was noisy and he became anxious and very tanned. While staying in the city, on the morning of 12 July 1954, he tried to get some larger perspective on his troubles.

Here's the dilemma, let's face it. I can't recover any nervous stability until I am able to work freely again, and I can't work freely until I recover a nervous stability.

Solution? – Much less clear.

Just not working doesn't solve the matter for the need to work, the blocked passion for it, continues to tear me inside.

Working against exhaustion bit by bit wears me down even further.

Then is there no way out? None except through some bit of luck – another name for God. Of course it is true that I go through these cycles repeatedly, constantly, but now the downward curve is fiercely relentless and the little upturns are very little indeed, relatively insignificant, little circles inside a great descending arc which is still descending.

On it went: up, then down, and down again. A loving phone call with Frank, from one European city to another. A panic attack in a cinema, stemmed when he staggered into a bar, pale and terrified, and knocked back two double Scotches in quick succession. A few weeks later, in Sicily, he sat in his friend Franco's bar till closing time and then walked with him down the main street, reassured by the music drifting from a nearby club. But when he turned for home alone, the club had closed and panic rose in him as he strode faster and faster down a road that seemed to stretch on endlessly, his chest constricted and his breath coming in gasps. On the hill up to the sanctuary of the Hotel Temio it reached a climax, and he stopped and grabbed a leaf of wild geranium and looked up at the stars, which he'd heard somewhere were supposed to be an antidote to fear. His lungs were whistling and when he got into his room and took a Seconal he wrote: 'someday, I fear, one of these panics will kill me'.

After that, there's only one more European entry, written the next morning. Then there's a gap before the journal is resumed in America on Saturday, 27 November. Much of this entry and the longer one that follows the next day were written on aeroplanes, which filled Williams with such unholy terror he had to knock himself almost senseless with alcohol and drugs. His condition at Tampa airport, a few legs into the arduous journey from Key West to L.A., was not exactly good to start off with. In recent days, he'd been experiencing:

> A *double* neurosis, 2-barrelled, the fear of speech, and the cardiac neurosis (augmented by fairly frequent palpitations, 'jolts', and general anxiety which made it necessary to carry a flask of whiskey with me wherever I went). Wakings at night, usually after 3 hours sleep and oppressive dreams, with that feeling of being near panic, sometimes just going downstairs for a drink seemed like a challenging, perilous undertaking.

He carried on writing aboard the plane, recording every flinch in mood. ('After all, what older friend than anxiety do I have? Or should I say acquaintance? Yes, I should!') Then the pilot announced the length of the flight. This was a nasty shock, since Williams had forgotten to factor in the time difference. He went to the men's room with a glass of water and his flask, two Seconals in his coat pocket, and continued his diary there. In it, he promised himself a haircut in New Orleans, and trade: 'The best I can get! And I promise myself I will get some. Okay? Sure.' The impression is of a man so desperate for reassurance he's split himself in two.

The next morning, after the promised night in the Quarter, he boarded yet another plane, priming himself with two and a half martinis before take-off. The flight was very turbulent, and he went into the lavatory again to drink, recording from inside his regret at having forgotten to bring any books by Hart Crane, the writer he most loved. Mid-afternoon found him grounded again, this time in the lounge at Dallas airport. 'I wonder if they serve liquor in El Paso? or sell it? Not sure my flask will serve 5 more hours,' he asks anxiously, before recording the answer: no.

Hurtled into the air once more, he returned to his old refuge: 'for a nip of my most precious elixir, which must be husbanded most prudently now'. He gazed at his face in the mirror, the 'old puss', and then out at the mountains visible from the window against the setting sun. At last they reached Los Angeles. 'Never again take a plane without a *full bottle* on me!' he instructed himself, adding: 'See you later – after 2 martinis at the airport bar, I trust.' Two days later, ensconced in the Beverly Hills Hotel, he got up and wrote that impassioned letter to Elia Kazan, which asks 'Why does a man drink?', and answers, with a kind of reflexiveness that should be impossible: '1. He's scared shitless of something. 2. He can't face the truth about something.'

In 'Three Players of a Summer Game', the first Brick makes a telling statement. 'A man that drinks,' he says, 'is two people, one grabbing the bottle, the other one fighting him off it, not one but two people fighting each other to get control of a bottle.' I'm not sure they're always so active, but the idea that a drinker contains two people is a way of approaching what is otherwise baffling or miraculous: the fact that this listing man locked in the lavatory three thousand metres above the mountains of Southern California, lost in contemplation of his own image, could retain in some unobliterated part of himself the necessary clarity to set down on paper what he saw there, which is to say the self-deceiving nature of the alcoholic. How else to explain that in the midst of such confusion and self-harm, he was able to produce a play like *Cat on a Hot Tin Roof*, with its uncompromising portrayal of the drinker's urge to evade reality?

You can know, and you can not know, all at once. You can vote for truth and still let what Maggie the Cat once described as a fire in a locked house rage inside yourself, unchecked and all-consuming. Put it down to the drinker's doubleness, like the first Brick said, or else to something Williams wrote in another letter that winter, while sitting at his desk in Florida: 'the startling co-existence of good and evil, the shocking *duality* of the single heart'.

★

I was beginning to feel a little dizzy. The conference room was very humid. Dr. Karcioglu had finished now and when the conversation turned to immigrant experiences in *The Rose Tattoo* I slipped out and went round the corner to the Hotel Monteleone. There's a famous bar there called the Carousel, which revolves around a central axis, wobbling as it goes. Tennessee used to drink there and so too did William Faulkner and Ernest Hemingway and Williams's cherubic sometimes-friend and sometimes-enemy Truman Capote. I ordered a lime daiquiri, and I sat on my own in the midday gloom and drank it very slowly.

People don't like to talk about alcohol. They don't like to think

about it, except in the most superficial of ways. They don't like to examine the damage it does and I don't blame them. I don't like it either. I know that desire for denial with every bone in my body: capitate, hamate, pisiform and triquetral. It is that intimate a part of me; that deeply implicated in my articulation, the architecture of my being. When I think back to my childhood what I see most often is a set of brass monkeys my granny kept on her mantelpiece, their hands clamped down over eyes, ears and mouth. *Hear no evil, see no evil, speak no evil*: the holy trinity of the alcoholic family.

I first read *Cat on a Hot Tin Roof* when I was seventeen, at the sixth-form college to which I'd begged to be allowed to go. It had been built in the 1960s, an unprepossessing snake of low-lying buildings, with a glassed-in cafeteria and an overspill of portakabins by the rugby pitch. The English A-level class met in an upstairs corner room that looked down into a little courtyard. It was autumn and before class started I'd sit on the radiator with my nose to the window and watch the rain sluicing crisp packets and drinks cartons towards the drains.

We read the play out loud and I still remember now the pleasure of speaking Maggie's lines. *One of those no-neck monsters hit me with a hot buttered biscuit. I wish you would lose your looks. It would make the martyrdom of Saint Maggie a little more bearable. You look so cool, so cool, so enviably cool.* The boy who played Brick had dark hair and pale skin and was going to be an actor. All his movements were economical and graceful, and it was apparent, though never publicly discussed, that he was gay.

The play poured out into the ugly little room, moving very quickly, like something that had ruptured and could no longer be contained. Brick limped back and forth to the liquor cabinet, wearing pyjamas and using a crutch. Maggie pushed on her bracelets and made her tough, gambler's bid for a child, and in the Broadway version of the final act Brick went along with her, and in the original he remained ambivalent and unconvinced. I remember loving the lines of direction between the dialogue, which seemed so much more fiercely felt and honest than anything I'd ever read.

In the copy I was given then, and which I've now owned half my life, I scribbled a list in royal blue Quink ink with what would have been a cheap fountain pen with silvery teeth-marks at its end. MENDACITY, it reads. ILLUSIONS/REALITY. ILLNESS/CURE. On the title page I added in Biro another note that said: *false cures versus real cures. Real involve spiritual/emotional growth.* Dear God. Hardly any wonder I latched on to the play so strongly. It might as well have been a mirror for the situation I'd only just escaped.

In 1981, when I was four, my father left and shortly afterwards my mother met a woman through the personal column of *Time Out.* Diana came to live with us in our house on the common in Chalfont St. Peter, a stone's throw from the convent where I went to school. She was warm, vivacious and funny, with the upturned collars and quick-fire charm of Cagney from *Cagney and Lacey.*

She joined our household, which at the time comprised my mother, my sister, our Swedish au pair and two cats, Catkin and Pussy Willow, both of whom came to sticky ends. She was an alcoholic, though none of us knew that then. After a while – three years, four years – we moved to Hampshire, staying temporarily in a rented bungalow on the outskirts of a housing estate. It was the ugliest house I'd ever seen. There was a field outside with a copse of trees and every day I thought about climbing the barbed wire and going out there with a book and a flask. It snowed more heavily that winter than it had for years. One day my cat disappeared and much later my mother admitted hitting her while reversing the car on the icy drive.

At school everyone hated me and my plummy voice. I read constantly, burying myself in *Little Women* and pony stories from the 1930s. I'd never been an especially happy child, but this degree of isolation was not something I had any idea how to deal with. Then we moved again. All the houses we had after we came south were new, some of them surrounded by raw seas of mud that had until recently been open fields. This one was called Tall Trees. It had oaks in the garden, though later they were blown down in the storm of 1987. There was a huge glass window above the front door and in the morning we'd sometimes find the corpses of small birds that had flown into it, mistaking the glass for sky.

In this house, alcohol began to take on a physical presence in our lives. Diana was often drunk then; often enraged. At night, over dinner, there'd be raised voices, and the arguments would continue rumbling into the small hours, while my sister and I listened, our stomachs tight with panic. It wasn't just the fights that frightened me, but rather the terrifying sense that someone was no longer inhabiting consensual reality.

Years later, I recognised the climate of that period when I first read *Brideshead Revisited*. Charles Ryder describes the effect of his beloved Sebastian's drinking on the household in which he lives in terms like Maggie's:

> . . . the subject was everywhere in the house like a fire deep in the hold of a ship, below the water-line, black and red in the darkness, coming to light in acrid wisps of smoke that oozed under hatches and billowed suddenly from the scuttles and air pipes.

Sebastian Flyte, who uses alcohol as a way of escaping – what, exactly? The terrible weight of his family? He suckles like an infant, the bottle as much of a nursery prop as the bear he totes around. Drunk, he even talks like a child. 'Been drinking whisky up here. None in the library now party's gone. Now party's gone and only mummy. Feeling rather drunk. Think I better have something-on-a-tray up here. Not dinner with mummy.'

I think of that line about the fire often, because it describes so exactly the house where I grew up: the atmosphere of the air, the condition of the rooms. I think sometimes I can still smell smoke, perhaps on my skin or deep in the fabric of an old sweater. It was the tail end of the 1980s, the era of Section 28, when the Local Government Act forbade councils from 'promoting the teaching in any maintained school of the acceptability of homosexuality as a pretended family relationship'. Towards the end of that period I remember looking through an album with a friend and panicking because I knew there was on the final page a photograph of my mother and Diana with their arms around each other. We weren't supposed to tell anyone about the practicalities of the family setup. Keeping someone else's secrets is a dreadful burden, though I understand why it was necessary. I still remember the rush of terror at the thought of her passing the information back to the girls at school. I knew the sort of things they'd say, the poisonous whispers – *lezza*, *gaylord* – and I suppose I must have had a sense that there were larger, more substantial repercussions to be had.

The crisis came – when? I must have been eleven or twelve. Late eighties, Thatcher still clinging on. What I remember – though this memory is as blurred as if I too am looking through a glass – is waking to the sound of screaming. Each time, it was like witnessing a possession.

Shakespeare spotted that. When Iago gets Cassio drunk, he falls into the sort of quarrel that is wholly foreign to his nature. The next day, sobered, he cries out in shame and horror: 'O God, that men should put an enemy in their mouths to steal away their brains! That we should with joy, pleasance, revel, and applause transform ourselves into beasts!'

The hall in that house was large, with an open flight of stairs and a gallery with a railing, so that you could look down to the front door. In my memory of this scene I'm in pyjamas, huddled on the landing with my sister. Diana is on the stairs, screaming curses at us all. Then, abruptly, the police are there, and they take her and our air rifle into custody – the only detail from that night that has stayed in any way clear to me.

After they leave we pack overnight bags and run away. We stay in a bed and breakfast on Southsea seafront, and at some point the next day, presumably while we're at school, my mother finds us another house: our seventh in ten years. It's on an estate near Portsmouth, already furnished, the walls thin as paper. That's where we start our lives again, among a stranger's books, a stranger's discarded things.

★

What the hell was I doing in a bar? I paid the check and took a streetcar back to my hotel. But the combination of the drink and the heat and the things I'd been thinking conspired to fuddle me so badly I got on the wrong line. The car was very busy, and among the passengers there was a small family: a mother and father with two shaven-headed boys, maybe three or four years old, with open sores and abrasions on their faces that looked like impetigo. They were dirty

and unkempt, both trailing reins. The father was on heroin, his eyes
drooping and vacant, his face and arms covered with a scrollwork of
tattoos. One of the boys cuddled into his lap, though even from where
I sat I could feel the coiled violence of his presence.

I saw many things in New Orleans that week. I saw a cemetery
hidden away amid flowering backstreets, where sweetpeas and roses
flourished among the jasmine and hibiscus. There were smashed
kumquats on the sidewalk and a dense carpet of weeds had grown up
between the graves. It was composed of many different plants, among
them scarlet pimpernel, melilot, wild geranium, yellow vetch and banks
of clover. There were no bees, and on either side of the path I saw
great marble mausoleums and plaster tombs, some broken open to
reveal interiors that resembled bread ovens, with two brick shelves
lying empty in the dark. The names on the headstones were mostly
German: *Koenig, Tupper, Faulks, Vose* and *Scheu*.

I saw a bride in the soft evening light outside Popeye's Chicken and
Biscuits, red-headed and very pretty, grinning across at the passers-by and
clutching a bouquet of creamish flowers. I saw a man painted blue
accosting a woman in a wheelchair. I saw an enormous grey-pink mushroom cloud fibrillating into its component parts above the roof of the
Super Bowl. I saw clouds of black butterflies and a furred red moth
crawling across the floor of a streetcar, one wing crushed beyond surviving,
about half the size of a dollar bill. I saw a performance of *The Glass
Menagerie* and everywhere I went I heard the sorrowful cry of mourning
doves, but of all these things it was the two shaven-headed boys who
stayed with me most strongly: a warning, as if I needed it, that addiction
is never an abstract matter, but one that brings – and here the small word
hurt came into my throat and stuck there for a second.

5

THE BLOODY PAPERS

I WAS BEGINNING TO UNDERSTAND Tennessee Williams's addiction to travel; to the quickening of energy that comes when one is about to shift location. At the end of my week in the city, I packed a swimsuit and a few clothes into a canvas bag and called a taxi to the airport. I was going to Florida, and as soon as I slammed the gate to the garden I began to feel buoyed up on the currents of departure. The live oaks were throwing a tracery of shadows on to the sidewalk, and when I looked up their branches were looped with strings of Mardi Gras beads: green and purple and gold, like the flashing on a starling.

In the departure lounge at Louis Armstrong a well-dressed woman was working her way through a stack of resumés. She had her phone crooked to her ear. 'Oh, I'll show it to you,' she said. 'I'll show it to you. Well, I will tell you that cooked my goose. Well, she is not head of a graduate faculty. She might be vice president of a graduate faculty, but that is not the same thing. She's trying to distort . . . Well, tomorrow I'm going to slip into your office at some point and show it to you.'

To get to Key West, I had to fly to Charlotte and then on to Miami, where I'd pick up a car and drive the last hundred or so miles. The sense of motion excited me. Stop too long, and you begin to marinate in your own thoughts, to soak up their vinegar and gall. Better to move, and if you're moving anyway why not veer south, where the water's warm and you can carry out, off-season, those summery rites of anointment and immersion?

The plane was small, and up in the air before I knew it. All around me people were falling asleep in their blue leather seats as we tacked sharply east and New Orleans was lost beneath a reef of cloud. I drank a ginger ale in a plastic cup. The wires were cut. No one would call; there was nothing now that couldn't wait. I could pick over the litter of the past or fret away at the cuticles of the future, but the present was out of my hands, slack as a paid-out line.

A long while back, working on John Cheever's papers in the Berg Collection at New York Public Library, I'd stumbled across a statement about the eeriness of air travel. He described the temporal sleight of hand that comes from watching the sun rise at half past one over the Atlantic, adding a little later: 'One does not travel so much as one seems incised – a picture cut out of a magazine and pasted onto another landscape.'

I'd copied these phrases down because they seemed to catch at a persistent attribute of his work: a kind of uncanniness produced by radical disruptions in space and time. Now, shuttling through the thin air above Louisiana, I turned them over again, and this time they sparked a different association. In the early 1970s Cheever began to be plagued by spells of what he described as *otherness*, though one could also use the term depersonalisation or fugue states or transient amnesia. These episodes had two components: olfactory, auditory or visual hallucinations and a simultaneous sort of brain freeze that left him unable to access words and names. Sometimes he'd feel he was being swamped by the past, and sometimes, frighteningly, that he'd lost his place in time altogether: 'I am not in this world; I am merely falling, falling.'

In 1972, the year before he went to teach at the University of Iowa, he wrote:

> With a hangover and a light fever I distinctly get the impression that I am in two places at once. I am aware of my surroundings here – rain and the beech trees and I smell the coal gas and see the furniture in the old house in Quincy. Have I gone mad?

Not exactly. What he was experiencing was the legacy of all those years of drinking: the scoops of gin and hookers of bourbon he'd knocked down in their thousands. By 1972, Cheever had been drinking chronically for almost forty years. He was living in a beautiful house in Ossining, with his beautiful wife, three more or less charming children and his delightful dynasty of golden retrievers: a writer who had by almost all the measures he cherished achieved success. And yet in her memoir *Home Before Dark*, Susan Cheever recalled that it had become 'clearer and clearer that my father was the worst kind of alcoholic. He seemed intent on destroying himself.' As early as 1959, Cheever was using the word *alcoholism* to describe his behaviour, writing grimly:

> In the morning I am deeply depressed, my insides barely function, my kidney is painful, my hands shake, and walking down

Madison Avenue I am in fear of death. But evening comes or even noon and some combination of nervous tensions obscures my memories of what whiskey costs me in the way of physical and intellectual well-being. I could very easily destroy myself. It is ten o'clock now and I am thinking of the noontime snort.

Alcohol affects the brain in many ways, but one of the most tangible, even to the casual drinker, is the havoc it wreaks on one's ability to recollect the past. In a single night, if you hit it hard enough, alcohol can overwhelm the brain's ability to lay down memories – a kind of anterograde amnesia known universally as blackouts. Blackouts, which are common especially in those who drink too fast or on an empty stomach, fall into two categories: *fragmentary* (partial loss) or *en-bloc* (total loss). After an en-bloc episode, the drinker will be unable to recall anything that happened during intoxication, no matter how coherent or engaged they appeared at the time.

Blackouts occur as a consequence of alcohol's interactions with the hippocampus, the memory centre of the brain. Research suggests that drinking suppresses hippocampal activity by making the cells responsible for memory formation both less active and less responsive to external signals. As such, though short-term memories are still formed, their translation into long-term memories is prevented.

This kind of patchiness of memory – an uncertainty as to what exactly did transpire the night before – had been afflicting Cheever for decades, making mornings in particular a time of blurry and uncertain guilt ('I cannot remember my meanness,' he wrote in 1966, 'because my recollections are damaged by alcohol'). The spells of otherness, on the other hand, were new and far more troubling, though they too were probably related to alcohol's effects on memory and cognition. Over time, heavy and continuous exposure to alcohol badly damages cognitive function, causing reduced capacity for concentration, aphasia, emotional instability and, at its most extreme, alcohol-induced dementia. These distressing changes are the result of what is known as *diffuse cerebral atrophy*, or shrinking of the brain, which affects all regions, including those concerned with the laying down and preservation of memory.

What's more, because of poor nutrition, impaired digestion and reduced or disrupted liver function, alcoholics are often deficient in thiamine, vitamin B1, an essential nutrient for nerve cell function. Thiamine deficiency causes severe cognitive impairment and is responsible for Korsakoff syndrome, a neurological disorder seen almost exclusively in alcoholics. Its symptoms include amnesia, confusion, confabulation (so-called 'honest lying' or false memories) and hallucinations caused by disruptions in the brain's ability to access long-term memory. Korsakoff syndrome affects in particular episodic memory, the faculty by which an individual locates themself chronologically.

According to Blake Bailey's lovely, intricate biography, a CAT scan performed just before Cheever went into recovery in 1975 revealed severe alcohol-induced atrophy of the brain. This damage was undoubtedly implicated in his attacks, in all likelihood causing both the aphasia and the hallucinations. (Later, he had several seizures.) But one of the strangest things about Cheever's spells of otherness is the way they seemed to allude to some buried trauma in his past – an event that might potentially have set the whole grim mechanism spinning in the first place. The most unsettling among his hallucinations was a recurrent vision of two friends on a beach, one of whom was singing a song he could never quite place, though he had a sense that if he did he'd be plunged into the deepest, darkest reservoir of unrecovered memory – what, he figured dolefully, 'psychiatrists would call a traumatic rejection'.

The possibility that his past was somehow indicated in his present plight was not exactly news to Cheever. Over the years he'd submitted to therapy several times, though he had little respect for the formal delvings of analysis. In the same box of papers in which I'd found the lines about flight, there were multiple references to *clinicians* and their tendency to misunderstand the elegant workings of his mind. Each of these relationships, with the exception of the last, was politely terminated when it became clear that the clinicians intended to dismantle the house of fiction he'd built up around his life.

Take David C. Hays, his psychiatrist in 1966. In 1963 Cheever had written 'The Swimmer', a story that judders forward, gaining its rhythm and its force by way of blackouts. It's these dead zones of memory that convey more powerfully than anything the depths of Neddy Merrill's ruination. While working away at it, a brilliant idea had struck Cheever. 'Might the seasons change?' he asked himself in his journal.

> Might the leaves turn and begin to fall? Might there be snow?
> But what is the meaning of this? One does not grow old in
> the space of an afternoon. Oh well, kick it around.

Kick it around he did. Speaking a few years later to the *Paris Review*, he commented: 'When he finds it's dark and cold, it has to have happened. And, by God, it did happen. I felt dark and cold for some time after I finished that story. As a matter of fact, it's one of the last stories I wrote for a long time.' As to its relationship to alcoholism and memory loss in his own life, one might note that in a preceding entry of the journal he'd noted ruefully: 'My memory is full of holes and craters,' and in a subsequent one: 'In church, on my knees before the chancel, I see, with a crushing force, how dependent I am on alcohol.'

In 1966, 'The Swimmer' was turned into a movie, with Burt Lancaster as Neddy. Filming took place not far from Ossining, and so in the summer of 1966 Cheever regularly bucketed over to join the fun, obliterating an attack of first-day nerves with a pint of whiskey, some martinis, a few glasses of wine and a Miltown for good measure. To his delight he was given a cameo role, and so it's possible to see him as he was that year: a tanned, elfin man of fifty-four, in a blue shirt and white jacket, shaking hands with Lancaster and kissing (*bussing*, he called it) a pretty girl in a bikini by the glinting waters of one of the location's thirteen swimming pools.

As that alarming first-day prescription suggests, his drinking had passed well beyond normal measures now, even bearing in mind the mores of the time. When he wasn't on location, he wrote in the early hours of the morning (*Bullet Park*, mostly), and by half past ten could be found twitching in the kitchen, waiting for his family to disperse so he could administer the first self-soothing scoop of Scotch or gin. If they didn't leave quickly enough he'd drive himself to the liquor store, where he'd buy a bottle, motor on to some pretty back street, and sit there suckling, inevitably spilling a good slug all down his chin.

This was the climate in which he made his first appointment with Hays, and yet on arrival he announced piously that he'd come for help with his wife's black moods, which he'd decided were responsible for his insufferable loneliness, misery and depression. His journals are crammed with complaints about Mary: her chilliness, her cutting comments, her habit of putting on a large wash whenever amorously approached. Hays, however, was unconvinced. After interviewing Mary, he informed Cheever on their second meeting that he was neurotic, narcissistic, egocentric, friendless, 'and so deeply involved in my own defensive illusions that I had invented a manic-depressive wife', a diagnosis he reproduced furiously in his journal that night.

The ensuing sessions proceeded along classically Freudian lines ('When I told him I liked swimming he said: Mother. When I told him I liked the rain he said: Mother. When I told him I drank too much he said: Mother'). By the end of the summer he'd had enough. He broke off relations, though not before he'd presented Hays with an inscribed copy of his first novel, *The Wapshot Chronicle*, which the man had inexplicably not yet found time to read.

It was the banality of Hays's analysis that offended him, the heedless predictability of its assertions, and yet Mother was clearly in there somewhere. In all his writings, Cheever returned repeatedly to the troublesome matter of his origins and its role in his latter-day distress, sometimes in letters, sometimes in novels and sometimes in journal entries that lie in a mixed region between actuality and imagination. Real events are cast in the protective casing of anecdote, with pseudonyms – *Estabrook* and *Coverley* – that are recycled bewilderingly throughout the published fiction.

One of the richest sources of his musings on the subject is a piece of writing he called the Bloody Papers. It was filed away in the Berg Collection in New York too, tucked into a creamish box of typewritten journal entries and drafts of stories, most of which had been shuffled so conclusively that to find two consecutive pages was a novelty. In contrast, the Bloody Papers presented a reasonably coherent and intact account of Cheever's early years.

On the first page, he describes the precision and dexterity with which Laurie Lee captured his mother in *Cider with Rosie*. 'When I think back to my parents,' he concludes wistfully, 'I find nothing so lucid and controlled. This troubles me because the disjointedness of my recollections seems to imply that I have never been willing to admit the facts of my own beginnings.'

He steels himself, setting down a clutter of vivid scenes. He remembers that when war was declared on Germany his mother, Mary Cheever, took his father's collection of beer steins into the back yard and smashed them with a hammer. He remembers being asked to sweep the kitchen floor, and having the broom snatched out of his hands because he 'swept like an old woman'. He remembers carving his name on to his mother's sewing machine and being thrashed with a belt till he bled. He remembers the gift shop she opened after her husband lost his job. 'After this I was to think of her, not in any domestic or maternal role but as a woman approaching a customer in a store and asking, bellicosely, "Is there something I can do for you?"'

How the gift shop smarted, though it's hard to tell whether what he most resented was the fact of his mother working or what he describes as 'the odour of failure' that clung to her affairs. Spitefully, he lists her other business ventures: the restaurants in Hanover and Jaffrey where the lobster would spoil for want of customers; the factory that manufactured bags; the bizarre phase in which she painted roses:

. . . on almost everything that came her way. She painted roses on match-boxes, tin trays, table tops, chair backs, soap dishes and toilet paper containers. She was growing old and this extraordinary explosion of ungainly roses seemed to exhaust her tremendous energies. Almost no one wanted to buy the tin boxes on which bloomed her grisley and primitive roses. Her enthusiasm was immense but the gall and chagrin of failure was on it all.

All the while he keeps taking little jabs at the clinicians, with their pained smiles, their air of infinite condescension, their insistence on making heavy weather out of even the most innocent of his dreams. Then he comes abreast with the figure of his father. He remembers Frederick Senior threatening to drown himself at a funfair in Nangasakit; remembers him shooting at his firstborn son with a loaded pistol he kept in his handkerchief drawer. He remembers being taken out of school unexpectedly one day to go to Brockton Fair and watch the trotting races. His father placed illegal bets under the bleachers and probably won; he often did. He remembers him blowing on his wife's neck; remembers his sensuality and the romantic excesses of his speech. 'Oh what a burden of light that cobweb holds,' he'd once exclaimed. Sensing, or perhaps just seeking kinship, his son adds: 'It was his style and also mine.'

A few soft, typewritten pages later, he returns to the amusement park, which he'd previously claimed left him neither angry nor bitter, only bewildered. For a minute or two he spins his wheels, gathering momentum by venting a little spleen.

Not only do I find it difficult to write; I have this morning a mild nausea. Why can't I put down the things about my father. The clinicians, as they say have mined my past. I have spent a fortune recounting my autobiography. One of my difficulties is that the clinicians find my sufferings entertaining . . .

Item: I came in one night for dinner and found my father was not there. When I asked where he was my Mother sighed and said: I can't tell you. I sensed a crises and said that she must tell me. He left here at around five, she said. He said he was going to Nagasakit to drown himself. I left the house and raced the car to Nagasakit. It was late in the summer, the sea was calm and I had no way of knowing if it contained, full fathom five, his remains. The amusement park was open and I heard some laughter from there. A group of people were watching the roller coaster where my father, waving a pint bottle, was pretending to threaten to leap. When he was finally grounded I got him by the arm and said Daddy you shouldn't do this to me, not in my formative years. I don't know where I got that chestnut. Probably from some syndicated column on adolesence. He was much too drunk for any genuine remorse. Nothing was said on the way home and he went to bed without his supper. So did I. I mention this because one clinician, when I told the story, chuckled.

Cheever often told this troubling story, each time with a subtle embellishment of detail, though the ironic, distancing tone remains remarkably consistent. Towards the end of his life, he put it in his fourth novel, *Falconer*, and in another disjointed story, 'The Folding Chair Set', both of which add, with a certain grim relish, that the missed supper that evening consisted of red flannel hash and poached eggs. But even in this private account he fabricated the location. There is no Nagasakit or Nangasakit on any map, though they presumably conceal some real, no doubt long since defunct amusement park near his boyhood home of Quincy.

★

In such a situation one looks instinctively for fellow travellers, and so it's not perhaps surprising that in the late stages of his own alcoholism Cheever developed an intense interest in the life of F. Scott Fitzgerald, a writer whose background and sensibilities resembled his own. In the same journal entry in which he recounted his first session with Hays, he described an afternoon spent on the terrace reading about Fitzgerald's *torments*. 'I am, he was,' he wrote warmly, 'one of those men who read the grievous accounts of hard-drinking, self-destructive authors, holding a glass of whiskey in our hands, the tears pouring down our cheeks.'

This sense of tearful kinship is palpable in a sketch Cheever was asked to produce for *Brief Lives: A Biographical Companion to the Arts*. Writing out of the common currency of their unhappy childhoods, he observed that as a boy Scott 'considered himself to be a lost prince', adding for reasons that are all too hopelessly apparent: 'How sensible of him.'

Both men felt an acute, and in Cheever's case physically scrotum-tightening sense of shame about their origins. 'Straight 1850 potato-famine Irish,' Fitzgerald said of his mother's family, the McQuillans, though they'd been successful enough since their arrival in the new world to work their way squarely into the mercantile middle class. Both were unpopular children: unsporty and painfully conscious of being among the poorest boys at private school, though each also possessed a compensatory gift for telling stories that could spellbind a room.

As a biographer, Cheever isn't entirely to be trusted. There's no evidence, for example, that Fitzgerald's mother was ever 'ruthless', and in the mention of 'a serious writer working to support a beautiful and capricious wife' one suspects him of working off some dark resentment of his own. Nonetheless, he apprehends Fitzgerald's inherent goodness, peering past 'the drunken pranks, pratfalls and ghastly jokes', 'the appalling lapses in discipline', 'the years of expatriation, booze-fighting, debt, sickness' to alight on the ways in which he maintained his seriousness and grace, his 'angelic austerity of spirit'. In the stories, he discovers hopefulness, depth and moral conviction, an ability at once to conjure history and convey the hot thrill of being alive.

Unlike Cheever, Fitzgerald was very much a wanted child. He was born on 24 September 1896 in St. Paul, a couple of months after his sisters, Mary and Louise, died in quick succession during an epidemic of summer influenza. His father, Edward, was from an old Maryland family (the most famous of whom, Scott's namesake Francis Scott Key, wrote 'The Star Spangled Banner'). In 1898 the company where Edward was president, the American Rattan and Willow Works, had gone under in a precursor of the Depression, and so the family moved from St. Paul to upstate New York in search of work. For the next few years they shunted back and forth between rented houses in

Syracuse and Buffalo; the same geographic instability that marked Tom Williams's childhood.

Edward's new job was as a wholesale grocery salesman at Proctor & Gamble, though in Fitzgerald's *Ledger* entry for August 1906 there's an ominous mention of him drinking too much and playing tipsy games of baseball in the back yard. Still, Scott liked his elegant, courtly father better than his mother, poor Mollie McQuillan with her mismatched shoes. Mollie was passionately concerned with her son's health (as one would be, having lost two infants) and in later life Fitzgerald felt in his self-pitying, blameful way that he'd been spoiled. There's a wincing reference in the *Ledger* to the times she'd made him sing in public, all gussied up in a sailor suit. 'A neurotic, half insane with pathological nervous worry,' he described her later, and avoided contact whenever he could. When she died in 1936 he didn't attend her funeral, though five years earlier he'd travelled by ship from Paris to pay his last respects to his father.

Struggling up through the murky waters of his thirties, Fitzgerald once told a journalist a story he'd been carrying around since he was eleven, living in Buffalo in the spring of 1908. Mollie had given him a quarter to go swimming and he was on his way to the Century Club when the telephone rang. I imagined him bopping idly along the hall in stockinged feet, licking the coin and listening in the distracted way a boy listens when his mother's voice abruptly shifted in pitch. 'He remembers the day,' he wrote in the *Ledger*, in the third person he almost always used there: 'and that he gave his mother back his swimming money after he heard her on the phone.' Sure enough, his father came through the door soon after and announced he'd lost his job. 'He came home that evening,' Fitzgerald told the reporter, 'an old man, a completely broken man. He had lost his essential drive, his immaculateness of purpose. He was a failure the rest of his days.'

In the wake of this catastrophe the Fitzgeralds returned to St. Paul, leaving their children (after another baby who'd died soon after birth, they'd had a daughter, Annabel) with Mollie's parents for nine months before reclaiming them. Supported by her family, they carried on the restless cycle of moves through nearly-smart addresses, pouring what remained of the McQuillan money into their children's education. Edward was from that point on virtually penniless, though he maintained at least the semblance of a tradesman. According to Andrew Turnbull's biography, 'he kept his samples of rice and dried apricots and coffee in a roll-top desk in his brother-in-law's real estate office, but his wife was so clearly the source of all revenue that he was known to charge postage stamps at the corner store'.

Later, Fitzgerald came to wonder if the buried wreckage of his childhood had somehow influenced his adult career. In an essay he wrote in 1936 (two years after 'Sleeping and Waking' and likewise published in *Esquire*), he approached the subject directly. 'Author's House' is a magnificently bizarre piece of writing, in which the narrator offers the reader – a *you* who's evidently in the room beside him – a tour around his own house. He starts in the cellar, a damp, gloomy space crammed with boxes and empty bottles festooned in spider webs. Playing his flashlight over this melancholy cod-Freudian detritus, the author explains:

> It's everything I've forgotten – all the complicated dark mixture of my youth and infancy that made me a fiction writer instead of a fireman or a soldier . . . Why I chose this

God-awful metier of sedentary days and sleepless nights and endless dissatisfaction. Why I would choose it again.

He draws *your* attention to a corner, adding: 'three months before I was born my mother lost her other two children and I think that came first of all though I don't know how it worked exactly. I think I started then to be a writer.' Then *you* spot a mound of dirt in another grimy corner and give a great start. Unwillingly, the author confesses: 'That is where I buried my first childish love of myself, my belief that I would never die like other people, and that I wasn't the son of my parents, but the son of a king, a king who ruled the whole world.' This grave, it might be added, is recent; 'too recent'.

Back upstairs, he spots some little boys playing football on a lawn and so gets to recounting a story about the day he was pulled from a football game at school. He was playing in the position of blocking back, and didn't like the cold. Also – also! – he felt sorry for the opposing end, who hadn't made a tackle, so he decided to let him catch a pass and then at the last minute changed his mind, but didn't intercept it either, out of some misplaced notion of fair play. The author remembers the desolate bus ride home, 'with everybody thinking I had been yellow', and that afterwards he was inspired to make a poem for the school paper, which made him as much of a hit with his father as if he'd actually been a football hero.

Mulling this shift in fortune, he says something Cheever would have understood entirely. He says: 'It was in my mind that if you weren't able to function in action you might at least be able to tell about it, because you felt the same intensity – it was a backdoor way out of facing reality.' Later, of course, he'd find a different *backdoor way out*, the one hinted at by the list of drinks the author reels off in the dining room: 'Clarets and Burgundies, Chateau Yquems and Champagnes, Pilsener and Dago Red, prohibition Scotch and Alabama white mule. It was very good while it lasted, but I didn't see what pap lay at the end.'

If he stopped to think about it, Cheever could generally convince himself that the desire to *tell about it* was a positive and noble thing. 'The tonic or curative force of straightforward narrative is inestimable,' he wrote on an undated page I'd come across in the Berg:

> We are told stories as children to help us bridge the abyss between waking and sleeping. We tell stories to our own children for the same purpose. When I find myself in danger – caught on a stuck ski-lift in a blizzard – I immediately start telling myself stories. I tell myself stories when I am in pain and I expect as I lay dying I will be telling myself a story in a struggle to make some link between the quick and the defunct.

This is true, and true in particular of the marvels he produced. The idea that storytelling was a panacea, a route out of pain and danger, is reflected in a letter he wrote in 1962 to a grad student working on his books. He said that he'd become a writer 'to give some fitness and shape to the unhappiness that overtook my family and to contain my own acuteness of feeling'. In darker moments, though, he'd begun to wonder if telling stories wasn't in some muddled, mysterious way related to his desire to drink. Pondering in his journal of 1966 Fitzgerald's long voyage into self-destruction, he wrote anxiously:

The writer cultivates, extends, raises, and inflates his imagination . . . As he inflates his imagination, he inflates his capacity for anxiety, and inevitably becomes the victim of crushing phobias that can only be allayed by crushing doses of heroin or alcohol.

Writers are indeed under unusual strains, and yet what this statement really conveys is an unwillingness to accept responsibility that is apparent in all alcoholic excuse notes. It was discernible in those slippery phrases *inevitably* and *can only be* – words used to give the impression the drinker is at the mercy of forces too vast and global to be resisted.

Two years on, and perhaps more conscious of the seriousness of his situation, he wrote carefully:

I must convince myself that writing is not, for a man of my disposition, a self-destructive vocation. I hope and think it is not, but I am not genuinely sure. It has given me money and renown, but I suspect that it may have something to do with my drinking habits. The excitement of alcohol and the excitement of fantasy are very similar.

Both excitements seemed related to their ability to lift him out of reality, vaulting away from a baggy and dispiriting past; an increasingly disorderly and dismaying present. Trying to work out the details was like unsnarling fishing line, though. And, thinking that, I remembered again what Cheever had done with his own memories in *Falconer*. The novel is set in a prison and concerns a well-bred heroin addict called

Farragut. While in the throes of withdrawal, a prison guard asks Farragut: 'Why is you an addict?' The question provokes a flood of memories that end with Farragut at fifteen, driving to Nagasakit to stop his father from killing himself by jumping into the sea. He runs along the beach, hearing all the while the sound of the clack of cars on rail-joints. At the amusement park a laughing crowd had gathered to watch Farragut's father on the rollercoaster, pretending to drink from an empty bottle while pantomiming that he's about to leap. Farragut asks the boy at the controls to bring him down and so Mr. Farragut stumbles out and rejoins his son, 'his youngest, his unwanted, his killjoy'. 'Daddy,' says Farragut, 'you shouldn't do this to me in my formative years.' And there the monologue ends, with Farragut's own heavily ironic repetition of the prison guard's question: 'Oh Farragut, why is you an addict.' This time, though, he doesn't bother with a question mark. The story says it all.

★

There were rocking chairs at Charlotte airport and one of the concession stands sold barbecue. The flight to Miami was delayed and by the time we boarded it was already evening. The runway was marked out in glowing dots of green and blue and larger splashes of red, the dark bulk of the city beyond a scattering of gold. A swift sense of pressure in the feet, then we were up in wispy cloud the colour of smoke, and then out into the unencumbered ink-blue of night. I had a sense of being cut loose from all my body's usual routines, and yet I was deeply relaxed, both physically and in my heart.

We were circling back to the south now, to Florida, that swampy, subtropical peninsula where the rich come to luxuriate and the poor to make their fortunes. Hemingway country. There are many regions of America associated with Hemingway, among them Michigan, Wyoming and Idaho, but Florida – or rather the ocean that surrounds it – is where he spent some of his happiest days, fishing for marlin from his black-hulled boat *Pilar*, all the friends he could muster aboard. Florida was the first place he came to after Europe, and he remained based there throughout the decade of his marriage to Pauline Pfeiffer.

They left Paris together in March 1928. Pauline was six months pregnant and in an endearing letter to his new wife written aboard ship he expressed the impatient hope that they would soon stop bouncing around on the bloody Atlantic: 'Only lets hurry and get to Havana and to Key West and then settle down and not get in Royal Male Steam Packets any more. The end is weak but so is Papa.'

In Key West they took an apartment while waiting for their new Ford coupé, a present from Pauline's rich Uncle Gus. On the morning of 10 April, an unexpected reunion occurred. A few weeks back, Hemingway's parents had written to him in Paris, telling him of their upcoming holiday in St. Petersburg, Florida. The letter hadn't yet recrossed the Atlantic, and so Hemingway had no idea his parents were near by, while they assumed he was still in France. Partway through their vacation, they'd gone to Havana for an excursion. They were coming back into Key West on the ferry when Hemingway's father spotted a hunched-over figure fishing on the pier.

Like Vassya in Chekhov's story 'The Steppe', who can see hares washing themselves with their paws and bustards preening their wings, Dr. Clarence Edmonds Hemingway was blessed with remarkably good vision. Recognising his son's stocky form he whistled like a bobwhite quail, the familial call. Ernest jumped up and ran to meet them. Grace – 'the all-American bitch' – was glowing, but Ed had lost weight, and looked old and exhausted, his neck scrawny inside the wing collar shirt he always wore. All the same, he was delighted to see his son. 'Like a dream,' he wrote a day or two later, 'to think of our joyous greeting.'

Hemingway rushed his parents off to meet Pauline, though neither had been exactly thrilled when they heard of his divorce. ('Oh Ernest, how could you leave Hadley and Bumby?' his father had written on 8 August 1927. 'I fell in love with Bumby and am so proud of him and you his father.') According to his sister Marcelline's soapy and not always reliable memoir *At the Hemingways*, their surprise encounter went some way to salving this wound. 'Daddy wiped a tear from his eye as he told me about it,' she wrote. 'This meeting with Ernest meant much to our parents, especially to Dad, for he had missed Ernest during the estrangement.'

There's a photo of the two Hemingway men taken that afternoon, standing by a flashy car that looks black against the sun. Ernest is leaning into it, in socks and light trousers, a jaunty Argyle vest and a shirt so white his shoulders merge in with the sky. His hands are clasped in front of him and he looks somehow both naughty and angelic, smiling knowingly at the photographer, his dark hair Brylcreemed back. There's a little dark object under his arm that resembles a hot water bottle cover – a sweater, perhaps.

Dr. Hemingway isn't looking at the camera. He's turned to gaze intently at his son. He's wearing a three-piece suit and tie, warm clothes for the climate, and holding in his hand a sailor's cap. His nose and chin look very sharp, eyes deeply set, just like the famous description of Dr. Adams, the man he both was and wasn't, that would soon appear in 'Fathers and Sons'. It's all there: 'the big frame, the quick movements, the wide shoulders, the hooked, hawk nose, the beard that covered the weak chin,' the famous eyes, that saw 'as a big-horn ram or as an eagle sees, literally.'

If you asked Ernest, he'd say Dr. Adams, the father in the Nick Adams stories, bore no relationship to Dr. Hemingway beyond the coincidence of their professions, their place of residence and the miracle of their vision. In fact, three years back, on 20 March 1925, he'd written his father a letter explaining just that. 'I'm so glad you liked the Doctor story,' he said. 'I've written a number of stories about the Michigan country – the country is always true – what happens in the stories is fiction.'

Maybe. Maybe not. In a letter written in 1930 to Max Perkins, he changed his tune, saying of *In Our Times*, the collection that included 'The Doctor and the Doctor's Wife': 'The reason most of the book seems so true is because most of it is true and I had no skill then, nor have much now, at changing names and circumstances. Regret this very much.'

Either way, the events in 'The Doctor and the Doctor's Wife' play off the dynamic Hemingway most hated in his parents. It opens with Dr. Adams down on the shore of the lake, trying to organise a team of Indians to saw and split some logs that have washed up on the beach. They've broken loose from the big log booms and the doctor assumes they'll rot there and never be reclaimed. One of the men, Dick Boulton, who is what Hemingway calls a 'half breed', accuses the doctor of stealing the logs. He has his men clean off the sand and find the mark of the sealer's hammer, which identifies it as the property of White and McNally. The doctor tries to bluster his way out, but he isn't nifty enough and eventually he makes the mistake of challenging Dick to a square fight. Then he backs down and walks away. The men on the beach watch as he retreats, stiff-backed, up the hill to his cottage.

In the second phase of Dr. Adams's humiliation, he has a conversation with his wife through the wall that separates their rooms. She's in bed with a headache, blinds down, playing swift hands of martyrs' cards. Henry cleans his shotgun, while his wife quotes homilies from the Bible and denies the reality of everything he says. 'Dear, I don't think, I really don't think that anyone would really do a thing like that,' she calls through the wall, as he spills yellow shotgun shells on to the bed. He goes out then and the screen door slams behind him and he hears his wife's aggressively muted intake of breath. He apologises and walks into the woods, where he finds Nick sitting against a tree, reading a book. He tells the boy his mother wants to see him, but Nick doesn't want to go. 'I know where there's black squirrels, Daddy,' he says. 'Let's go there,' Dr. Adams replies, and with this consoling exchange they disappear together over the threshold of the page.

Despite its ending, something dangerous was flickering in that story, and it surfaces again in 'Now I Lay Me', the Nick Adams account of trout fishing and sleeplessness that I'd been brooding over on the night train down through Carolina. 'Now I Lay Me' was written the summer before Hemingway arrived in Key West and was published in *Men Without Women* a few months later.

On the nights when Nick can't manage the trick of fishing in his mind, he stays awake by remembering everything he can muster about his early years. First of all, he thinks of everyone he's ever known, so that he can say a Hail Mary and an Our Father for them. He begins this process with the earliest thing he can recall, which is the attic of the house where he was born. There are two things he says about this attic: that his parents' wedding cake hangs from a rafter in a tin box and that there are jars of snakes and other specimens up there that his father collected as a boy. The snakes are preserved in alcohol, but the alcohol has begun to evaporate and the exposed backs are turning white. He says there are many people he can remember and pray for, but he doesn't name them. The only things present are the cake in the tin box and the whitening snakes.

At other times, he continues, he tries remembering everything that has ever happened to him, which means working back from the war as far as he can get. This takes him immediately into the attic again. From there he works forward, remembering that when his grandfather died his mother designed and built a new house, and 'many things that were not to be moved' were burned in the back yard. What an ambiguous phrase this is. 'Were not to be moved', as in too precious to be moved, a prohibition that might be given to a small boy, or 'were not to be moved' as in too insignificant to bother transporting to the new house, the sort of command a child might overhear a parent giving to a servant?

He remembers, he continues, the jars being thrown into the fire, where they popped in the heat, the alcohol going up in little flares. He remembers the snakes in the back-yard, but there are no people in this memory, only things. He can't, he says, remember who was responsible for burning the snakes, and so he goes on wandering through his past until he encounters people for whom he can pray.

In the next paragraph he remembers his mother 'cleaning things out' and 'making a good clearance', which leads him directly to another fire. This time Mrs. Adams burns things in the basement that 'should not have been there'. Dr. Adams returns home and sees the fire burning in the road beside the house. 'What's this?' he asks.

> 'I've been cleaning out the basement, dear,' my mother said from the porch. She was standing there smiling, to meet him. My father looked at the fire and kicked at something. Then he leaned over and picked something out of the ashes. 'Get a rake, Nick,' he said to me. I went to the basement and brought a rake and my father raked very carefully in the ashes. He raked out stone axes and stone skinning knives and tools for making arrow-heads and pieces of pottery and many arrow-heads. They had all been blackened and chipped by the fire. My father raked them all out very carefully and spread them on the grass by the road.

Nick is told to take the game-bags and the gun into the house, and bring a newspaper back out. He finds one in the pile in his father's office. His father spreads all the blackened bits of stone on to the paper and wraps them up.

> 'The best arrow-heads went all to pieces,' he said. He walked into the house with the paper package and I stayed outside on the grass with the two game-bags. After a while, I took

them in. In remembering that, there were only two people, so
I would pray for them both.

Recently I'd read in an essay by Paul Smith called 'The Bloody
Typewriter and the Burning Snakes' that in an early draft of this story
the mother says two sentences, not one. The second is 'Ernie helped
me' – the only time, apparently, in all the typescripts of the Nick
Adams stories that Ernest's name is used in place of Nick's. This isn't,
as Smith is at pains to explain, to say that 'Now I Lay Me' is necessarily autobiographical, or that it really happened, though it has a
tendency to be quoted in Hemingway biographies as gospel fact. Not
so. It's fiction, with all the wonderful, ungraspable fluidity that suggests.
But even without the anchoring presence of Ernest's name, the scene
is overwhelmingly articulate about the effects a corrosive dynamic
between parents might have on a small child.

There was a great fashion, a while back, for making the burned
and broken arrowheads a metaphor for castration, and in some way
it's undeniable, although doing so takes away from Hemingway's refined,
ferocious attention on objects-as-they-are. There's such a note of grief
in the description of those damaged snakes and damaged arrowheads
and knives, a conjuring of the child's marvellous gift for attention (and
thinking this I remembered a line in Edwina Williams's curious memoir
of her son, in which she recalled how his powers of observation were
much stronger than other children's, and that he could stare mesmer-
ised at a single flower long after another boy would have flung it
down). That one person can wilfully damage or exert power over
another, and that this damage can be enacted not so much symbolically as materially, in the beloved, consoling world of things, can leave

a child with impossible, indigestible sadness and rage – a feeling not dissimilar, I'd guess, to having a shard of blackened stone lodged within one's chest.

It seems at least some of this unhappy relationship was drawn from life. In her son's estimation, Grace Hemingway was a bustling, domineering woman, while her husband was gentle and evasive; sometimes overcome by depression and sometimes by fits of rage. Ed was a lifelong teetotaller and suffered until his death an intense anxiety about money. He made his wife and children keep account books and even when they were almost grown was still enforcing petty rules about dancing and library cards. 'Excited and exacting', his daughter Marcelline put it; 'irritable and exacting'. He spanked his children, but he also had a sense of honour and a love of the outdoors that were immediately infectious. Grace, on the other hand, exerted her personality in ways her son had baulked against since boyhood – as well, of course, as having dressed him in infancy as a girl. 'Isn't that old River Forest woman terrible?' Hemingway once wrote to Hadley, long after their divorce. 'I don't know how I could have been whelped by her but evidently was . . . a winner in any all time Bitchshow.'

It was all coming apart, anyhow. After that week in Florida Hemingway only saw his father once more. In October 1928, a few weeks after the birth of his son Patrick, he visited his parents in what had been his boyhood home: 600 North Kenilworth Avenue, Oak Park, Illinois, the house his mother had both designed and paid for. During the visit Ed seemed tired, irritable and not at all well, though he didn't discuss the worries that had begun to bear down on him like a ton of bricks. He'd planned on retiring to a practice in Florida, and had bought up land during the real estate boom as an investment.

But now the crash was under way, and his finances as well as his health were precarious. He'd been diagnosed with angina pectoris and diabetes – 'a touch of the sugar', as he told his colleagues.

After Hemingway left, Ed wrote him a brief, fond note. In with the letter was another envelope, addressed 'To My Son'. Inside there was a poem, written in Ed's slanting hand:

> I can't seem to think of a way
> To say what I'd like most to say
> To my very dear son
> Whose book is just done,
> Except give him my love
> and 'HOORAY'.

He'd put the same odd quotation marks around the word 'Dad' in the letter, too.

A month went by. Then on 6 December, he woke with a pain in his foot. The doctor in him immediately foresaw diabetic neuropathy, gangrene, amputation: an unspooling ticker tape of grim eventuality. In pain and increasingly frantic about an unpayable debt, he told Grace that he was scared. She suggested he talk to a doctor, but he didn't. He went out and returned to the house before noon, going down to the basement, where he burned a few papers. Then he called up to his wife that he was tired and would rest before lunch. He went into his bedroom, closed the door and shot himself in the right temple with his father's .32 calibre Smith & Wesson.

At that moment, Hemingway was eating lunch in the Breevort Hotel in New York, where ten years later Cheever would drink whole afternoons away. His companion was his five-year-old son Bumby, who'd just arrived from Paris. After lunch, they went to Penn Station and boarded the Havana Special to Key West. Just outside Trenton a porter delivered a telegram from Oak Park. It read: FATHER DIED THIS MORNING ARRANGE TO STOP HERE IF POSSIBLE.

Reeling, he got off the train at Philadelphia, leaving his small son to travel on in the care of the porter. He only had $40 in cash; not enough to get home. He telegrammed Max Perkins, asking him to wire money by way of Western Union. Then, figuring Max had probably already left the office, he telephoned Fitzgerald, who was living at the time in Delaware. Scott answered the phone immediately; immediately agreed. A few days later Hemingway wrote from Oak Park:

> You were damned good and also bloody effective to get me that money . . . My father shot himself as I suppose you may have read in the papers. Will send you the $100 as soon as I reach Key West . . . I was fond as hell of my father and feel too punk – also sick etc. – to write a letter but wanted to say thank you.

Punk: a word a woodsman might use to describe a tree that's rotten; that looks all right until you realise you can tear into it with your bare hands. To Max Perkins, a week later, he added more details:

> Various worthless land in Michigan, Florida etc. with taxes to pay on all of it. No other capital – all gone . . . He had angina pectoris and diabetes preventing him from getting any more

insurance. Sunk all his savings, my grandfather's estate etc. in Florida. Hadn't been able to sleep with pain etc. – knocked him temporarily out of his head.

Dr. Hemingway, who sometimes washed his son's mouth out with soap, sometimes beat him with a razor strop, who was sometimes implacable, turned temper on a ha'penny, who drove into his boy a principle of honour and sportsmanship that never wholly left him, who passed on from hand to hand those nourishing loves for the Michigan woods, for clear water, jacksnipe, wild geese, dead grass, new corn, deserted orchards, cider mills and open fires. Open your mouth, boy. One more stone to swallow down.

★

The plane was passing through a region of turbulence. We hiccupped up; bounced down. A mood of mild tension filled the cabin. The stewardesses were smiling their determined smiles. The air was chilly and smelled of banana chewing gum.

I'd fallen into a world of fathers and sons. By some grisly coincidence, the Florida land boom also played a role in the death of the poet John Berryman's father. As an adult, Berryman was grimly aware of the loss he shared with Hemingway. He once wrote a poem for them both that began 'Tears Henry shed for poor old Hemingway', before pleading to some unspecified force:

> Save us from shotguns & fathers' suicides.
> It all depends on who you're the father *of*

if you want to kill youself –
a bad example, murder of oneself

Over the course of his life, Berryman served as an impassioned teacher and fine scholar, a husband, father, philanderer and drunk. 'The most brilliant, intense, articulate man I've ever met,' his student, the poet Philip Levine, remembered: 'at times even the kindest and most gentle.' His own writing began tight and tense, staccato, and then, as his drinking got under way, it changed, blooming by degrees into the Pulitzer Prize-winning Dream Songs, a sequence of extraordinary intensity situated sometimes in life and sometimes in death. These poems are narrated by another not-quite self: Henry House, sometimes Henry Pussycat, Huffy Henry or else Mr. Bones, a white, middle-aged American in black-face (layers upon layers of borrowed identity) who 'has suffered an irreversible loss' and who, while emphatically not the poet, seems to share all the elements of his excruciating biography.

One of the odd things about this compulsive play with names is that Berryman himself experienced a grave and dislocating name change in childhood. Strictly speaking, it isn't possible to say John Berryman was born on 25 October 1914 in Oklahoma, since as an infant he was christened with his father's name, John Allyn Smith. His parents' marriage was by all accounts unhappy from the start. In an autobiographical fragment his mother Martha wrote in old age, she claimed that Allyn Senior raped her and then blackmailed her into marriage. Whether this grotesque story is true or not, it seems that it was her firstborn son and not her husband who received the full intensity of both her love and need.

Smith was a loan officer in the First State Bank, but he lost his job in 1924, and in the autumn of the following year relocated to Florida, where the land boom was then under way. He was accompanied by his wife and mother-in-law, but the children – John Jr. and his younger brother Robert – were left behind at a Catholic boarding school where, over the course of the next few months, John was systematically bullied. Eventually a neighbour apprised Martha of the situation, and she took a train from Tampa to reclaim her boys, who waited for her in the principal's office, clutching their possessions in paper bags. By Christmas the Smiths were reunited, and all three adults were working in their new restaurant, the Orange Blossom.

For John Jr., it seemed like life was about to improve. In the early 1920s, Florida was a place where fortunes were made daily, and for a brief moment the land rush favoured the Smiths. But in the spring of 1926 the crash occurred, precipitated when a schooner sank in the turning basin of Miami harbour, blocking access for the boats bringing in building supplies. Then, as Martha put it in a letter a long time later, 'everything went like snow in the sun'. As boom turned to bust the Orange Blossom became untenable and was sold at a loss. The family moved into cheaper lodgings, renting an apartment on Clearwater Beach owned by an older couple, John Angus and Ethel Berryman.

You can figure the rest out from the name. Martha and John Angus began what sounds like a spectacularly ill-concealed love affair. Ethel tried to persuade her husband to move to New York; instead he sold off all his holdings, gave her half, threw in the car as a bonus and asked her to move out. Meanwhile, John Allyn was taking solace in drink and had entered what would turn out to be an abortive liaison with a Cuban woman who later cut and ran with what little remained of his money. John Angus was often in the apartment, and sometimes all three would engage in tortured discussions as to their future.

As divorce proceedings got under way John Allyn took to spending his days strolling the beach with a gun in his hand, or taking long, distracted swims. One day he apparently went out into the Gulf with Robert tied to a rope, heading so far out into the ocean that John Angus had to be dispatched to bring them back. The negotiations grew more ugly after that, and at some point Martha took five of the six bullets from her husband's .32 and buried them in the sand. On 25 June 1926, the three spent another interminable night in talk. At midnight or so Martha fell asleep on the couch. A little later she rose and saw that John Angus had left and John Allyn was sleeping in what had once been the marital bed. At six she woke again and discovered her husband had left the house and was lying sprawled on the steps in the sun, a bullet hole in his chest. The note he'd left on her dresser read: 'Again I am not able to sleep – three nights now and the terrible headaches.'

Hundreds of people were shooting themselves in Florida that summer, and the death was not investigated by the police, though there are suggestions in both Berryman's biographies that it didn't resemble an ordinary suicide owing to an absence of the powder burns that tend to be visible with self-inflicted gunshot wounds. As for Martha, ten weeks later she married John Angus and bestowed his name upon her sons, taking, at her new husband's request, *Jill Angel* for herself. Little wonder then that the adult Berryman, tottering in and out of rehab, drinking himself halfway to death and back, might set down in Dream Song after Dream Song the story of the bullet and the swim, concluding: 'That mad drive wiped out my childhood.'

★

A line came into my head then. It was from another Dream Song. What was it? Something about pieces. 'The pieces sat up and wrote'? Yes.

> Hunger was constitutional with him,
> wine, cigarettes, liquor, need need need
> until he went to pieces.
> The pieces sat up & wrote.

The overwhelming infantile wail of that *need need need*, too urgent even for punctuation. If you carry that sense of starvation – for love, for nourishment, for security – with you into adulthood, what do you do? You feed it, I suppose, with whatever you can find to stave off the awful, annihilating sense of dismemberment, disintegration, of being torn apart, of losing the integrity of the self.

These are the terrors of the infant waiting for the breast, or they are if you read Freud and Melanie Klein; and these are also the terrors of the adult whose childhood sense of security was ruptured before they'd managed to build a sturdy enough skin with which to face the world. Hardly any wonder that the Dream Songs are so obsessively interested in the state of being skinless or of having one's pelt ripped off or stripped away. Indeed, Berryman once joshed bleakly to his editor about having them bound 'blue-black' in scraps of his own skin.

It struck me then that Berryman's pieces might have some kind of kinship with the objects raked out of the fire in 'Now I Lay Me': the broken knives and broken arrowheads, the blackened, blunted parts of things that were once whole and useful. The mood of that whole story radiates outward from the fire (in fact I'd read in one biography that its forcefulness as an image meant it must have literally happened; a statement that seems gravely to misunderstand the novelist's art). Nonetheless, I wondered if its extraordinary intensity derived in some way from a child's sense that in the silent, smiling war between his parents, there was a terrible heat, and in that heat things that should be kept entire were broken or struck apart. And then of course Nick fetches a newspaper to wrap up the relics: containing them in a false skin made literally of words.

Hunger, liquor, need, pieces, wrote. Something about that list of words was crucial. I could feel it, but I couldn't quite crack it. Linear A. I'd been banging my head against these questions for months, years. The three-way relationship between childhood experience, alcohol and writing. I'd read paper after paper about early life stresses and mediating factors, about the hand-me-down catastrophe of genetic predisposition and the unearned luck of genetic resilience. I'd read about castration complexes and death drives and how Hemingway's mother was the dark queen of his internal world and in the midst of all these things I could hear the stripped-down elements of Berryman's poem: five words, clicking like beads on an abacus.

Hunger, liquor, need, pieces, wrote. A sense was building in me that there was a hidden relationship between the two strategies of writing and drinking and that both had to do with a feeling that something precious had gone to pieces, and a desire at once to mend it – to give it fitness and shape, in Cheever's phrase – and to deny that it was so. Hence those obsessive retellings: hence Nagasakit, Nick Adams, Henry Pussycat, Dick Diver, Estabrook and Coverley.

Writing about Marguerite Duras, another alcoholic writer who liked to rake over the live coals of her own experience, Edmund White once observed:

> Perhaps most novels are an adjudication between the rival claims of daydreaming and memory, of wish-fulfilment and the repetition compulsion, Freud's term for the seemingly inexplicable reenactment of painful real-life experiences (he argued that we repeat them in order to gain mastery over them). And as with music, the more familiar the melody, the more elegant and palpably ingenious can be the variations.

If I had to answer the question, I guess I'd say that fiction might – in addition to all its other functions – serve as a kind of storehouse, a way of simultaneously expelling something while keeping it close to home. And if I had to elaborate on this, I might say that when Ed Hemingway shot himself, the coroner took the gun, a Civil War .32 pistol, but later Grace managed to facilitate its return. At his request, she posted it to her son in Key West, along with a couple of her own paintings, adding in the accompanying letter that it was not to be considered a permanent gift. One version of this story says Hemingway defied her by throwing it in a lake. Perhaps. But what certainly did happen is that just over a decade later, married by now to a third wife, Martha Gellhorn, and living between Cuba and Sun Valley, he went to his desk – early in the morning, to judge by his habits – and wrote the following words:

> Then after your father had shot himself with this pistol, and you had come home from school and they'd had the funeral, the coroner had returned it after the inquest . . .

He had put the gun back in the drawer in the cabinet where it belonged, but the next day he took it out and he had ridden up to the top of the high country above Red Lodge, with Chub, where they had built the road to Cooke City now over the pass and across the Bear Tooth plateau, and up there where the wind was thin and there was snow all summer on the hills they had stopped by the lake which was supposed to be eight hundred feet deep and was a deep green color, and Chub held the two horses and he climbed out on a rock and leaned over and saw his face in the still water, and saw himself holding the gun, and then he dropped it, holding it by the muzzle, and saw it go down making bubbles until it was just as big as a watch charm in that clear water, and then it was out of sight.

How pleasurable it must have been to write that long second sentence, riding up in one's mind into the high clean country of Montana. Down goes the gun, getting smaller and smaller, until it's disappeared from view: lost in one of those immaculate landscapes that Hemingway loved to reconstruct on the page. There's some funny intensity about the action needing to be witnessed, too. Robert Jordan – both the 'he' and the 'you' of this passage and the hero of *For Whom the Bell Tolls* – doesn't drop the gun until he's seen himself holding it reflected in the green glass of the water, which is to say that there's a brief moment of *mise en abyme*, as if even the semblance's own mirror self has to be implicated in the act: another kind of *watch charm*. Finally, the incident is capped with silence, just as the hills are capped in snow.

'I know why you did that with the old gun, Bob,' Chub said.

'Well, then we don't have to talk about it,' he had said.

As to the role of alcohol in all this: imagine the mixed relief and terror of getting that sequence down. Imagine pressing the words, letter by letter, into the page. And imagine getting up, closing the door to your study and walking downstairs. What do you do, with that sudden space in your chest? You go the liquor cabinet and you pour yourself a shot of the one thing no one can take from you: the nice good lovely gin, the nice good lovely rum. Click in a cube of ice. Lift the glass to your mouth. Tilt your head. Swallow it.

6

GOING SOUTH

WE CAME IN ABOVE MIAMI at half past ten. First the lights, in their beautiful switchboard patterns, and then things passing in the space beneath the plane: diffuse dark shapes that must have been clouds, but which looked for a moment like the shadows of something gigantic swimming overhead. We swung out over the Atlantic, descending fast. My ears popped. A woman behind me switched on her phone as soon as the wheels hit tarmac. 'Guess who's on this plane? My dad and his ex-wife. When I saw them at the airport I nearly freaked out.'

It was the first time I'd caught an internal flight, or flown without checked baggage. There was nothing to do. I just lifted my bag out of the locker and walked away. The airport was brightly lit and almost deserted and for a long time I went back and forth between levels, trying to find the stop for the hotel shuttle. It was very hot, and I went in and out, riding down on escalators and back up in lifts, my tiredness shot through with little fibrillations of alarm. Eventually I called the hotel, but the answering service was stuck on a loop. 'Dial 5 to speak to a hotel service representative,' a mechanised voice kept repeating. At last, when I was almost sobbing with frustration, the minibus appeared and swept me away to the Red Roof Inn.

The next morning, I collected the car. The day was overcast and very warm, and there were clouds of vultures circling the city. I drove out on Route 1, past strip malls and strip joints, signs for psychic readings and computer repairs. Then the buildings thinned and beyond the alligator fencing there was nothing but mangrove swamps and pools of standing water, where little white egrets dipped for fish. After a while the land narrowed in like a neck and there beyond the swamp was the sea. It was shallow and seamed with sandbars and deeper channels, the colours shifting musically from turquoise to green to a rich purple like spilled grape juice.

I parked by the bridge to Fiesta Key. There were two elderly black women fishing on the jetty. I said hello, and one turned to greet me. 'Y'all going to Key West?' she asked, and when I said yes she nodded at the pilings running out to sea, and said: 'That the old road.' I asked her what she was fishing for and she replied: 'Snapper. Drum. Whatever comin' through here on the way to the Gulf.'

In Marathon I stopped for lunch at the Cracked Conch Café, drank a beer, ate a chicken quesadilla, drove on. Conch, pronounced *Konk*, the name for Key natives. Within minutes I was at the start of the Seven Mile Bridge. I've had dreams of crossing over water all my life, and as I drove up on to it I had a funny, overwhelming sense of realities collapsing into one another. The road was made of pinkish concrete, and the old bridge ran beside it, handrails rusted. There were mangrove islands far out to sea, and a single white boat in the east. I could still feel it days later: the enormous proximity of water, and the sensation of flying above it, weightless and unimpeded.

Languages were sliding together; the Gulf sluicing into the Atlantic. Bahia Honda Key, *deep bay*, Spanish Harbor Channel, Norfolk Island Pine. In Key West I lost my way and found myself on the estate by the Navy Yard, where Hemingway once kept his boat *Pilar*. I backed out and consulted the map. At first glance the town seemed enchanted, the little clapboard houses overwhelmed by the lusciousness of their gardens. I'd never been anywhere so dense with flowers, so gigantically, preposterously fertile. Banana trees, lignum vitae, cockerels and chickens meandering down the road. There were cats everywhere: cats and little lizards and larger lizards, and people slopping home in flip-flops or weaving bikes through pools of shade.

At the guesthouse my room was painted primrose yellow and the air-conditioning made a reassuring hum. As soon as I'd unpacked I went out to the pool. Two couples were drinking beer in plastic cups and talking about Cuba. 'They're a horrible people,' one said. I sat on in the sun, reading a book about Hemingway's haunts, and when at last I got up the design of my swimsuit was emblazoned into my skin, white on fiery pink.

★

For more than ten years Key West was a place that Hemingway returned to: a place to recuperate, to set new things going or finish old ones off. After his father died and he'd dealt with the fallout in Oak Park, he returned to the town to revise *A Farewell to Arms*, leaving only the ending uncertainly set. Then, exhausted by the upheavals of his American year, he went to Paris with Patrick and Pauline, spending almost the whole of 1929 at large in Europe.

They sailed back into town on 9 January 1930. Almost immediately afterwards he began *Death in the Afternoon*, his beautiful, unclassifiable and sometimes maddeningly dull treatise on bullfighting. This time he worked in a rented house on Pearl Street, within spitting distance of the marina. In June he took the book away with him to Wyoming, where he spent the summer on the Nordquist ranch, writing mornings and riding and fishing in the afternoons.

This period of good solid work came abruptly to an end the day after Halloween. Driving a friend to Billings to catch the night train, he wrecked the car in the dark, spilling into a ditch and smashing his right arm. They had been passing a bottle of bourbon back and forth, but he figured afterwards his poor night vision had been to blame. When, weeks later, the hospital released him he chose Key West to recuperate, spending the first few months of 1931 waiting irritably to see if the damaged nerve would regenerate or not. 'I'm still in bed most of the time,' he told Max, 'but count on Key West to fix everything up finely.'

It was towards the end of this painful and frustrating period that the Hemingways finally bought a house of their own. On 29 April, Pauline's Uncle Gus paid $8,000 for the Tift property, a big, well-situated wreck at 907 Whitehead Street. The house with balconies opposite the lighthouse, Hemingway described it to a friend, adding happily to Max: 'this is really going to be the hell of a fine house.' The garden was full of figs and coconuts and limes, and he wrote dreamily about how he'd like to plant a gin tree.

The next morning I went to see it for myself. It had rained before dawn, but by ten the streets were sweltering. I took a shortcut through the cemetery, where I disturbed a bearded green iguana the size of a cat. The graves were decorated with bunches of faded plastic flowers and painted angels the boiled pink of baby dolls. On Whitehead Street I joined a queue running the length of the wall Pauline had built to dissuade tourists.

Toll paid, I went straight to the pool, palm-shadowed, the trees arching up above it. 'You'd always be picking out leaves,' an English man muttered. In the shop there were earrings with six-toed cats and posters of Papa beaming next to a giant marlin. 'He's a very famous writer, honey,' a woman said pleadingly to her teenaged son.

The house was very stately, with yellow shutters and a wrought-iron verandah that ran right round the second floor. I ducked inside and made a beeline for the bookshelves. *Poise: How to Attain It. Danger is my Business. Buddenbrooks.* Hans Christian Andersen's *Fairy Tales. On the Eve* by Turgenev. Two copies of *The Adventures of Tom Sawyer.* There were bits of Africana dotted here and there: horribly caricatured boys with hands like paws, their eyes sorrowful and swollen. Jade ashtrays; a chandelier made of opaque glass flowers in wonderful seawater colours.

At the back there was a smaller building that had originally been a coach house. Shortly after he moved in, Hemingway converted its upper storey into a writing studio, connecting it to the master bedroom by way of a catwalk. It was closed to visitors now, but you could peer in through a wrought-iron gate. The room was big and book-lined, with pale grey walls and a red tiled floor. It was decorated with mementoes of old trips: a model bull, a decoy duck, a marlin. 'Hey Mom,' a different boy called out, 'is that a typewriter?'

I wished I could slip inside. It reminded of my grandfather's flat. On the far wall there was a trophy head of a big Grant's gazelle, its neck long and lovely, its ears alert. I thought it might have been shot on Hemingway's first trip to Africa, one of the hundred and two corpses itemised in Pauline's expedition diary.

The trip had been in the planning for a very long time. Before the accident in Billings, Uncle Gus had promised $25,000 for an African safari on the understanding that a good book could be wrung from it. Hemingway initially figured on an all-male group, but by the time his arm was strong enough to shoot only his pal Charlie Thompson was still on board. In the end Pauline made up numbers, though she never enjoyed hunting with quite the zeal of her husband.

On 20 December 1933 they travelled from Nairobi to the Masai game reserve in the Ngorongoro Crater, west of Mount Kilimanjaro. From the beginning, Hemingway was out of sorts. He missed a gazelle, missed a leopard, then wounded and failed to find and kill a cheetah. He had frequent attacks of diarrhoea, and by January was evidently suffering from a serious case of amoebic dysentery. In *Hemingway: The 1930s* (the fourth volume in a wonderfully detailed and novelistic five-part biography), Michael Reynolds observed: 'By January 11, he was taking chlorine salts continuously, but his evening drinking undermined any good the medicine might have done.'

Eventually their guide telegraphed for a plane. Hemingway spent that day in bed, going to the campfire in the evening to eat a bowl of mashed potato. The plane was promised for the following morning but all day it failed to arrive. Then at ten the next day they spotted it glinting in the sky. It whisked him off to Nairobi, where he was treated with the anti-protozoal emetine and ran up a spectacular bar bill in the New Stanley Hotel. Returned to the field, his shooting improved, but now every kudzu, every rhino he brought down was markedly smaller than those bagged by Charlie. Not a man not to mind, he drank whiskey in the evenings and brooded, becoming sour and aggressive, and sometimes, in the mornings, visibly sad.

Back in Key West, he wrote his account of the trip, *Green Hills of Africa*, in a great tumbling rush, finishing the first draft in six months. But Africa lingered in his mind, and a year or so later he turned to it again. 'The Snows of Kilimanjaro' is the story of a writer, Harry, who's dying of gangrene on an African hunt, incurred by failing to take proper care of a little thorn scratch on his knee. The plane that's supposed to take him into town hasn't arrived, and all day he lies on a cot in the shade of a mimosa tree, insulting his wife while drinking whiskey and sodas, though she begs him to lay off. ('It said in Black's to avoid all alcohol.') 'You bitch,' he says to her. 'You rich bitch.'

In the space between fights he dreams of the stories he hasn't written yet, the ones he's been saving up and now will never start. 'Snows' has the same doubled, riddling structure as 'Now I Lay Me'. It's packed with fictions within the fiction; landscapes within the landscape. These italicised paragraphs are dense and impressionistic, dark rivulets that cut right through the central frame. Many of them are about Paris, and one is about Harry's grandfather's guns, which were burned in a fire, the lead melting in the magazines.

Hemingway pulled off a similar feat in the last chapter of *Death in the Afternoon*, which starts 'If I could have made this enough of a book it would have had everything in it', and then rises to its own challenge, listing a swelling tide of images and memories that ought to be there, that should have been there, that are not there, but somehow magically also are: the smell of burned powder and the noise of the traca and the last night of the feria when Maera fought Alfredo David in the Café Kutz and the trees in the forest of the Irati that are like drawings in a child's fairy book.

All his life, Hemingway possessed a genius for packing, for assembling trunks and fishing boxes; for stowing the things he needed on his travels in the most elegant and ingenious of ways. There's something of the same facility here, in this knack for building secret layers, for filling his fictions up with more than you'd think they'd bear. 'I put all the true stuff in,' he said of 'Snows' in the *Paris Review*, 'and with all the load, the most load any short story ever carried, it still takes off and flies.'

All the true stuff. The story is clearly freighted with objects and incidents from his own trip – the cot, the missing plane, the bowl of mashed potato, the insistence on drinking despite medical advice. Harry keeps having visions of his death and in the last of these the plane arrives, and he flies up above the bush just as Hemingway did, seeing the zebra and the wildebeest moving in long fingers across the yellow-grey of the plains, and then the square white summit of Mount Kilimanjaro itself, as wide as the whole world.

Before this final dream, Harry asks himself why he failed as a writer. 'He had destroyed his talent,' he answers, 'by not using it, by betrayals of himself and what he believed in, by drinking so much that he blunted the edge of his perceptions.' The woman, Helen, gets a portion of the blame. She's very rich, and he feels that he let himself be bought, for comfort's sake, and that the proximity of money rotted him hollow, just like the gangrene in his leg. 'You were equipped with good insides so that you did not go to pieces that way, the way most of them had,' he thinks, but even good insides don't last forever.

Both of these characters are fictional, but the scornful reference to *most of them* had its roots in true stuff of a different sort. Hemingway began 'Snows' in the summer of 1935, and was working on it all through the first quarter of 1936. His insomnia was bad that winter, and he often got up in the small hours and crept into the studio to work – because, as he told Pauline's mother on 26 January, when he worked on a book his brain would get to racing at night. Come morning the words he'd written in his mind would all have vanished and he'd be 'pooped'.

It was the same spell of insomnia that he'd described to Fitzgerald in the letter about non-sleeping being 'a hell of a damned thing'; the one he'd sent to Baltimore on 21 December 1935, when Scott was still living at 1307 Park Avenue. The letter was supposed to be an olive branch, but a few weeks later Fitzgerald did something that effectively torpedoed the remaining elements of their friendship.

In February, *Esquire* ran the first of three instalments of 'The Crack-up', a long, painful essay in which Fitzgerald admitted publicly to having a breakdown. It's circuitous and rambling, a combination of speechifying and savage self-exposure. In it he revealed the depths of his depression; his exhaustion; his profound and incapacitating despair. He confessed to disliking all his former friends, writing: 'I saw that for a long time I had not liked people and things, but only followed the rickety old pretense of liking.' Though not everything he says is strictly true (he denies, for example, being 'entangled' in alcoholism, swearing that he has 'not tasted so much as a glass of beer for six months'), he leaves the reader in no doubt as to the extent of his emotional and creative debilitation.

Hemingway was horrified. On 7 February he wrote viciously to

Max that if Scott had actually made it to France in the First World War (a regret he'd mentioned yet again in the *Esquire* essay) he would have been shot for cowardice – though he also added that he felt awfully about him and wished that he could help. To Sara Murphy, their mutual friend and one of the inspirations for Nicole Diver in *Tender*, he observed grimly that it seemed like they were all on the retreat from Moscow. 'Scott is gone the first week of the retreat. But we might as well fight the best god–damned rear guard action in history,' he concluded, trying vainly to boost both their spirits (this letter, one might add, was written with a giant hangover and is composed largely of a long, bragging story about a drunken brawl with Wallace Stevens that ended when Hemingway punched him repeatedly in the face until he fell down in a puddle of water).

It got worse. In the March instalment, Fitzgerald made a pointed statement about the breakdown's prelude:

> I saw honest men through moods of suicidal gloom – some of them gave up and died; others adjusted themselves and went on to a larger success than mine; but my morale never sank below the level of self-disgust when I had put on some unsightly personal show.

The man who gave up and died was probably the alcoholic writer Ring Lardner, who'd been one of Fitzgerald's dearest friends and was the model for Abe North in *Tender*. The man who adjusted himself, on the other hand, was in all likelihood Hemingway, who when he broke with Hadley in the autumn of 1926 had suffered a black period of suicidal depression.

In the boxing ring, Hemingway never fought quite clean, and there's something of the sucker punch to his next move. The angry letters continued, but he also used 'Snows' to broadcast his disappointment and contempt. In the version published that August, also in *Esquire*, he made a scornful reference to 'poor Scott Fitzgerald', who venerated the rich. 'He thought they were a special glamorous race,' Harry thinks, 'and when he found they weren't it wrecked him just as much as any other thing that wrecked him.'

This time it was Fitzgerald's turn to be appalled. He wrote to Hemingway from the Grove Park Inn in Asheville, where he was spending yet another purgatorial summer, saying:

> Please lay off me in print. If I choose to write *de profundis* sometimes it doesn't mean I want friends praying aloud over my corpse. No doubt you meant it kindly but it cost me a night's sleep. And when you incorporate it (the story) in a book would you mind cutting my name?

Hemingway agreed, replacing *Scott Fitzgerald* with *Julian*, but the sentiment remained, along with the contemptuous reference to people who went to pieces.

Cruel as all this sounds, I don't think Hemingway was motivated entirely by malice. He'd been having a rough time of it that winter. 'Never had the real old melancholia before and am glad to have had it so I know what people go through,' he told Pauline's mother, not quite truthfully. 'It makes me more tolerant of what happened to my father.' But whatever tolerance for poor old Ed he'd managed to locate was mixed with less admissible feelings of terror, shame and rage. It seems plausible from the violence of his reaction to 'The Crack-up' that Fitzgerald's confession had churned up some of this darker soil. A few days after the third instalment was published in April, he'd written again to Max, saying this time: 'I wish he would pull out of that shamelessness of defeat. We're all going to die. Isn't it time enough to quit then?'

I suppose, thinking these threads through, that you could read 'Snows' as playing two games at once. On the one hand, it's motivated by a kind of rage at death and defeat and people too weak to stand up straight and do their duty. Harry doesn't want to die and is disgusted by the waste of work he's left undone. His feelings are mirrored by the sinister and surreal ways his death presents itself to him. It comes first as an evil-smelling emptiness, with a hyena slipping at its edges. It comes in pairs, on bicycles, in absolute silence, like the policemen in one of his never-to-be-told stories. By evening it's climbed on to his chest, breathing its foul breath in his face.

And yet, despite all this, Harry's passage out of life is ecstatic. There's something nearly triumphant about his last dream flight, in which he passes first above a pink sifting cloud of locusts and then through a rainstorm, before emerging in front of the vast, annihilatingly white peak of Kilimanjaro itself. In the updraft of these paragraphs, one senses the presence of another Hemingway: the one who knew all too well the voluptuousness of despair; the gravitational pull death exerts upon its subjects. After all, it was he, not Scott, who'd been threatening suicide in his letters for years, long before Dr. Hemingway closed his bedroom door and pulled the trigger.

Was that, I wondered then, what lay behind the years of drinking? Was that how he employed alcohol: to simultaneously ward death off and lure it in? I thought again of *For Whom the Bell Tolls*. Hemingway began the book in 1938, when he'd already begun to drift away from the security of Key West and his marriage to Pauline, edging instead towards Cuba and the woman who'd become his third wife, the journalist Martha Gellhorn. In this time of unsettlement and change, he began a new novel about an American man, Robert Jordan, who is fighting for the Republicans in the Spanish Civil War. There's nothing rotten about Jordan, but part of his struggle is, like Harry, to remain courageous in the face of death. He worries particularly about pain, and that one day he might be in so much pain that he'll be forced to kill himself. It's what his father did, the shameful thing he both can and cannot understand.

Early on, Robert tells the guerrillas that his father is dead. 'He shot himself,' he says. 'To avoid being tortured?' Pilar asks. 'Yes,' says Jordan. 'To avoid being tortured.' His father wasn't tortured, or not in the way Pilar thinks he means. There's a kind of sympathy in his lie, a willingness to admit to the black undertow that gathered his father in. But later, thinking of his grandfather, the Civil War hero, he realises that they would both be acutely ashamed of his father, who he describes then, distancingly, as 'the other one'.

> Anyone has a right to do it, he thought. But it isn't a good thing to do. I understand it but I do not approve of it.

A minute or two later, he forces himself to admit that his father was a *cobarde*, a coward. 'I'll never forget how sick it made me the first time I knew . . . Because if he wasn't a coward he would have stood up to that woman and not let her bully him.' At the very end of this internal monologue, he concludes: 'He understood his father and he forgave him everything and he pitied him but he was ashamed of him.'

Robert is possessed of admirable strength of mind, but it must be admitted that he helps his courage along with libations of what he calls 'the giant killer' – that same substance Hemingway once said he couldn't live without. A friend of Robert's employs a similar turn of phrase, knocking back a great draught of wine and exclaiming: '*That is what kills the worm that haunts us.*'

Just as he'd later do in *A Moveable Feast*, Hemingway counterpoints these good drinkers with a weaker character, a man who's almost destroyed by alcohol. Pablo was once the leader of the guerrillas, but now he's a *cobarde* who nearly brings the whole band down with his fear. 'Of all men the drunkard is the foulest,' his wife Pilar says to him in disgust: 'the drunkard stinks and vomits in his own bed and dissolves his organs in alcohol.' Later, Robert describes Pablo's state of mind as being 'a deadly wheel . . . it is the thing that drunkards and those who are truly mean or cruel ride until they die.'

There was something sickening about that last image. I imagined what it might be like to ride such a wheel: the confusion, the gathering sense of entrapment. I thought of it and then I thought of Hemingway in Africa, early in the morning, gripping his gun and looking down the sights at the Grant's gazelle. I thought of what Pauline had said, about how sad he looked, and how she took to staying behind to avoid his vicious swings in temper. I thought of how things are handed down in families, and how hard one can try to dislodge them, or bury them, or drown them, or palm them off on someone else. And then I went down the rickety stairs and into the garden, where Hemingway once joked about planting a gin tree. By the pool, I ran into a tour. The guide must have been winding up, because the first words I heard were 'manic depression'. 'Well, that ran in the Hemingway family,' he said, in a purposeful drawl. 'Papa checked himself into the Mayo Clinic. They gave him ECT and he lost his memory and never wrote again. Castro had taken over Cuba. He lost his house and his fishing boat. He lost his work, his manuscripts. He said it was as if he'd lost his life. He shot himself in Idaho, nineteen days before his sixty-second birthday.' There was a scattering of applause, and then as I stood there gaping the crowd began to hand him dollar bills.

★

There are so many currents of exchange, some benign, some toxic, some exalted. Berryman, hearing on the radio the fact but not the manner of Hemingway's death, thought of both their fathers and announced to a friend with complete certainty: 'The poor son-of-a-bitch blew his fucking head off.' As for Cheever, he'd been reading Hemingway since boyhood, as his early writing couldn't help but show. After learning of his death he noted tenderly: 'He put down an immense vision of love and friendship, swallows and the sound of rain.' Almost a decade later, he was still thinking it over, writing in his journal: 'I remain mystified by his suicide.'

Tennessee Williams was also an admirer. His notebooks are full of late-night observations about Hemingway's novels, which he read with pleasure in hotel rooms across the world. And then there was the Key West connection. He first visited the town in February 1941, three months after Hemingway divorced Pauline. In a letter from 'the most fantastic place that I have been yet', he observed that Hemingway's signature was still on a bar stool in Sloppy Joe's, where a dungaree-clad Tennessee was now consorting with B-girls, transients and sailors. Later, he made friends with Pauline herself, who'd stayed on in town after her husband left her for Martha Gellhorn and the Cuban sun.

He only met Hemingway once, in a Havana bar called the Floridita. The encounter took place late one April morning in 1959. They were accompanied by mutual friends: the critic Kenneth Tynan and George Plimpton, the legendary editor of the *Paris Review*. Afterwards, both men recorded catty versions of the day's events. Tynan claimed Tennessee was wearing a yachting jacket, in an attempt to convince Hemingway that 'although he might be decadent he was decadent in an outdoor way'. Plimpton added a yachting cap to the ensemble, and had Hemingway ask in a puzzled voice: 'Is he the commodore of something . . . that yachting cap?' before concluding firmly: 'Goddam good playwright.'

Williams's own account is softer, less aggrandising, less mannered. He said they talked about bullfighting. In Spain he'd become friends with Antonio Ordóñez, one of the bullfighters Hemingway most admired. They spoke of him, and later Williams remembered simply: 'He was exactly the opposite of what I'd expected. I had expected a very manly, super-macho sort of guy, very bullying and coarse spoken. On the contrary, Hemingway struck me as a gentleman who seemed to have a very touchingly shy quality about him.'

What did he see that day? In 1959, Hemingway was sixty, married for the fourth and final time to Mary Welsh. In photographs he looks old and pained, bloated in the belly and frozen in the face, though I've also seen one of him kicking a can of beer on a snowy track in

Idaho, his whole weight poised on his left toe, his right leg scissored out at ninety degrees, balletic and limber as a boy. Sometimes, on a good day, he looks like a man in charge of himself, interested and glad to be alive. But then there are photographs in which he's drunk or drinking, or sat at a table surrounded by empty glasses. In these pictures he seems bewildered, somehow buried, a little smile, more often than not, stuck into his face.

Then there's the description given by Andrew Turnbull, Fitzgerald's biographer, who also met Hemingway that year. By coincidence they travelled back from Europe on the same boat. Hoping to discuss Fitzgerald, Turnbull sent over a letter of introduction. At first there was no reply, and so he strolled up to First Class, intrigued to see what Papa looked like. He spotted him a few times walking on his own, dressed in a plaid shirt and sleeveless leather jacket. Hemingway didn't speak to anyone, and looked 'furtively away when another glance met his'. On the last day out he agreed to a drink with Turnbull, though he didn't want to be pumped about Fitzgerald. Writing the encounter up in the *New York Times*, Turnbull remembered being struck by his skinny forearms and 'sad mask of a face', adding that Hemingway 'seemed shy and wistful, with something inexpressible in his glance'.

In the winter of 1979, two decades after the morning in the Floridita and eighteen years after Hemingway's death in Ketchum, Idaho, Williams put Papa in a play. *Clothes for a Summer Hotel* is set in Highland Hospital, the asylum in Asheville, North Carolina, where Zelda Fitzgerald lived from 1936 until she was killed in a fire there in 1948. Madness, alcoholism, incarceration: those recurring, returning themes. A ghost play, he called it. It centres on the Fitzgeralds' marriage, and takes place in a kind of afterlife, with everyone except Scott aware that they're dead and much preoccupied by the mode of their dying.

It wasn't a success. The critics loathed it, and it was the last of his plays to be staged on Broadway, a humiliation he never quite forgave. In a way, they were right. It's clumsy, badly constructed and absurdly didactic, showing in all its seams and creases the debilitating effect of alcohol on Williams's ability to think. And yet it's also touching, and so deeply felt that it's doubly painful to read.

In the scene with Hemingway, the two men circle one another at a party: Hemingway confident and insulting, Scott gentle and confused. Insinuations of homosexuality pass back and forth. It seems to be another version of Skipper and Brick in *Cat on a Hot Tin Roof*, the one willing to confess his feelings and the other boarded up and sick about it. A stage direction, italicised:

> [*He approaches Scott. For a moment we see their true depth of pure feeling for each other. Hemingway is frightened of it, however.*]

They talk and talk, quoting great chunks of their own history back and forth, as people generally don't but ghosts may do. In the closing minutes, Hemingway turns to his betrayal of Scott in *A Moveable Feast*. Scott listens; replies: 'I suspect you were lonelier than I and possibly you were even as lonely as Zelda.' They stare at one another, and then Hemingway says:

> *Fuck it! Hadley, Hadley, call me, the game's gone soft, can't play it any longer.* [*Offstage, a woman's voice sings 'Ma biond.'*] – That's Miss Mary whom you never knew, a good, loving friend, and

a hunting, fishing companion – at the end. We sang that song together the night before I chose to blast my brains out for no reason but the good and sufficient reason that my work was finished, strong, hard work, all done – no reason to continue . . . What do you make of that, Scott?

The reference to the song is drawn from life. In Mary's memoir, *How It Was*, she recalls that on the last night in Ketchum, she and her ailing husband slept in separate rooms. They called between the walls to one another, using the familiar endearment *kitten*. Then Mary began to sing a song, and after a while her husband joined in. The song was called 'Tutti mi chiamano Bionda' ('They Call Me Blonde'), not 'Ma biond', and it was about a woman's hair, a subject that had excited Hemingway his whole life.

Perhaps he was thinking then of Martha's taffy-coloured locks, or of Garbo peering past her fringe. Or perhaps he was thinking of Maria, Robert Jordan's lover in *For Whom the Bell Tolls*; the girl he calls *rabbit*; *little rabbit*. Her head was shaved by the Fascists, and has grown back in like corn. It's the colour of grain burned dark in the sun, and short as a beaver's pelt, so that when he runs his hand across her scalp it flattens beneath his fingers, causing his throat to thicken.

If he was thinking of Maria, perhaps he also thought of Robert Jordan, who once said to himself of the things he had done: 'But my guess is you will get rid of all that by writing about it . . . Once you write it down it is all gone.' At the end of the novel he waits alone in the pine trees, his leg smashed beyond repair, trying to persuade himself to stay alive long enough to shoot a Fascist patrol leader, so that Maria and the little surviving band of partisans can make their getaway. He's weakening, and he feels himself slipping, as you sometimes feel snow slipping on a mountain. He keeps thinking about shooting himself, before he faints and gets caught and tortured by the Fascists. 'It would be all right to do it now,' he tells himself. 'Really. I'm telling you it would be all right.' Then, having given himself permission, he finds he can wait a minute or two more, until the soldiers come riding up the trail and he has finished the strong, hard work he came for.

★

It wasn't so easy to find traces of Tennessee Williams's life in Key West, though he lived in the town for almost four decades. He arrived on 12 February 1941, during the peripatetic, poverty-stricken period before *Menagerie* changed the contours of his life forever. On that first visit, he stayed in the slave quarters of a sea captain's house called 'Trade Winds' to convalesce after an operation to remove the cataract in his left eye. His play *Battle of Angels* had just failed in Boston, and he needed somewhere to recover his confidence as well as his vision. 'I chose Key West,' he wrote in *Memoirs*, 'because swimming was practically a way of life for me, and since Key West was the southernmost point in America, I figured I would be able to swim there.'

So it proved. In addition to swimming, there were the alluring possibilities of cruising (the naval base meant swarms of sailors), as well as the quiet mornings, conducive to work. 'Sponge and deep sea fishing are the main occupations and the houses are mostly clapboard shanties which have weathered grey with nets drying on the front porches and great flaming bushes of poinsettia in the yards,' he wrote to a friend from 'Trade Winds', adding enthusiastically: 'I shan't do anything for the next few weeks but swim and lie on the beach till I begin to feel human again.'

He kept coming back. In 1949 he rented a cottage on Duncan Street, setting up house with his partner Frank Merlo and his grandfather, the skinny, stork-like Reverend Dakin, by now widowed and far from happy living in St. Louis with his daughter and increasingly aggressive son-in-law. The next spring, Tennessee bought the house and over the years extended it, adding a pool and a beautiful writing studio, with framed photographs of Chekhov and Hart Crane on the yellow walls. The palms and banana trees made wonderful sounds as he worked, he wrote happily to his friend Maria St. Just, 'like ladies running barefooted in silk skirts downstairs'.

Saturday night dances at Sloppy Joe's, where a good band played on the stage and Frank would perform his wild version of the lindy hop. Swimming at South Beach, before the motels and car parks sprang up. The reassuring routines of work. For a long time, Key West represented an ideal kind of life, lulling and thrilling all at once. Take this statement, written early in the morning of the first day of 1954, when Tennessee was incarcerated in the hospital outside New Orleans with what he thought was cancer:

> Oh how I long to be loose again, entering the Key West studio for morning work, with the sky and the Australian pines through the sky light and the clear morning light on all four sides and the warmth of coffee in me and the other world of creation. And driving out to the beach in the afternoon, the slow, easy, meditative drink on the pink terrace there, the long easy swim in the buoyant, pleasantly cool water.

How lovely it sounds. Listen to that stream of adjectives – *slow, easy, long, easy, buoyant, cool*: a place that nourishes, that facilitates the transition to whatever other world it is the writer co-inhabits. And again, a few years later, in a letter: 'I am going . . . to rest and recuperate in a sweet, sweet place, the little house in Key West with Horse and dog.'

I went down to the little house one morning, when the sun was still low, and pale in the sky. It was on the corner of Duncan and Leon: a white clapboard cottage with freshly painted red shutters and a tin roof, almost hidden beneath giant palms and cactuses stuck at their tops with scraps of flowers like red silk. It looked like a more benign version of the jungle garden in *Suddenly Last Summer*, fecund and not wholly under human control.

Tennessee lived here on and off until his death in 1983, though not always in the company of his grandfather and Frank, whose surname, I remembered then, meant *blackbird*. It was their relationship that was preoccupying me that morning. By all accounts, Frank Merlo was a thoroughly decent man. 'He was just plain good,' Christopher Isherwood observed: 'a man who kept cool, even when he and Tennessee were exposed to the most appalling pressures of social and professional life.'

From the beginning there were tensions in the relationship – as, I expect, there are tensions in every relationship that's ever been. Frank wanted monogamy, but though he brought harmony and structure to Tennessee's life, exclusivity never seems to have been an option. Still, they kept house together in Florida and New York, spent summers bustling around in Europe, and though there were frequent bouts of cruising Frank remained the lynchpin of Tennessee's life. In 1949, he wrote with amazed pleasure: 'I love F. – deeply, tenderly, unconditionally. I think I love with every bit of my heart.'

Things started to change in the latter half of the 1950s. After Cornelius Williams died in 1957 Tennessee went into psychoanalysis, and also spent a spell in what he described as a 'plush-lined loony-bin' – drying out, or trying to. The seriousness with which he approached this endeavour can be gauged from his notebooks, in which he confesses day after day to 'drinking a bit more than my quota'. One laconic itemisation includes: 'Two Scotches at bar. 3 drinks in morning. A daiquiri at Dirty Dick's, 3 glasses of red wine at lunch and 3 of wine at dinner – Also two seconals so far, and a green tranquillizer whose name I do not know and a yellow one I think is called reserpine or something like that.'

The therapist, Dr. Kubie, was also attempting to cure him of homosexuality, 'and has succeeded in destroying my interest in all except the Horse, and perhaps the Horse will go next'. There were other issues, too. In his notebooks and letters of the time, he referred often to a growing distance between him and Frank, though as late as August 1958 he was writing wistfully: 'I miss the horse & dog that I live with in Rome.'

Squinting back at this confusing period from the 1970s, Tennessee thought that both men's drinking and drug use had been getting out of control, though the testimony of their friends suggests that the belief Frank was taking drugs was pure paranoia. He also liked to accuse his lover of sexual infidelity, though this too seems to have been at least partly projection: the maddening suspicion and unclarity of the chronic alcoholic. Weigh it up against his own self-confessed behaviour: four-somes with drag queens; running away for a weekend with a creamy-skinned boy he called the Dixie Doxy. Then home to tight silences, slammed doors, a plate of meatloaf hurled at the kitchen wall – the sort of behaviour Cheever found so baffling in his wife Mary, though an onlooker might see a fairly obvious connection between a sloppy, unfaithful drunk and the desire to sleep alone at night.

Tracking events into the 1960s grows progressively more difficult. The letters become less frequent, while the notebooks, which Tennessee kept more or less faithfully from 6 March 1936, run out entirely in September 1958. We're left with *Memoirs*: that strange, untrustworthy document. The dates are often wrong, and incidents tend to be collapsed together or recounted out of sequence. As his one-time confidant Donald Windham observed, possibly resentfully:

> There is probably not an episode described in *Memoirs* that did not happen at some time, to some one, in some way, but more likely than not to a different person, at a different time, with different details. Curtain after curtain of ambivalence has descended in his life.

Not forensic evidence, then, but instead a very precise record of the kind of stories an alcoholic tells himself: confused, self-lacerating and resolutely bedded in denial.

According to this lubricated testimony, in 1960 Frank began to lose weight and suffer from mysterious spells of tiredness. While he was in New York for tests, Tennessee invited a young painter to stay at the Duncan Street house. A friend of Frank's warned him about the interloper, and so he flew home from hospital, and sat in the corner of the living room, watching the two men with what Tennessee described as great, baleful eyes. Then, without warning, he dashed across the room 'like a jungle cat' and grabbed the painter by the throat. The police were called, and took him to a friend's (Frank was as popular with the Key West police force as he was with everyone else he ever met). The next morning he returned as Tennessee was loading all his papers into the car. 'He watched in silence for a while and then as the motor started ran down the path I was standing on, saying: "Are you going to leave me without shaking hands? After fourteen years together?"'

It's dreadful, reading this, reading between the lines, imagining someone tearing out the foundations of their life. It seems to me a classic example of the alcoholic's desire to self-harm by hurting those who are most dear, demonising and then banishing them, as if that will achieve anything at all. An undated letter to Maria St. Just sounds the same punitive note: 'The Horse has done just about all in his power to shatter me and humiliate me, so I must find the courage to forget and put away a sick thing.'

In the spring of 1962, Frank insisted on a meeting in New York. Tennessee brought his agent, and it was agreed that Frank would remain on salary – an unpleasant word in the context of the end of a fourteen-year relationship. Ten minutes after he left the building, Frank rang and begged to continue the conversation in private. They went to a nearby bar, and Tennessee said something he claimed to remember word for word more than a decade on. He said: 'Frank, I want to get my goodness back,' though if that was true it's hard not to feel he was going cold turkey on precisely the wrong thing.

Silence for a while. Then – in this version of events at least – in 1963 a friend rang to say Frank had been diagnosed with lung cancer. He had surgery in New York but the tumour was too close to his heart and so the doctors sewed him up and sent him home to Key West. For a few months he was full of beans. He went out dancing

– that wild lindy hop – and was accompanied everywhere by Gigi, Tennessee's bulldog. When he got weaker he moved back into Duncan Street, sleeping in his and Tennessee's old bedroom, while Tennessee and his new boyfriend, a poet nicknamed Angel, took the room downstairs. At some point they returned to New York, leaving Angel alone in the south. Frank's weight had dropped below a hundred pounds, and he looked 'like the skeleton of a sparrow', though he remained fiercely independent. At night he locked his door, and in the afternoons he watched television, side by side on the love seat with the old dog, their expressions, Tennessee observed, almost identically stoical.

All that summer he kept going in and out of hospital. Tennessee visited most days, displaying the exquisite generosity and tenderness that was as much a part of his nature as the lodestone of depression, the crushing paranoia. On 21 September Frank had trouble breathing, and there was a delay before anyone brought oxygen. When he finally fell asleep Tennessee went out to a gay bar with some friends and got drunk and when he came home the phone rang and Frank's best friend told him the Little Horse was dead. 'As long as Frank was well, I was happy,' he wrote in *Memoirs*. 'He had a gift for creating a life and, when he ceased to be alive, I couldn't create a life for myself.' And in a letter, written to Windham early in 1964: 'next to my work, Frankie was my life.'

★

The hell with it. I walked away from the Duncan Street house then and down to the beach. I wanted to swim, to wash away some of the sadness these stories stirred in me. A red-faced man with a ponytail called out: 'I hope your day is as beautiful as you are,' which made me bark a laugh. There was something calming about walking through the quiet streets, full of the sound of mourning doves and starlings chattering invisibly in the trees. Around the corner there was a school, and then a community garden, planted with nasturtiums, ruby chard, fennel and bright blue stars of borage.

On South Street a man was out painting his house, and further down someone was coaxing a motorbike, muttering 'son of a bitch' when it coughed into life. The sound of a chainsaw, the *sussshsh* of leaves, the smell of jasmine, there for a moment and then gone. On the boardwalk at Clarence Higgs Beach there was a stretch of shining black stone. As I got closer I realised it was the Key West Aids Memorial. It was engraved with a map of the islands, and underneath were the names of the dead – Richard Cahil. Steve Vanney. Edgar Ellis. Troy Aney.

It was very hot. The sea was slapping right against the boardwalk, the sun splintering off it in quick, dangerous sparkles. A homeless woman made a feint towards a glossy green cockerel. I slogged on past the big hotels to Dog Beach, stripped down to my swimsuit, and waded out past a raft of black seaweed. There were a few sharp rocks – coral, maybe – and then sand packed in hard ripples that felt very pleasant beneath my feet. Little twigs and branches of kelp kept floating by. The water was warm and opaque, addled with sand. I waded out until I was chest deep and then let go into it, pulling hard towards the buoys.

Everything was looser out here, more dissipated. The stories I'd been turning over scared me, because I sensed in some small part of myself how pleasurable it might be to let alcohol unhinge you, to take you down into an unreachable, sunken place, where sounds are very muted.

Drowning your sorrows, that's the phrase. And I remembered then, floating on water the exact greenish-yellow of Gatorade, that one of Tennessee's most persistent fantasies was about being buried at sea. In *Memoirs*, he described a codicil to his will in which he asked to be 'sewn up in a clean white sack and dropped over board, twelve hours north of Havana, so that my bones may rest not too far from those of Hart Crane'. Hart Crane, the alcoholic poet. Something about that fantasy of liquidity, of deliquescence, underpinned the story about Frank, though once again I wasn't sure I knew how or why. None of it was clear to me, but when I got back to the guesthouse I rang round all the boat companies until I found one that would take me out the next morning and let me swim in the deep, mixed waters of the Gulf, where Tennessee had hoped his body would end up.

I got up just after dawn and went into town by way of Harry Truman's Little White House. There was an ice cream shop open by the harbour, and I bought coffee and a bagel, and sat in the sun eating it and trying not to think about sharks. The night before, in a frenzy of anxiety, I'd Googled 'shark attack Florida' and come up with a man in Marathon who'd died after his thigh was bitten to the bone. I'd been reading through the plays too, looking for sea-burials, and I steered myself back to them now, swerving forcibly away from the image of a fin breaking water.

In the final scene of *Streetcar*, Blanche is in the bathroom, preparing herself for a departure she's disastrously misunderstood. She's been through the worst of it now: been raped by Stanley, been rejected and exposed by Mitch. She comes out into the bedroom, hair freshly washed, barely footed in reality, and gets to rattling on about a dirty grape.

I shall eat an unwashed grape one day out on the ocean. I will die – with my hand in the hand of some nice-looking ship's doctor, a very young one with a small blond moustache and a big silver watch. 'Poor lady', they'll say. 'That quinine did her no good. That unwashed grape has transported her soul to heaven. [*The cathedral chimes are heard.*] And I'll be buried at sea sewn up in a clean white sack and dropped overboard – at noon – in the blaze of summer – and into an ocean as blue as [*chimes again*] my first lover's eyes.

The same image, borrowed loosely from a short story by Chekhov called 'Gusev', is repeated in *The Night of the Iguana*, one of Williams's last critical and commercial successes. All that bad year of 1961, when Frank was starting to deteriorate, and he was responding by whirling away into affairs and drinking himself silly, he was at the same time hard at work on his most compassionate and explicitly hopeful play. It's strung with painful, almost embarrassingly urgent questions about appetite and punishment, sex and corruption; about the cost of making art, and whether one can be good, or find a way of living that doesn't mean being torn to pieces – a counter, in that respect at least, to the profoundly bleak *Suddenly Last Summer*, the play he'd written during his analysis, in which the predatory poet Sebastian Venables is torn apart and eaten by a gang of urchin children he's been buying for sex.

I'd watched the film of *Iguana* in bed in my own flat, not long before I left England. Ava Gardner as Maxine, in her tight jeans, playing the role Bette Davis had on stage: a widowed hotel proprietor, tough, broke and cheerful, though she's freefalling without any kind of safety net. Richard Burton as Reverend Shannon, the defrocked priest, alcoholic and seducer of teenaged girls, teetering into a breakdown while leading a tour party of church ladies through the tropics of Mexico. He's terrified of a thing he calls 'the spook', and Deborah Kerr as Hannah Jelkes sits with him through the long hot night on the hotel terrace, teaching him by her own hard-won calm that there are demons inside us with which we can learn to co-exist.

It's all very close to the bone. Hannah's version of the spook is 'the blue devil': a term Tennessee had been using in his journals since his early twenties, and which he once compared to 'having wildcats under my skin'. Like Cheever's cockroach or *cafard*, the blue devil signified anxiety, depression, an intolerable swamping of fear and shame. Asked how she won the battle, Hannah says simply: 'I showed him that I could endure him and I made him respect my endurance . . . Endurance is something that spooks and blue devils respect.' Later, she delivers one of the most beautiful lines in all Williams's work: 'Nothing human disgusts me unless it's unkind.' So much of him is in that statement: tolerant, non-judgmental, determined to drag out into the light all the shameful clutter of psychopathology our species has evolved.

The line about the burial comes around the midpoint of the play, which runs over a twenty-four hour period with the same unity of setting that made *Cat* so claustrophobic and compelling. Maxine is telling Shannon about her husband's recent death. His last request, she says philosophically, was 'to be dropped in the sea, yeah, right out there, in that bay, not even sewed up in canvas, just in his fisherman's outfit'. A few years after writing that line, Tennessee reiterated his desire for the same thing, noting in his journal:

I wish a Greek Orthodox service: then a return to the States and the burial at sea (a day North of Havana) where my idol Hart Crane, feeling his work finished (as did Mishima at the end, and as do I), found refuge only in that vast 'mother of life'.

I looked out at it, anxiety mixing with the usual swimmer's lust. The cat was riding light, bouncing a little on the waves. People were gathering on the quay. It was time to board. I joined the crowd weaving in single file across the ramp. Right away there was a hitch. The dreadlocked captain announced that we wouldn't be going to the coral reefs. The weather was off, the waves too big. Instead we'd be heading south-west, in the rough direction of Havana. 'We're getting what Mother Nature has for us,' he said irritably. 'It's what you make it, guys. So everyone knows what they're getting into? A nice boat ride out, a nice swim, a nice boat ride back in the afternoon?'

Fine by me. It was rough. As soon as we left the harbour the swells started up. I sat on the starboard deck, watching the water rushing out from under the prow, the light scattering in the wake. The air smelled of gasoline and salt. I leaned over, looking down at the glossy blue-green water and then out, towards the horizon. No sign of Cuba, sixty miles away, through water that swarmed with sharks. A flying fish breached and flagged impossibly upward, crashing down in a spurt of foam.

It was somewhere out here that Hart Crane drowned in 1932. One night, travelling back by steamer from Mexico to New York, he was beaten up by a sailor he'd tried to seduce. The next morning, he jumped from the fantail, 275 miles north of Havana and ten miles off the coast of Florida, and though the captain stopped the engines immediately his body was never recovered. Williams often travelled with copies of Crane's books and letters, and liked to use his poems as dipping pans for titles, though he wasn't sure he understood so much as a single line. No matter. He got the impact, the heady sense of being glutted by imagistic language. One of the last plays he ever wrote, *Steps Must be Gentle*, was a two-hander in which ghost versions of Crane and his mother Grace air their grievances, just as Hemingway and Fitzgerald did in *Clothes for a Summer Hotel*. In it, Crane recounts the events on the *Orizaba*: how his face was disfigured in the row and how he came out on to the deck in pyjamas and a coat, which he folded neatly over the stern rail before stepping out.

Beneath the biographical dressing, the play is recognisably a rearrangement of the old bones of *The Glass Menagerie*, written forty years before. There's something profoundly distressing about realising that even in the very last years of his life Williams still felt compelled to write about young men desperate to escape their mothers. This time, though, there's no coffin trick, no whirling through cities like dead leaves. Even five fathoms beneath the sea, Crane has not travelled beyond the reach of his mother's suffocating devotion and need.

By coincidence, Crane also played a role in Cheever's inner life. As a young man he'd met the poet, who was friends with his old mentor Malcolm Cowley. Cowley's wife Peggy was Crane's travelling companion on the *Orizaba*, and Cheever liked to tell a bitchy story in which Crane killed himself because Peggy had been too busy in the ship's beauty parlour to comfort him after the attack. Despite his flippancy, the poet's death loomed large in Cheever's mind. It represented all too clearly the consequences – violence, rejection, humiliation, death – that might follow a public admittance of homosexual desire.

Both of these stories seemed to move beneath the surface of the water; both freighted with the kind of sorrows one might wish to drown. The boat had anchored seven miles from shore. The crew were tossing boxes of facemasks and flippers on to the deck. I pulled on my gear and staggered down the yellow steps into rocking glass-blue waves that were smashing against the sides, tossing streamers of spray into my face. The ropes tensed then slackened. I stepped off, gasping, and kicked my way out.

There wasn't much to see. Sand, a few plants, some lumps of reddish coral in balls like polystyrene. The sun fell in shafts. I breathed audibly, as slowly as I could. Tiny grains of debris were raining past my mask, like static on a screen. 'Liquor and swimming,' Tennessee said in an interview in the 1960s, 'is all that keeps me going: Miltown, liquor and swimming.'

It had struck me a long time back that the dream of letting go into water is prevalent in the work of alcoholic writers. I'd been collecting them up, these little fantasies of cleanliness, purification, dissolution and death. Some were healthful: antidotes to a kind of felt dirtiness gathering elsewhere. In a fairly weak mid-period short story called 'The Swimmers', Fitzgerald wrote about immersion as a literally life-saving practice for a man trapped in an unhappy marriage.

When difficulties became insurmountable, inevitable, Henry sought surcease in exercise. For three years, swimming had been a sort of refuge, and he turned to it as one man to music or another to drink. There was a point when he would resolutely stop thinking and go to the Virginia coast for a week to wash his mind in the water. Far out past the breakers he could survey the green-and-brown line of the Old Dominion with the pleasant impersonality of a porpoise. The burden of his wretched marriage fell away with the buoyant tumble of his body among the swells, and he would begin to move in a child's dream of space. Sometimes remembered playmates of his youth swam with him; sometimes, with his two sons beside him, he seemed to be setting off along the bright pathway to the moon.

This pleasant activity recalls John Cheever, who made Neddy Merrill say in 'The Swimmer' what he himself so ardently believed, that: 'To be embraced and sustained by the light green water was less a pleasure, it seemed, than the resumption of a natural condition.' It sounds delicious, but in that story there's an explicit link between the desire for buoyancy, and the need to drive away difficulties with a measure of gin. Even the phrase 'resumption of a natural condition' bears some hint of regression: recalling the naked swimmer of the womb, irresponsible and free-floating in his purely liquid realm.

By the end of Neddy's journey home, he's exhausted and ill from the two kinds of plunges he's been taking. Even the structure of the story is swimmy, jolting uncertainly through time, like the party scenes in *The Great Gatsby*, which proceeds in a surge of unconnected frames, made jazzy and modern by the splicings of Nick Carraway's blackouts.

As for the mapping of an alcoholic's descent by way of his ability to move through water – wasn't that repeated in *Tender is the Night*, where Dick Diver begins as the graceful, competent king of the Riviera beach and ends by nearly killing himself while tumbling off an aqua-plane, botching a trick he could pull off perfectly two summers before?

I was drifting away from the boat. I took two or three sharp strokes, let go again. There was more. A letter Hemingway wrote in 1950, in which he described diving off the deck of *Pilar*, somewhere in this same luminous region of the Gulf. He'd gone way down in waters that were a mile and a half deep, and on some black impulse emptied his lungs of air. Suspended in the warm half-light, he thought about letting himself drown, and it was only the memory of his three boys that made him kick fiercely to the surface.

Another. In the Dream Song 'Henry's Understanding', John Berryman recalled a night on holiday in Maine, aged thirty-two or so. His wife is asleep, his friends Richard and Helen are asleep, but he – or rather the Henry-he, that ever-diminishing mask – is wide awake and reading. He thinks of putting down the book, undressing, climbing into bed, and then it occurs to him:

> that *one* night, instead of warm pajamas,
> I'd take off all my clothes
> & cross the damp cold lawn & down the bluff
> into the terrible water & walk forever
> under it out toward the island.

This isn't quite a fantasy of death. You don't walk forever, dead. Instead, it's a dream of entering some other realm, both protective and destructive: an underwater world, where you are naked, unreachable, and entirely alone. The island at the end of the lawn was P'tit Manan, visible from Richard's house, though it's not perhaps irrelevant that when his father shot himself they were living on Clearwater Island, out in the Gulf of Mexico.

I swam back to the boat then and struggled up the steps, dumping my gear on the deck and showering under a hose of sun-warmed water. The sky was blue, whitened with little scuds of cirrus. A few snorkellers were still in the sea, splayed like starfish, their arms akimbo. 'Let's go!' the captain shouted. 'Come back to the boat!' and they herded obediently in.

As we sailed back to Key West the crew handed round trays of beer. I took a cup, the plastic beaded with condensation. People were sprawled all over the deck, their bodies glistening with sunscreen, palpably relaxed after their swim. My hair had worked itself into spectacular tangles and I was unravelling them with my fingers when all of a sudden there were three, four, five fins in the water. 'Dolphins! Dolphins! Dolphins!' the prettiest cabin boy shouted. Atlantic bottle-noses, leaping beside the boat, lifting their clean, beaming faces to the sun. They shot back under, leeing east, and as they ducked I remembered another line, this time Fitzgerald's, which riddled in with the rest: 'All good writing is *swimming under water* and holding your breath.'

★

There was one last thing I wanted to do in Key West. I'd been walking past St. Mary's Star of the Sea two, sometimes four times a day. It was on Truman Avenue, a big Spanish-looking building with two spires like pointed hats. On my final morning in town, I went inside. All of the doors were open, and the big room was flooded with light. The prayer book was open on Psalm 139: 'Oh Lord you have searched me and known me.' Underneath was the Spanish: 'Señor, tu me examinas y conoces.'

Hemingway's youngest son, Gregory, was baptised here on 14 January 1932, and it was here too that Tennessee Williams made his conversion to Catholicism, slap-bang in the worst period of his life. After Frank died in 1963, he went to see Max Jacobson, the infamous Dr. Feelgood, who treated his patients with intramuscular injections of vitamins, painkillers and amphetamines, the so-called 'miracle shots'. This was the beginning of Tennessee's Stoned Age, which lasted right through the 1960s. During that whole irredeemable period, he was far gone and out, barely perpendicular against the current, buoyed on a diet of coffee, liquor, Doriden, Mellaril, barbiturates and speed. Hardly any wonder he found it hard to speak and kept toppling over in bars, theatres and hotels. Each year, he put on a new play, and each year it failed, rarely lasting more than a month before it closed.

In January of 1969, his brother Dakin came to visit and became convinced Tennessee was about to die. A Catholic himself, he organised the conversion, hoping at the very least to ensure his brother didn't wind up in hell. Years later, in the *Paris Review* interview of 1981, Tennessee recounted a hazy memory of meeting a Jesuit father who seemed 'very lovely' and who decided, probably wisely, that Mr. Williams was not capable of learning catechisms. Instead, he received extreme unction, which is reserved for the very sick, before being pronounced a Catholic. The baptism took place in this airy blue and white room. I imagined him listing up the aisle, supported by his housekeeper and Dakin, parroting the responses beneath a stained glass image of Our Lady, standing in the midst of the ocean, the sun setting behind her in bars of red and gold.

It didn't help, perhaps because he was barely conscious of where he was or what he was saying. Dakin's next intervention was more extreme. In September of the same year, Tennessee got up to make himself coffee and somehow either sat on the stove or fell down and spilled the Silex of boiling water over his body, getting what he recounted at different times as either second or third degree burns. He rang a friend, raving, and she contacted Dakin. This time he took his brother back with him to St. Louis, the place Tennessee hated most on earth, and had him admitted to St. Barnes Hospital, where he remained on a locked ward for three months. Tennessee never forgave Dakin for this realisation of his greatest fear, though it undoubtedly saved his life.

Dakin . . . just threw me into Barnes Hospital (St. Louis), right into the psychiatric ward, which was *incredibly* awful. They suddenly snatched away every pill I had! The injections went too. So I blacked out. It was cold turkey, baby. They tell me I had three brain concussions in the course of one long day, and a coronary. How I survived, I don't know. I think there were homicidal intentions at work there. I was in that place for three and a half months. The first month I was in the violent ward, although I was not violent. I was terrified and I crouched in a corner trying to read. The patients would have terrible fights over the one television set. Someone would put on the news, and another patient would jump up, yelling, and turn on cartoons. No wonder they were violent.

Writing to a friend from this uncertain sanctuary, he recalled the Silex and the fits but seemed bewildered as to how they fitted together: 'The rest is not blank but is too fragmented and chaotic to be sorted out so far . . . I can only lie on my right side these interminable nights without sleep for more than an occasional lucky bad dream hour. ("Death, how do you like your beautiful blue-eyed boy?") It's sort of fun writing you. This typewriter haunts me.'

Immediately after his release he went on the David Frost show. You can see a clip on YouTube. Tennessee looks thin and dapper in a sweater and dark trousers. He's still very handsome, his moustache neatly trimmed. 'Ah'm on the wagon now,' he says, so drunk he can hardly work the words free. Everyone laughs, and he pokes his tongue out coquettishly and drawls: 'I allow myself o-one drink a day.' Frost asks him about his homosexuality, as if it's another affliction he might have overcome, and Williams gets off a one-liner that has the audience eating out of his hand. 'But I've covered the waterfront,' he giggles, and flings himself back in the chair to a great storm of applause.

Back at liberty, he resumed the obsessive cycle of production. In the course of the 1970s there were six new plays, one novel, one volume of poems, one collection of stories and *Memoirs*, which became a bestseller. In the spring of 1979, he took up his long-neglected diary again, this time titling it *Mes Cahiers Noir*. It begins with a long, raving entry full of disconnected aphorisms.

Did I die by my own hand or was I destroyed slowly and brutally by a conspiratorial group?

The best I can say for myself is that I worked like hell.

I am old and ugly and that is abhorrent, but in a different way. My disease is abhorrent, but in a different way.

I remained a kind person, or at least a person who respected kindness and struggled to retain it, for a long, long time.

It was around this time that Truman Capote satirised him in his wicked, sometimes wickedly funny, novel *Answered Prayers*, which he never finished, despite all his boasts, and which was published after his death, though sections of it ran in the late 1970s in *Esquire* and led to the exodus of a great number of his friends. The Williams character is a playwright called Mr. Wallace, who lives in a disgustingly filthy room at the Plaza hotel, with laundry everywhere and 'dog shit all over the place, and drying puddles of dog piss marking the rugs' – a picture Tennessee's journals confirm as accurate. He has 'a way-down-yonder voice mushy as sweet-potato pie . . . a voice jingling with gin-slurred giggles', and he shivers as he bolts his Scotch. 'Alcoholics,' the narrator P.B. Jones confides, 'really despise the taste of alcohol' – a fact Capote, of all people, ought to know.

Mr. Wallace talks in looping circuits of paranoia, hypochondria and self-pity, a tone instantly recognisable from the last hundred pages of the diaries. Musing blearily to the naked stranger in his bed, he comments that he feels safe:

> As safe as a hunted man can feel. A man with murderers on his trail. I'm liable to die very suddenly. And if I do, it won't be a natural death. They'll try to make it look like heart failure. Or an accident. But promise me you won't believe that. Promise me you'll write a letter to the Times and tell them it was murder.

In fact, Tennessee did write a letter very similar to this to Dakin. Then there's a lot about how Mr. Wallace is in love with his own heroines, who are basically versions of himself, and how he's self-obsessed and incapable of taking in the existence of anybody else. It ends with him asking Jones, who is a kind of failed-writer-cum-rent boy, to strip and spread himself. When he demurs, Mr. Wallace says in his sloppy, sugary voice, 'Ohhh, I don't want to cornhole you, old buddy. I just want to put out my cigar.'

I hated that story, though perhaps it says more about Capote than Williams. It didn't sound like his style: not the cruelty, anyhow, though it's true he objectified trade and was capable of violent fits of temper, often cutting friends and lovers out of his life for minor, imagined slights. Still, if you read it you need to hold for balance the version of Williams reflected back by Marlon Brando, who played Stanley Kowalski in *A Streetcar Named Desire*. Tennessee never thought Brando liked him, but he did, and this is what that big, silent man, who had his own problems in life, had to say about him. He wrote:

> You have been as brave as anybody I've known, and it is comforting to think about it. You probably don't think of yourself as brave because nobody who really has courage does, but I know you are and I get food from that.

It was still true, even in the last years of his life. In January 1979 he was attacked in the streets of Key West by what the town police blotter records to have been four or five white males in the 500 block of Duval Street. They punched his friend in the jaw (the same friend, as it happens, who interviewed him for the *Paris Review*), then threw

Tennessee to the ground and kicked him. A lens fell out of his glasses, but he was otherwise unharmed. They knew who he was, but he didn't let it bother him. 'Why not?' an interviewer asked a few months later, and he replied, stalwart as ever: 'Because, baby, I don't allow it to.'

That summer, he wrote *Clothes for a Summer Hotel*, which was staged at the Cort Theater in New York the following spring. On the opening night the audience leapt to their feet for Williams, dapper and grizzled in the royal box. It was his sixty-ninth birthday, and he attended the cast party in a blaze of pleasure. For a buoyant moment it seemed like the play might be a success, though it had already failed two preview runs in Washington and Chicago. Then the reviews trickled in. 'Structurally wasteful', the *New York Times* reported, concluding: 'the finest playwright of our time has spent his evening trying hard, much too hard, to sound like other people.'

It got worse. At the end of March, a blizzard hit Manhattan, and at one minute past midnight on 1 April, the city's transport workers went on strike. The vast, intricate mechanism of New York seized up and theatre takings crashed. At the end of each performance the producer went on stage to rally the crowd, begging them to come again, to bring their friends. This play will run forever, he promised, but on the evening of 16 April he didn't appear and the cast understood their play was finished. Miserably, they gathered their things. Geraldine Page, who had been playing the hawk-eyed, unlovable Zelda, even took the flowers from her dressing room and packed them in her suitcase.

A day or two later, the set was taken to an incinerator in New Jersey and burned. Among the props were a tent made of silk streamers; a set of black gates; the façade of a triple-storeyed building, the upper windows barred; and a bush hung with leaves of red cellophane, designed to look as if it was licked with flames. There's something immensely distressing about this fire, for a play so obsessed with the burning out of promise, the conflagration of both hope and talent. Horribly ironic, too, that the simulacrum of Zelda's madhouse should also be incinerated, when days before Geraldine Page had stood in front of it and described her death, her transformation into a little heap of indistinguishable ash.

While the fire was taking place, Tennessee headed back to Key West, to swim out his disappointment and distress. I imagined him padding past the church on his way to the beach, thinking about the ghosts he'd summoned so briefly to the stage. Not easy, raising the dead – or, for that matter, looking in the mirror and recording what you see there. I thought about what lay ahead: two more years of incessant travel, and then the night in the Elysée. He never actually set down the codicil to his will, and so Dakin buried him in the cold ground of St. Louis, next to his mother, the armfuls of yellow roses on his coffin insufficient compensation for the loss of that last, long-cherished dream.

Sometimes it's better to look back. And for a second I saw him very clearly: the Tennessee of the early 1950s; on a good day, Frank at home. A short, handsome man with a slight paunch, tanned brown as a nut, his Ray-Bans on, in madras shorts and tennis pumps. The day's work is done, the afternoon clear and clean, all his. I imagined him cruising the pretty boys on Dog Beach, and then walking out past them into the little greeny waves, giving himself up to the current, tomorrow's words just starting to rise, to bite.

7

THE CONFESSIONS OF MR. BONES

IT TOOK ME SIX DAYS to get from Key West to Port Angeles, slogging from the south-eastern corner of America all the way up to its north-western extremity, a journey of almost 5,000 miles. I drove to Miami, flew to New Orleans to reclaim my case, slept a night there and then got on a train bound for Chicago. From the plane I'd watched the weather coming in, the flocks of cumulus driving hard across Carolina. I'd overtaken them, but now the sky was darkening and the forecast promised T-storms.

On the outskirts of New Orleans we passed a run of boarded-up houses, all derelict, and then a boat wedged into the branches of a tree, a relic of Katrina. We followed the Mississippi north as the after-noon ebbed away. For miles the plain was filled with burned or poisoned trees, their bark blackened, rising out of a swamp that caught the sky and gave it back in little flustered eddies. I ate applesauce from a plastic carton and watched a heron capped with bright blue feathers pick its way through brackish water. There was a turtle down there too, and as soon as I noticed it I saw there were hundreds of them, crammed on every floating branch. Then houses again, and a billboard extolling the virtues of LASER LIPO.

Beehives in the forest, grazing horses, red earth. The wind had gotten up, driving the dust in chutes. The light pulsed, electric. Big clouds were gathering, and there was a yellowish cast to the west, the colour of old piano keys, old teeth. The streetlights clicked on, and then the overhead lights in the carriage. 'Nobody hit the Powerball, I guess,' a man said. 'Well, that's good. It's up to 30 million.' Then the clouds clamped down like a lid, the sky turned a funny burnished green and rain started pummelling against the windows until the glass was corrugated. In a few seconds the world outside was obliterated. Low rolls of thunder, and every few seconds a flicker of lightning.

I hadn't seen rain in the longest time. I could smell it; the sweet, replenished scent of earth. 'A heck of a rainstorm,' someone said into their phone. 'Is it raining there? It really got dark and then it came down . . . I'm pretty close to Jackson.' By six it was light again. The rivers were brown with mud and the streets were brown too and slick with water. I watched the day unfold, flare out. We ran for a long time across a single field, the red mark where the sun had set small as a hearth fire against the acres of ploughed earth.

That night I ate dinner with two strangers, both very shy. 'I hope you two ladies don't mind,' the man said, 'but where I was raised we ate fried chicken with our fingers.' Then, exhausted by the mileage I was clocking up, I went back to my seat and fell asleep, rocked to and fro by the train.

I woke at five, just as the sun was rising. We'd crossed by night into the Grain Belt and now we were running up Illinois, through mile after mile of stubbled corn, punctuated by metal grain silos and graveyards for abandoned trucks and cars. I put Sufjan Stevens on my iPod and watched the colourless world well up with light. The fields seemed endless, a sea that shifted as the sun rose from lead to pewter and then to gold.

People were waking, passing up and down the aisle with cups of coffee. There are moments in a journey that can never be predicted in advance: not their richness, nor the effect they have on one's heart. The light fell equably, agreeably, on Harvey Christian Bookstore, Stewart Roofing and Harvey Fire Department; on children waiting for yellow school buses; on wooden houses, brick churches and country platforms. Hope, it said, unmistakably, and as the train wailed its low, harmonious cry I lay back in my seat and opened a book with the cheerful title of *Recovery*.

★

Recovery is an unfinished novel by John Berryman, the poet whose father shot himself on Clearwater Island on 26 June 1926. In the wake of that catastrophe John's mother and his new stepfather moved the family to New York to start their lives afresh. Two years on John was sent to South Kent, a spartan Connecticut boarding school, of which he remembered later an entire class being made to crawl on their knees across a gravel terrace, reading their history books as they went. He didn't mind that particular punishment, but school in general was a torment. As a boy, Berryman was gawky and scrawny, in thick glasses, his face livid with acne. Useless at football and far too clever to be well liked, he didn't thrive until he left at the age of seventeen for Columbia, New York's Ivy League university.

Academia was at once a refuge and an intoxication. In his first year he was far too excited by the social possibilities, particularly the proximity of all those beautiful Barnard girls, to pay much attention to his classes. Dating, dancing and writing poetry ate up his time and he did poorly in almost all his first year courses. He took a leave of absence and returned with renewed seriousness in the spring. A friend at the time, Dorothy Rockwell, remembered him then as:

> . . . thin and gratingly intense – kind of grim-jawed but every now and then his face would split into a fiendish grin. He was going to be a poet and was Van Doren's protégé, and this put him a cut above the rest of us if we thought about it.

He was a nervy boy, and sometimes threatened suicide (Lionel Trilling, who was teaching at Columbia at the time, recalled considering him affected). There was no doubt, though, as to his brilliance. By 1935, he was regularly publishing poems in the *Columbia Review*, one of which was reprinted in the *Nation*. His academic work also sharpened, helped by his habits of obsessive nocturnal study. In 1936 he was rewarded with a scholarship to Cambridge. The habit was set. For the rest of his ranging life, he'd remain anchored in academia.

In Cambridge he attended lectures by T.S. Eliot and Auden, met Yeats and Dylan Thomas, and worked on Shakespeare late into the night. After a period of 'unwilling monkhood', he fell in love with an English girl with the appropriate name of Beatrice. But despite what would be a lifelong Anglophilia, he returned to America in 1938, leaving Beatrice behind. He wanted to get a job as a professor, though it didn't prove as easy as he'd hoped. In the end, his old professor Mark Van Doren supplied a reference ('he is to my certain knowledge both brilliant and promising: a fine poet, a fully equipped critic, and insatiable reader, and – though you must know this – an engaging person'), and with that in hand he finally swung a job in the English department of Wayne State University.

The workload was heavy and that year he suffered badly from insomnia. He often spent whole nights walking around Detroit, going into university gaunt and smelly to teach what were by all accounts inspired classes, in which he held forth on Shakespeare or poetry, quoting great gouts by heart. He trembled as he talked, and paced the room, his voice getting higher and higher as his excitement grew. When he returned to the apartment he shared with a married couple, he'd frequently faint as soon as he walked through the door. Coming to Wayne had been, he began to think: 'an insane mistake, and I am paying – in health, in temper, in *time*'. He was barely eating and sometimes suffered hallucinations and yet he refused to stop his frantic programme of reading, teaching and study. A doctor made a tentative diagnosis of *petit mal* epilepsy, while a psychiatrist thought he was neurotic and in imminent danger of complete nervous collapse.

Slowly, he pulled himself together. In 1940 he took up a post as an instructor in English literature at Harvard, where he spent a great deal of time with the poets Robert Lowell and Delmore Schwartz, both of whom drank heavily and also suffered from turbulent mental health. In 1942, he married Eileen Mulligan, a dark-haired, quick-witted girl who later became an analyst. After a few years of jobbing lectureships, they moved together to Princeton, where he taught creative writing while working on an analytical biography of Stephen Crane and a study of *King Lear*, as well as publishing his first volume of poems, *The Dispossessed*.

Until this point he'd drunk only socially, but in 1947 events precipitated a great shift in both his writing and his habits. He fell in love with a colleague's wife and began an affair, simultaneously anatomising it in a feverish sequence of sonnets. This was the moment, he figured later, when he began to drink seriously, both to choke back his guilt and to fan the flames of his desire. Eileen agreed. In her marvellously lively memoir of their life together, *Poets in Their Youth*, she remembered him at the time:

> . . . alternately hysterical and depressed, couldn't sleep, had violent nightmares when he did and, most disturbingly of all, was drinking in a terrifyingly uncharacteristic way . . . For John, who awakened guilt-ridden and exhausted from a battle with demons, a 'brilliant' martini became the cure for a hangover, a nightcap or two the cure for insomnia.

During this period he started a poem about Anne Bradstreet: at once a biography and a seduction in verse of the long-dead, pox-spotted New England poet. 'Homage to Mistress Bradstreet' almost killed him, but it was good: hot to the touch, exquisitely wrought. There's a verse in it I love, a homage at once to the magical facility of the biographer's art and to the intimate kinship one can feel for the long dead. The poet speaks directly to Anne's ghost, summoning her back by the magnetic force of his devotion.

Both of our worlds unhanded us. Lie stark,

thy eyes look to me mild. Out of maize and air
your body's made and moves. I summon, see,
from the centuries it.
I think you won't stay. How do we
linger, diminished, in our lovers' air,
implausibly visible, to whom, a year,
years, over interims; or not;
to a long stranger; or not; shimmer & disappear.

What followed on the poem was not good, however. In 1953, the year
of its completion, Eileen left Berryman, worn to despair by his anxiety,
drinking, promiscuity and toxic guilt. He moved to the Chelsea Hotel
in New York, where his old friend Dylan Thomas was also staying.
On 4 November, Thomas collapsed in his room after guzzling whiskeys
in the White Horse. He was taken to St. Vincent's Hospital in the
Village, where a few days later Berryman walked into the temporarily
unattended chamber to find him dead in his oxygen tent, his bare feet
sticking out from beneath the sheet. It was a warning – one perhaps
too demanding to translate.

In 1954, Berryman was hired to teach a semester of creative writing
at the University of Iowa, where two decades on John Cheever and
Raymond Carver would also struggle to balance their compulsions and
their duties. On his first day, he fell down the stairs of his new apartment,
smashing through a glass door and breaking his left wrist. He taught in
a sling, inspiring and relentless as ever despite a gathering depression. The
poet Philip Levine, one of his students that year, later wrote an elegy to

his former teacher entitled 'Mine Own John Berryman': a testament to his decency and commitment to literature.

> He entered the room each night shaking with anticipation and always armed with a pack of note cards, which he rarely consulted. Privately, he confessed to me that he spent days preparing for these sessions. He went away from them in a state bordering on collapse . . . No matter what you hear or read about his drinking, his madness, his unreliability as a person, I am here to tell you that in the winter and spring of 1954, living in isolation and loneliness in one of the bleakest towns of our difficult Midwest, John Berryman never failed his obligations as a teacher.

The work ended abruptly that fall, though, when he got into a drunken altercation with his landlord. He was arrested and spent a night in a cell, where the cops apparently exposed themselves to him. When news of this humiliating escapade seeped out he was summoned before the Deans and fired from his job. Luckily, a friend found him a post at the University of Minnesota, which would for the rest of his life serve as a home base. He took an apartment in Minneapolis and began a new sequence of poems he called the Dream Songs.

They're like nothing else on earth, these mixed messages of love and desperation. The closest comparison I can think of is Gerard Manley Hopkins, had Hopkins been a philandering alcoholic at large in the twentieth century, hip to its rhythms, its cobalt jazz. Three stanzas of six lines, speedy, impacted, full of *emphasis* and – gaps. Henry at the centre, Henry Pussycat, Huffy Henry, sometimes called by his unnamed companion *Mr. Bones*. The two men's voices range in ways no poetry had till then, soaring and slouching through dialect, baby talk, slang, the archaic gleanings of a Shakespeare scholar. As it grew, the poem gathered shape: passing Henry out of life to death and back again. All the while he complains, harping on about his dismal life, his lost father, his dead and living friends, his alcoholism and his troubles with the compact and delicious bodies of women. Henry is a man in a confession booth, hungry for solace of all kinds, berating, like Job, a God he can't quite admit either to or in.

Outside the poem, a period of domestic peace began. A week after his divorce from Eileen was granted in 1956, Berryman married Ann Levine, a much younger woman he'd met in Minnesota. That year, he was given a Rockefeller Fellowship, and in 1957 won the Harriet Monroe Poetry Prize for *Bradstreet*. Shortly after, Ann gave birth to a son, Paul, nicknamed Poo. 'He is getting a pot, his second chin is wicked to contemplate, his skin is ravishing all over, and he smells good,' the new father wrote dotingly, though he'd come rapidly to resent the division of Ann's attentions.

After months of fighting, she left him in January 1959, taking the baby with her. Berryman began drinking harder than ever then and a few weeks later, after an attack of delirium tremens, was admitted to Glenwood Hills Hospital on Golden Valley Road, Minneapolis, a closed ward for alcoholics. Despite being in the throes of what he described as 'mental agony, broken health and the double wreck of my marriage', he kept up the pace of work and study, writing and rearranging Dream Songs and staggering out by taxi to teach his classes. Released, he drank again; returned again. His sleep was wretched, even with sedatives, 'so I'm nearly dead all the time'.

The two things, writing and drinking, ran concurrently. Later that same year he spent a November day in the university library reading books on the history of minstrel shows, trying to see if he could work the Tambo and Bones routine into the Dream Songs. From this came the decision to give Henry his companion, his rueful witness and sparring partner. That same night, staggering drunk into the bath, he fell and twisted his right arm. Man down. Man going on.

In 1960, he took the opportunity to wheel south, accepting the offer of a spring semester at Berkeley. From this uncertain refuge he wrote gleefully to a friend: 'I get through the most marvellous quantities of liquor here, by the way. I dont drink as *much* as I did in Mpls, but I enjoy it much more, because I don't go to bars, I just order it in and settle down with it.' He'd been teaching with his usual flair and rigour, but in his free time suffered intensely from isolation and paranoia, though this lightened a little when he met a Catholic girl called Kate Donahue, herself the daughter of an alcoholic, who in 1961 became his third and final wife.

On it went. In 1962, he spent a summer at the Bread Loaf residency, writing Songs and drinking gin martinis. By fall his behaviour was erratic. He shouted, sometimes sobbed. In November he went unwillingly to McLean's Hospital outside Boston, where Robert Lowell was also treated. On the third day he promised never to combine liquor with writing poetry again. He was released on 1 December, dry seven days, and twenty-four hours later his wife gave birth to their first daughter, Martha, soon to be known as Miss Twiss.

Another injury, almost comical this time. The next day he visited Kate and the baby in hospital, then took a celebratory drink with friends. Somehow the cab home succeeded in running over his foot and breaking his ankle. When he missed an appointment with his psychiatrist, friends were sent to track him down. They found him holed up in bed, his foot already festering. Taken to the emergency room he bellowed: 'I feel like a minor character in a bad Scott Fitzgerald novel.' The next day, very drunk again, he accused Kate of neglecting him.

In 1964 he was hospitalised three times, spilling Dream Songs all the way. No wonder he described Henry grievingly as 'losing altitude'; no wonder he seemed to be 'out of everything/save whiskey & cigarettes'. And yet the good news kept coming; kept somehow failing to plug the gap. On 27 April, 77 *Dream Songs* was published. The reviews weren't as warm as he would have liked, particularly the one from his old friend Lowell ('At first the brain aches and freezes at so much darkness, disorder and oddness'), but there were critics – and better yet, poets – who got what he and Huffy Henry were about. Writing in the *Nation*, Adrienne Rich described it as 'creepy and scorching', observing 'his book owes much of its beauty and flair to a kind of unfakable courage, which spills out in comedy as well as in rage, in thrusts of tenderness as well as defiance'. There were other compensations too. That year he won the Russell Loines Award and the next he was awarded a Pulitzer.

In 1965, the combination of success and self-destruction accelerated. He broke his left arm walking in socks on a wooden floor; wrote to his friend William Meredith: 'I've been in & out of hospitals so often lately I'm dizzy.' He was awarded a Guggenheim Fellowship to continue work on the Songs, and in 1966 used the money to take his family to Ireland for a year. In Dublin he met the poet John Montague, who later felt moved to comment:

Berryman is the only poet I have ever seen for whom drink seemed to be a positive stimulus. He drank enormously and smoked heavily, but it seemed to be part of a pattern of work, a crashing of the brain barriers as he raced towards the completion of the *Dream Songs*. For he appeared to me positively happy, a man who was engaged in completing his life's work, with a wife and child he adored.

It was a half truth, at the very best. On New Year's Day 1967, he fell and hurt his back, damaging a nerve. In April he was committed to Grange Gorman mental hospital to detox. In May he flew back to New York to collect an award from the Academy of American Poets, staying at the Chelsea Hotel, never a safe place. When friends found him vomiting blood they took him to the French Hospital, 'all but dead'. He submitted to treatment, insisting on keeping a half pint of whiskey by his bed. Another Dream Song: 'He was *all* regret, swallowing his own vomit, / disappointing people, letting everyone down / in the forests of the soul.'

That autumn *Berryman's Sonnets* came out – the ones he'd written in Princeton in the white heat of his affair. In 1968 the second volume of Dream Songs, *His Toy, His Dream, His Rest*, was published, followed the next year by *The Dream Songs*, the collected volume. The honours, too, kept flooding in. *His Toy* was awarded the National Book Award for Poetry and the Bollingen Prize. He was appointed Regent Professor of Humanities at Minnesota and gave readings countrywide. And then, on 10 November 1969, he was admitted to Hazelden, a hospital in Minneapolis, with acute symptoms of alcoholism and a sprained left ankle, caused by tumbling over in his own bathroom.

This time he didn't just dry out, buoyed up on thorazidine. Hazelden was one of the pioneers of the Minnesota Model, the then radical, now commonplace technique of treating alcoholics as in-patients in therapeutic communities, where they follow the Twelve Steps of Alcoholics Anonymous, attend lectures and learn, through constant challenging and self-exposure, how to lay down the defences that perpetuate their disease.

It wasn't an easy process, undoing the habits of two decades, never mind the terrors that underlay them. On 1 December, a counsellor jotted down his impressions of Berryman.

> Pt. admits that he is an alcoholic . . . Indication of depression, anxiety, immaturity, lack of insight, high aesthetic interests, feelings of alienation, & dependency . . . Admitted he is full of fear.

Released, he stayed sober twelve days, then drank again. At the same time there was a spell of euphoric work: new lyrics, another shot at the Shakespeare biography. In a letter to William Meredith he sounded manic:

> I am having the best winter within memory – mostly very hard every day at Shakespeare scholarship & criticism, but also a new poem called 'Washington in Love', which advances spasmodically . . . my two slight interesting seminars at the University, one in *Hamlet*, the other on the American character, and reading Trollope's magnificent *Last Chronicle*, and *Genesis* daily, and Vaillant's *The Aztecs* in preparation for 3 weeks or a month in Mexico next summer.

Then, on 26 February 1970, he was taken back to hospital, his shins black with bruises, unable to walk or stand. He returned four times in the next six weeks, each time staying just long enough to detoxify before going back out to drink.

On 2 May he was rushed to the Intensive Alcohol Treatment Center at St. Mary's Hospital in Minneapolis, for his second stab at treatment. Here he took the First Step, in which an alcoholic admits they're powerless over alcohol and that their life has become unmanageable. Trying to get to grips with the enormous, terrifying implications of this sentence, Berryman wrote down and later read out to his treatment group this high-speed, seemingly no-holds-barred autobiography of his drinking self.

> Social drinking until 1947 during a long & terrible love affair, my first infidelity to my wife after 5 years of marriage. My mistress drank heavily & I drank w. her. Guilt, murderous & suicidal. Hallucinations one day walking home. Heard voices. 7 years of psychoanalysis & group therapy in N.Y. Walked up & down drunk on a foot-wide parapet 8 stories high. Passes at women drunk, often successful. Wife left me after 11 yrs of marriage bec. of drinking. Despair, heavy drinking alone, jobless, penniless, in N.Y. Lost when blacked-out the most important professional letter I have ever received. Seduced students drunk. Made homosexual advances drunk, 4 or 5 times. Antabuse once for a few days, agony on floor after a beer. Quarrel w. landlord drunk at midnight over the key to my apartment, he called police, spent the night in jail, news somehow reached press & radio, forced to resign. Two months

of intense self-analysis-dream-interpretations etc. Remarried. My chairman told me I had called up a student drunk at midnight & threatened to kill her. Wife left me bec. of drinking. Gave a public lecture drunk. Drunk in Calcutta, wandered streets lost all night, unable to remember my address. Married present wife 8 yrs ago. Many barbiturates & tranquilizers off & on over last 10 yrs. Many hospitalizations. Many alibis for drinking, lying abt. it. Severe memory-loss, memory distortions. DT's once in Abbott, lasted hours. Quart of whiskey a day for months in Dublin working hard on a long poem. Dry 4 months 2 years ago. Wife hiding bottles, myself hiding bottles. Wet bed drunk in a London hotel, manager furious, had to pay for a new mattress, $100. Lectured too weak to stand, had to sit. Lectured badly prepared. Too ill to give an examination, colleague gave it. Too ill to lecture one day. Literary work stalled for months. Quart of whiskey a day for months. Wife desperate, threatened to leave unless I stopped. Two doctors drove me to Hazelden last November, 1 week intensive care unit, 5 wks treatment. AA 3 times, bored, made no friends. First drink at Newlbars' party. Two months light drinking, hard biographical work. Suddenly began new poems 9 weeks ago, heavier & heavier drinking more & more, up to a quart a day. Defecated uncontrollably in university corridor, got home unnoticed. Book finished in outburst of five weeks, most intense work in my whole life exc. maybe first two weeks of 1953. My wife said St Mary's or else. Came here.

It didn't help. On 12 June he was discharged uncured. On 18 June he wrote another disturbingly glib letter to Meredith: 'I'm just out of

6 wks in hospital (alcoholism as usual) & my doctors say it will be a year before I'm all right. I've added 17 poems, some of them very important, to *Love & Fame*.'

The same day he started drinking again in a bar in St. Paul, though despite repeated lapses he kept going to AA. At the beginning of October he gave a reading, and then flew back to Minneapolis from New York. He rang Kate from the airport, telling her he was on his way home. Then he disappeared for two days, reeling in on Sunday shabby, wrecked and wretched. He remembered the phone call, remembered stopping at a bar for a nightcap. After that nothing, all data wiped. Confronted by his wife and friends in his own living room, he agreed to go back to St. Mary's and try, for the third time, to get dry.

★

All this awful history pours, barely altered, into *Recovery*. For years, in the Dream Songs, Berryman had been using Henry House to process and reconfigure various items from his own past, central among them the suicide of his father. Now he takes up a new mask, thinner and more transparent. Alan Severance is a public intellectual, a Pulitzer Prize-winning Professor of Immunology – 'twice-invited guest on the Dick Cavett Show (stoned once, and a riot)'. Their jobs diverge, as do some details about an aunt. Otherwise almost everything about Severance, from his messy room, hacking cough and roaring voice to his grandiosity, brilliance, kindness, arrogance, injuries and multiple delusions, is drawn from the real, well-weathered experience of Berryman himself.

It opens with a prelude. Alan is drunk. Lots of light, some inexplicable darkness. Ah, he's in his own entry-hall, familiar figures hard by. His wife is holding out a glass – not, he thinks to himself, nearly big enough. Also standing: two policemen and his Dean. His wife says, cold-eyed: 'This is the last drink you will ever take.' *Screw that*, he thinks, registering also the 'unnerving and apocalyptic' sense that this time it might be true.

The next thing he knows he's back on Ward W, a stand-in for Berryman's ward at St. Mary's. Third chance: deep in withdrawal, toxic with it, though as far as he's concerned his mind is clear as mountain air. He knows *exactly* what went wrong, or thinks he does. An error in the First Step, made in his last pass through recovery. He grins at himself in the mirror, staggers out to the Snack Room to meet his fellow sufferers. For the next God knows how many weeks he'll have access to nothing more potent than coffee, Eskimo Pies and cigarettes. Instead, he'll submit to the gruelling daily rounds of lectures, group therapy, dyads, counselling, private study and prayer.

In a letter to his friend Saul Bellow, written as the book bloomed swiftly, thrillingly, in his mind, Berryman wrote that it would contain: 'Encyclopedic data, almost as heavy as Melville's about whaling.' It's true. *Recovery* is like a crash course in the Minnesota Model, like being locked up in the ward of a treatment centre. It's saturated with the smells of recovery – cigarettes and coffee, mostly – and with its unique speech: a language created explicitly for mastery over this most slippery of diseases.

Reading it, I'd built up a rough glossary of alcoholic terms, some familiar, some new to me. *Denial*: the keynote of the alcoholic personality. The refusal to admit there's a problem. The willingness to say anything to ensure that drinking can continue. *Levelling*: the practice of challenging another addict's delusion. *Slips*: drinks taken after recovery. *Minimising*: a species of denial. The pervasive alcoholic tendency to pretend their drinking, their disasters, are ordinary, unexceptional, barely worth the effort of examination. *Sincere delusions*: delusions the alcoholic genuinely believes. *Regrouping*: the resumption of defences after a period of honesty and openness. *Seeking people*: a corrective to the alcoholic tendency to isolation, 'self-imposed solitary-confinement', self-pity, the belief that one is exceptional and suffers more than others. Indeed, the whole group structure of AA is designed to challenge this by making addicts confront the overwhelming similarities between their stories. *Projection*: reading into another person the feelings you deny in yourself. *Dry drunk*: not drinking, but not committed to changing the personality structures of alcoholism; getting by on will power alone. A very perilous position. *Playing Group*: another species of denial, in which the addict parrots the tenets of AA without having really accepted them or opened up.

For Alan Severance, the process is excruciating as well as exhilarating: tacking in a high wind, recovering his own spirit. He makes friends, submits to criticism, scrapes away at the encrusted layers of his own delusions. Sometimes it seems never-ending, the ability of his disease to defend itself. Still, he has hope. He decides on an impulse to become a Jew, spending hours in fervent study. He talks too much in Group, annoying everybody. Another patient describes him as a 'sick old *lion*' during a game of Animal-Vegetable-Mineral, and then they all jump in, telling him he's pompous, arrogant, disgusting. It's true; he often backs up his statements by commenting, preeningly, on his fame and sexual allure. The confrontation hurts. But he recovers, sees the help in it, shoulders on. Another day the counsellors tear into him, wringing out the confession that it's two, maybe three years since he's seen his son. They want him to understand that it's not just the drinking; that everything about his life is out of joint. 'This was hard, very hard. He couldn't think, just felt.'

Alan Severance isn't the most sympathetic of characters. In fact, I often had a strong urge to smack him round the head. He's grotesquely convinced of the magnificence of his illness, the extraordinary integrity of his brain – or, in other moods, the breathtaking worthlessness of his existence. 'Maybe it's easier to be a monster,' one of the counsellors says, 'than a human being.' And later: 'Alcoholics are rigid, childish, intolerant, programmatic. They *have* to live furtive lives. Your only chance is to come out in the open.'

Sometimes he does, and it's these moments – when he humanises, levels, lets down his guard – that give *Recovery* its extraordinary power. What's more, as Alan's treatment proceeds, it becomes increasingly apparent that he's not alone. The ward is full of people engaged in a Herculean battle with their own minds. Wilbur with his bullying parents. Jasper the poet. Pitiful Sherry, who Alan takes under his wing. It's captivating, watching this group of ordinary Americans attempting to change, to free themselves from addiction. And then, all of a sudden, on page 224 the book stops dead. There are a few pages of scratchy notes, but to all intents and purposes Berryman's *Recovery* is abandoned.

★

At Chicago I got on the Empire Builder to Seattle. Two days to go. I counted through the states ahead. Illinois, Wisconsin, Minnesota,

North Dakota, Idaho and Washington. Later that night we'd pass through St. Paul, Berryman's city and also Fitzgerald's. At the end of *The Great Gatsby* Fitzgerald gave Nick his own memories of travelling home from school. Gatsby has just died, and after the miserable funeral in the rain Nick gets to thinking about catching the winter train from Chicago to St. Paul as a boy. He remembers the dim lights of small Wisconsin stations, the murky yellow cars, and then he says to himself: 'That's my Middle West. Not the wheat or the prairies or the lost Swede towns, but the thrilling returning trains of my youth, and the street lamps and sleigh bells in the frosty dark.'

This time, at long last, I had a cabin: a tiny, pleasingly dinky room with two big blue chairs that slid together to make a bed. There were lots of Amish on the train, the women bonneted, the men in black hats, with great Berrymanish beards. At dinner that night I sat with a couple from Montana and a Michigan geologist who worked on the oil wells in South Dakota. He was morbidly obese, with a pallid face, his eyes sunk far down into mounds of doughy flesh. He drank two Pepsis while we waited for our food and showed me his wedding ring, a circlet of Celtic knots, adding regretfully, 'but I can't sleep in it at night'. We talked about Ireland for a long time, over grilled steaks in mushroom sauce. At La Crosse I looked up and saw an elderly black man on the platform selling red roses from a bucket. Just after I went back to my cabin we crossed the Mississippi and its floodplain, trundling eight feet above the bilgy water. God knows how wide it was. A mile, inset with islands? More?

I pushed the two seats together, settling down on the narrow bed. The abrupt end of *Recovery* had shocked me when I first read it, but it was worse now that I knew the circumstances in which it was written. Berryman was released from his second spell at St. Mary's in late November 1970, determined to stay dry. Some time that winter he wrote himself a Thirteenth Step: 'Avoid *all avoidable nervous & mental effort* for weeks to come. *Only teach*, & that *minimally*. (God can't help a nervous wreck: he'll drink, being physically alcoholic.) TAKE IT EASY!' Good advice, but he was already deep in the usual salt mine of work and self-improvement: a habit he'd had since he was a little boy, writing letters home to his mother boasting about his study. He read Emily Dickinson, underlining 'can't stay' in a line from her letters: 'I can't stay any longer in a world of death.' He read Freud's *Civilisation and its Discontents*, underlining: 'I could not point to any need in child-hood so strong as that for a *father's protection*.'

At the beginning of 1971 he started writing political poems, inflamed by a sense that society itself was out of joint, even crooked. Poems about Che Guevara, My Lai. On 27 January he gave a reading in Chicago, drunk. His dear friend Saul Bellow was there, and later wrote in an essay printed at the front of *Recovery* that he looked decayed and that the reading itself was a disaster. Berryman muttered inaudibly on stage. He vomited in the car, passed out in his room and slept through the party given in his honour. 'But in the morning he was full of innocent cheer. He was chirping. It had been a great evening. He recalled an immense success. His cab came, we hugged each other, and he was off to the airport under a frozen sun.'

Quickly he reined himself in, returning to AA and repairing his sobriety. In the spring he taught two courses: 'The Meaning of Life' and 'The Post-Novel: Fiction as Wisdom-work', which included Malcolm Lowry's classic take on alcoholism, *Under the Volcano*. In March he corrected the proofs of an interview with the *Paris Review* that had been carried out while he was in St. Mary's for the second time. He pointed out six instances of delusion, among them the claim that he had played a large part in the development of the nation, like Jefferson and Poe, and that he was not ashamed to hope that he'd be 'nearly crucified' in order to produce great poetry.

On 24 April, he decided to write *Recovery* as a novel. On 20 May, 'dry as a bone, nearly 4 months', he stayed alone in a hotel in Hartford, Connecticut. At some point that night he had the unnerving sense that Christ was somewhere in the room with him. He started a poem and carried it on, almost frantic, into the small hours. It ends:

> Let me be clear about this. It is plain to me
> *Christ* underwent man & treachery & socks
> & lashes, thirst, exhaustion, the bit, for *my* pathetic & disgusting
> vices,
> to make this filthy fact of particular, long-after,
> far-away, five-foot-ten & moribund
> human being happy. Well, he has!
> I am so happy I could scream!
> It's *enough*! I can't BEAR ANY MORE.
> *Let this be it*. I've *had* it. I can't wait.

Something badly awry in the perspective here. It's marked by the old alcoholic knack for self-pity, the conviction that nothing, not even God, is big enough to contain one's suffering – that Christ's happiness, in fact, depends on that of Berryman's. Terrifying, particularly if your recovery depends – Step Two – on believing that a Power greater than yourself can restore you to sanity, let alone – Step

Three – that you can turn your will and life over to a forgiving, beneficent God.

In his diaries that summer, the same phrases keep repeating. *Take it easy. Take it v. slow.* Hard to heed. He was rapt with the new book, the thrill of it, the enormous charge. He told his first wife, Eileen, in a letter: 'Of course I am determined to produce the most powerful and shapely work of narrative art since *Don Quixote* – what else.'

On 13 June, his mother, who had been displaying increasing forget-fulness and strange behaviour – perhaps dementia, perhaps not – was finally persuaded to move into an expensive apartment across the street, funded by her dutiful son. The same day Kate went into labour. A couple of weeks later Berryman wrote his ecstatic letter to Bellow about *Recovery* being packed with encyclopaedic data. He was boiling over with other plans, too. A scheme for teaching his children, including Paul, who was visiting that summer. New books, scads of them. The long-neglected Shakespeare study. A life of Christ for children. A book of essays about the omnipresent theme of sacrifice in literature and art. Gloatingly, he totted them up: thirteen books burning for completion.

'I admit,' he wrote to his old mentor Mark Van Doren:

> I am putting myself through a crash course this summer of 20 works I should have mastered as they came out, besides the very elaborate novel-related reading, medical lectures and so on. BUT I am insisting on 10 pp a week drafted-typed-revised-retyped; so I don't see how I can go far astray. I am also studying theology before breakfast and after 1 a.m. and keep up a fancy exercise-programme and spend two evenings a week

at hospital and am catching up on 60–70 unanswered letters (many with Mss., alas, including some from Eileen, who has taken to writing stories – not bad either – and some poems from former mistresses and various protégées scattered around the Western world) and supporting with vivacity & plus-strokes & money various people, various causes.

Unsurprisingly, he stumbled under the weight of these good works. In the last days of July, *Recovery* stalled. Writing to Kate from California, where he'd gone to escape the noise of his newly swollen household, he compared it to being 'in the Colosseum with the lionesses'. In the same letter he described a nightmare in which he found a decayed Russian aristocrat sleeping in front of his fireplace. Shooing him out, he realised the interloper had been clipping holes in his Shakespeare notes. Kate had been sympathetic to this bum, and her dream betrayal reminded him that he had other axes to grind.

> I was sympathetic to your 'depression' etc. God knows why. 'I've been in shock for ten years' – I haven't heard such crap since 'You've been drunk for nine years' (the aggressive delusion is succeeded by the defensive delusion) . . . I think you suffer from, among other things, the jealous hatred of the very weak for the decisively strong (yes, dear, that's me) . . . I want you in treatment before I return. I don't buy the 'busy every minute' either, in regard to letters. Christ you nurse the baby, cook meals, that's it . . . No doubt I am projecting.

So much for abandoning resentment and self-pity – which, as he knew and as he'd just made Alan Severance say in *Recovery*, are the number one reasons a recovering alcoholic goes back to the bottle. That summer, an old and very close friend, Ralph Ross, Berryman's chairman at the university and one of his most stalwart supports, observed 'no real warmth shown us, or anyone, no excitement of mind, no ardor. I concluded that the only John one could love was a John with 2 or 3 drinks in him, no more & no less, & such a John could not exist.'

All year he'd been worrying that his tentative return to Catholicism might be yet another delusion. During his first treatment at St. Mary's in May 1970 he'd had what he thought of as a conversion experience. He wanted to leave hospital for a few hours to teach a class, was given permission and then told at the last minute he couldn't go. A huge row ensued, which ended with him giving up in despair, stricken with guilt about his students. Then, unexpectedly, a counsellor offered to teach it for him. Something about this unlooked-for intervention tumbled him into a new sense of faith, and ever since he'd been writing religious poems, later published as *Delusion, Etc.* These might be described as addresses to the Lord: attempts to square himself with the God he felt had snatched his father and all his sense of security away more than forty years before. There'd been a period of blissfully renewed faith, but now it started pulling away, strips of paper from a damp wall.

On 13 December he wrote a long, unhappily ranging diary entry. 'All yesterday, terrible.' 'Don't *believe* gun or knife; *won't*.' He ticked through his anxieties, the little and the large. His cough made Martha grind her teeth. His house wasn't paid for, he was afraid of his new chairman, he was 20lb underweight and 'OLD'. He slept badly, had bad dreams, dreaded winter. His penis was shrinking into his groin. He wrote: 'Religious doubts come up,' added: 'wonder if Hell −' and left that queasy thought unfinished. He described days spent in bed, obsessed with Daddy's grave. In the same entry, he recorded giving up *Recovery* for good (*'gave up* novel. Bitter disappointment').

In December he was plagued by thoughts of suicide. On New Year's Eve, he went to a party, where someone took his photo: tense, suited, the light bouncing off his glasses. On 5 January, he bought a bottle of whiskey, and drank half of it. He wrote a poem that imagined cutting his throat after climbing the high railing of a bridge. 'I didn't,' it starts. 'And I didn't.' He scratched a line through it with his pen, tossed it in the bin, put the bottle away and called an AA friend, asking if someone else could take over at the next meeting, since he wouldn't be able to attend. Then, on Friday 7 January, he caught the morning bus to the Washington Avenue Bridge. He climbed the railing and let himself go, falling 100 feet on to a pier and rolling partway down the embankment of the Mississippi River. His body was identified by a blank cheque in his pocket and the name on his broken glasses.

Hardly any wonder *Recovery* was unfinished. What a title. What an insane risk. I looked out through the thick glass. We were coming into St. Paul. It was very late. There was a long pause while the train re-fuelled before we chugged out through Minneapolis, passing within half a mile of Berryman's old house in Prospect Park, and then curving by the university where he'd worked so hard, with such devotion, leaving his mark on many lives.

Skyscrapers, their windows glowing in the dark. Buildings that looked like factories, laboratories. Buildings without windows, mills, boarded-up warehouses, all lit by the same sickly orange. Then we headed into partial darkness, broken by streetlamps that dimly revealed offices and parking lots; a man in silhouette walking down a flight of stairs. There was water out there somewhere. I could make out smears of reflected orange, breaking and reforming. Then a road, a truck, and then the outer edges of the city, muddling and messy, with shapes that might have been chimneys, water towers and, surely, chainlink fences.

★

I woke again at dawn. This time, the world outside was white. North Dakota, flat as an unironed sheet. There were dun patches where the snow had melted. It was a landscape of minimal colour. Telegraph poles, farms, the horizon wiped clean by mist, the sky above so blue it took my breath away.

At breakfast I sat with my friends from the night before. We talked about oil: how many barrels there were in Dakota, how many barrels the Saudis had, whether wind power would be big out here. Doug used to work as a machinist, manufacturing chromium caps for pistons. The degreaser they used contained the carcinogen dichloromethane. Many of the men got prostate cancer, he said, including his dad. Then the plant closed down and part of its output moved to Colombia, part to India. 'Do they still use the degreaser out there?' Diane asked, and Doug said, shruggingly: 'I guess so. They have different labor laws out there.'

I spent the rest of the morning in the observation car, digging through *Recovery* again. In Bellow's essay at the front there was a statement about Berryman's drinking I found hard to swallow. He described the feverish production of the Dream Songs and then added: 'Inspiration contained a death threat. He would, as he wrote the things he had waited and prayed for, fall apart. Drink was a stabilizer. It somewhat reduced the fatal intensity.'

In the 1970s, a good deal less was known about alcoholism than today, either by doctors and psychologists or the population at large. It had only recently been classified as a disease, and most ordinary people had very little understanding of what it involved. It was also an era considerably more lubricated and less censorious than our own. In addition, Bellow may have been experiencing a species of the pervasive, insidious denial that tends to affect even the sharpest friends and family members of alcoholics. Nonetheless, it was a foolish thing to say. The poems weren't killing Berryman. They didn't cause delirium tremens, or give him gynaecomastia, or make him fall down flights of stairs, vomit or defecate in public places. Alcohol might have quietened his near omnipresent sense of panic on a drink by drink basis, but on a drink by drink basis it had also created a life of physical and moral disintegration and despair.

Why, then? Why did a man of such prodigious intelligence, such gifts, return over and over to a substance that was destroying the fabric of his life? In *Recovery*, Alan Severance keeps asking himself this question, despite the patient efforts of his therapists to draw him back to the present moment. The Minnesota Model is – or was, in 1970 – essentially pragmatic, steering clear of psychoanalysis, the search for *reasons*, in favour of tackling and treating the addict's behaviour in the present. Severance, though, is stubbornly obsessed with two items from his past: the suicide of his father and a period of puzzling blankness during his adolescence. He keeps harking back to them in Group, unable to see that this is a way of avoiding his current situation and his responsibility to change it.

Not everything about Alan Severance is drawn from life, and part of his power as a character derives from the ironic distance between his perspective and the reader's – which implies that Berryman possessed more insight into the disease than his stand-in (though reading the vain, deluded, boastful poems of 1970's *Love and Fame* you might not always think so). That said, the material about the father is directly lifted from reality. Berryman was convinced that John Allyn's suicide was the crucial event of his life. For years, he'd been worrying over it, trying to work out how grave a wound he'd been struck.

The problem was he could remember almost nothing about the events on Clearwater Island. Neither what had happened nor his own feelings at the time were at all clear to him, and so he had to depend on the precarious testimony of his mother. According to *Poets in Their Youth*, Eileen Simpson's memoir, these conversations took place repeatedly, in person and by letter, particularly at times when John was under strain. Each time, Mrs. Berryman's story changed, and though sometimes he found this funny, at other moments her unreliability plunged him into an access of despair.

When he was in St. Mary's for the last time, he wrote to his mother, asking her to set down once and for all her recollections of Allyn's death. His questions were numbered and painfully precise.

1. Did I *hear* Daddy threaten to swim out w me (or Bob?) or drown us both? or did you tell me later? *when?*
2. When did I first learn that he'd killed himself?
3. How did I *seem to take* his death when first told? Before the drive back to Tampa that morning? How did I *act* in the car? Back in Tampa? at the funeral parlour? At the graveyard in Holdenville?

in Minn? Gloucester? thro' the 8th grade? (in Was DC? — where
tho't I recognized him on the street one day — crushed?)

Mrs. Berryman answered with a long, circuitous letter. She said that
the subject was painful and that she'd rather not remember; that she'd
spent much of her life being tormented by what had happened to
her husband. She described the circumstances of his death, in a
confused and havering way. She said that she took five bullets out of
the gun and buried them, but that he must have secreted a sixth
somewhere, put it in and then clicked through the chamber so many
times that eventually he came upon it (the idea that Allyn's death
was an accident was a standard of her repertoire, most often wheeled
out for strangers and new friends). She didn't answer the question
about how her son behaved or seemed in that heartrending, pathetic
tally of locations.

Berryman's response, written a few days before he left St. Mary's,
is almost abject. He apologises for having distressed her. He tells her
that anyway he's decided to abandon the subject: that he left it for a
few hours and felt so much better he's resolved never to approach it
again. (This lurch from brief experience to extravagant commitment
is, incidentally, characteristic of his recovery, a kind of run before you
can walk grandiosity that made him dangerously prone to failure.
Sabotage, in short, since the inevitable disappointment would lead him
straight back to drinking.)

The subject wasn't abandoned, of course. Instead he handed it to
Severance to chew over — just as, for the last decade and a half, he'd
given it to Henry, who is also haunted by the suicide of 'the blue
father', 'this dreadful banker', and who spends much of the Dream

Songs either rehearsing the events on Clearwater Island or trying to dig down physically to his father's grave.

Trapped on Ward W, Alan spends much of his time pondering his loss. After an unsuccessful session of transactional analysis, he writes in his notebook:

> New problem. Did I myself feel any *guilt* perhaps – long repressed if so, and mere speculation now (defence here) – *about Daddy's death?* (I certainly picked up enough of Mother's self-blame to accuse her once, drunk and raging, of having actually murdered him and staged a suicide.) Lecturer lately on children's blaming themselves for father drunk (=What did I do to make Daddy angry and get drunk?). BLANK, probably odd. He *was* drinking heavily, all four of them were in those last weeks, nightmarish quarrels. Gun-death at dawn, like Hemingway's, imitating his father. Does my fanatical drinking emulate his, and my fanatical smoking (both 'manly')? So possibly it wasn't rage/self-pity, but guilt, that were simply driven underground for a year (Why? if so) to emerge after all and cripple my prep school years.

He continues in this vein for another paragraph, then drops his pen, baffled. 'Tall handsome Daddy,' he thinks to himself, 'adored and lost so soon!'

This statement is very close to one written in Berryman's own hospital diary, and the crippled prep school years were yet another item purloined from reality. At South Kent he'd been badly bullied and once, after being beaten up on a cross-country run, had tried very hard to throw himself under a train (poor impulse control, a psychiatrist might note here, sucking on his pen).

When he looked back at this period from adulthood what troubled him most was a pervasive sense of blankness. His boyhood self seemed fogged-in and weirdly ambitionless. Damn it, he couldn't even remember what he'd *read*. In *Recovery*, Alan returns often to this subject, even raising in Group the mystery of his 'uncharacteristic . . . wasted years'. (The counsellor, amused: 'Everybody wastes years.')

I sat back in my chair, chewing my own pen. We were passing Rugby, the cars wheel-deep in snow. Black earth, the ice like tarnished silver. There were rusting drums in the field. I could see for miles, the rolling hills scored with pines. All the time that regretful, admonitory sound: *Hoooo Hoooo! Hiiiii Hiiiii!*

Something about the spectacle of an ageing man picking at old wounds really got to me. I could see that in one respect it was just another avoidance technique, a way of refusing to face up to the role of drinking in the ongoing wreck of his life. And alcohol, as he well knew, is addicting for all sorts of reasons, some genetic and some merely circumstantial. The most urgent task isn't to find out why one drinks, but to get dry and then stay dry. Still, that period of blankness tugged at me. 'Missing someone who is loved and longed for,' Freud once observed, 'is the key to an understanding of anxiety.'

Recently, I'd come across a study that radically reaffirms the relevance of childhood experience to health in later life. The Adverse Childhood Experience Study was carried out in San Diego from 1995 to 1997, though its research is ongoing. It studied a cohort of 17,000 middle-class American adults of diverse ethnicity: a huge endeavour, and certainly large enough for its results to be statistically significant. Each participant was asked to complete a questionnaire asking whether they'd experienced eight different kinds of childhood trauma, among them parental addiction, violence, sexual abuse, loss, and disruption of other kinds. These scores were then correlated against the presence of a variety of mental and physical diseases in adulthood, including alcoholism.

The results were staggering. In every condition, from nicotine addiction to heart disease, there was an unambiguous relationship between the percentage of sufferers and the degree of childhood trauma. In a paper entitled 'The Origins of Addiction: Evidence from the Adverse Childhood Experience Study', one of the co-principal investigators, Dr. Vincent Felitti, summarised their findings in terms of addiction:

> In our detailed study . . . we found that the compulsive use of nicotine, alcohol, and injected street drugs increases proportionally in a strong, graded, dose-response manner that closely parallels the intensity of adverse life experiences during childhood. This of course supports old psychoanalytic views and is at odds with current concepts, including those of biological psychiatry, drug-treatment programs, and drug-eradication programs. Our findings are disturbing to some because they imply that the basic causes of addiction lie within *us* and the way we treat each other, not in drug dealers or dangerous chemicals. They suggest that billions of dollars have been spent everywhere except where the answer is to be found.

Beneath this statement there was a table displaying the results for ACE score vs. Adult Alcoholism. It was one of the most sobering things I'd ever seen. Five black bars, steadily increasing. On the far left the bar was tiny. Just over 2% of adults with an ACE score of 0 (meaning that they had answered no to all eight questions about traumatic childhood experiences) had become alcoholics. The next along was slightly larger. Almost 6% of adults with an ACE score of 1 had become alcoholics. The next was bigger again. Around 10% of adults with an ACE score of 2 had become alcoholics. Then up again. Just under 12% of adults with an ACE score of 3 had become alcoholics. The last was the biggest. 16% of adults with an ACE score of 4 or more had developed an addiction to alcohol.

In the conclusion to this paper, one of a great many published by the ACE team on its various findings, Felitti wrote:

> The current concept of addiction is ill founded. Our study of the relationship of adverse childhood experiences to adult health status in over 17,000 persons shows addiction to be a readily understandable although largely unconscious attempt to gain relief from well-concealed prior life traumas by using psychoactive materials. Because it is difficult to get enough of something that doesn't quite work, the attempt is ultimately unsuccessful, apart from its risks. What we have shown will not surprise most psychoanalysts, although the magnitude of our observations are new, and our conclusions are sometimes vigorously challenged by other disciplines.
>
> The evidence supporting our conclusions about the basic cause of addiction is powerful and its implications are daunting.

The prevalence of adverse childhood experiences and their long-term effects are clearly a major determinant of the health and social well being of the nation. This is true whether looked at from the standpoint of social costs, the economics of health care, the quality of human existence, the focus of medical treatment, or the effects of public policy. Adverse childhood experiences are difficult issues, made more so because they strike close to home for many of us. Taking them on will create an ordeal of change, but will also provide for many the opportunity to have a better life.

There are criticisms of the ACE study, particularly that its findings are retrospective, and depend on the assumption that those taking part are both telling the truth and in possession of accurate memories. It also raises all kinds of questions, none of them as yet fully answered, including the exact route by which childhood trauma leads to later ill health, and what protective mechanisms exist in the majority who suffer early life upheaval but do not go on to develop adulthood disease. Still, it stands as radical proof of the common sense assumption that where you end up has its roots in where you began.

Berryman's ACE score was 3. *It is difficult to get enough of something that doesn't work.* Christ. It made a different sense of all those poems. Dream Song 96, stanza 1:

> Under the table, no. That last was stunning,
> that flagon had breasts. Some men grow down cursed.
> Why drink so, two days running?
> two months, O seasons, years, two decades running?

I answer (smiles) my question on the cuff:
Man, I been thirsty.

That flagon had breasts. He was addicted to a false source of nourishment, but the thirst was real. Hardly any wonder he ended up, as the poem does, in hospital, his 'rum, his Cointreau, gin-&-sherry, his bourbon' all threatened by figures in white coats.

I thought back again to the prep school years. They came hard on the heels of three consecutive losses: first the awful period at the Oklahoma boarding school when he was eleven, then his father's death and then the remarriage of his adored mother, which swallowed up even her Christian name. After two years in his new home in Jackson Heights he was sent to South Kent, where he was abjectly unpopular. No one to confide to, and anyway an environment in which feeling itself was dangerous. His letters home bear little traces of his distress – quick, pseudo-casual mentions of the boys who smashed his glasses or locked him in a cupboard. In urgent need of a defence, he began to bury himself behind a false self, a mask evident in all his cheerful, phoney letters to his mother. ('And it's only 18 days until I go *home*! Imagine! I don't have an idea as to how the house will look. You're all settled by now, I guess, and I'll be a total stranger. Gee!') He was learning to absent himself, to deny and minimise his unhappiness: a technique that would serve him ill in years to come. And underneath, of course, the real feelings seethed: inadmissible, and as such impossible to discharge, except in wild moments like the day he flung himself down in the path of an oncoming train.

Something else came into my mind then. Perhaps it was irrelevant, perhaps not. Anyway, it seemed to belong amid this braid of need and attachment, separation and anxiety. In Dream Song 96 Berryman made explicit reference to the commonality between bottles and breasts, to the suckling nourishment he could draw from a flagon. In the published correspondence with his mother, *We Dream of Honor* (which one critic described as being of interest only to a psychiatrist) there's a small window into Mrs. Berryman's feelings on the same subject. The introduction quotes a fragment of a short story she wrote in August 1931, during her son's second summer home from South Kent. It's a fantasy about a woman breastfeeding her infant son, and matches the ardent, seductive tone she often took in letters to John, though whether it's drawn from life or not is impossible to know.

> They were alone . . . He pushed at the bottle with his tongue, hunger assuaged, sleep hanging on his lids. Yearning over him, she dribbled milk on her breast and thrust the hardening nipple into his lax mouth; once, twice, he spit it out and then as the flesh-feel aroused him, he closed and tugged, drawing long arduous pulls, ceasing only to wail aloud at failure, nuzzling again for the nipple, pulling and drawing, whimpering and crying at the unnatural nothingness. Needle pain was stilled in her by the ecstasy of his need; futility closed iron claws upon her at the anguish of her sterile breast . . . As presently he relaxed, the bitterness of grief grew less keen.

It reads like a nineteenth-century seduction scene. *The ecstasy of his need*: what a dangerous thing to inculcate. And the breast is empty, while the real nourishment comes from a bottle. What's more, it's sexualised – *as the flesh-feel aroused him* – and mixed with a punishing lack of satisfaction.

If this has any bearing on the real relationship between mother and son, then it might explain at least in part why as an adult he would want complete control over his source of nourishment and comfort, and why he might suffer lifelong from an appalling sense of thirst.

★

The land changed again after Minot. Now there were closed river valleys, partially covered in scrubby trees, and little houses with bright red barns. I watched a falcon havering above the ruined grass. When the sun came out the cataracts of ice shone blue, silver, grey, pewter and sandy brown, the colours entwined like marble. Outside Stanley I saw a fox cantering through snow, its coat the dry brownish-yellow of winter grass. There was a wrecked goods train on its side by the tracks. An oil well, distant fires burning. 'Attention please,' the tannoy said. 'Williston, North Dakota will be coming up very soon. Williston, North Dakota is the next stop.'

I ate lunch that day with a man called Bob, who'd been the foreman electrician on Bill Gates's house. Two women joined us, both in their sixties. One was very dippy, the other stern, and they chattered away as we worked through our macaroni cheese and peanut butter pie. The stern one described how she raised her children and then the layout of her ranch. 'I have two hundred acres,' she said. She wasn't boasting, just walking us through it. 'A well, water a little hard, three springs, so I have water even if the pump fails. Stands of p-pine, ponderosa, so the cattle can get shade, and on the other side of the property, the north side, you get the moose and elk, they calve down there. I don't let the coyote and mountain lion on my property. If I

257

see them I fire a warning shot in the dirt. My husband doesn't like that, but I was raised around guns. My father's half-Wolf. He could catch a brook trout with his bare hands.' Then she told us a story about her mother walking to school in button-up boots in the 1920s, crushing big brown tarantulas all the way.

After coffee I went back to my cabin. Since Glasgow we'd been following the Milk River. It had burst its banks, and here and there fences were submerged to their topmost rung. I napped a while, and woke again to a different world. We were heading into the Rockies. Snow was billowing past the window. I figured from the map that we must be in East Glacier Park, almost 5,000 feet above sea level. I gummed my nose to the glass. Loose formless clouds. Only the nearest trees looked green. The mountains were covered in pines, the black on white translating to the monochrome grey of newsprint.

Talking to those people over lunch had reminded me of something else. In John Haffenden's compassionate and exacting biography of Berryman, he points out that one of the ways in which *Recovery* parts company with the poet's lived experience was in his relationships with the other inhabitants of the ward. Alan Severance is generally well liked, though at times his educated diction and self-important claims, delivered at a roar, repel his fellow patients. They think he's arrogant and deluded, but that's par for the course, and many of the sweeter scenes involve him engaging warmly with the others.

In reality, this wasn't quite the case. Berryman apparently found it very hard to see himself as part of this collective of poorly educated, unhappy people. For example, in *Recovery*, Severance makes mention of a 'great friend of his' from a good background, with whom he hoped to establish a more exclusive AA group. Unhappily, according to Haffenden, the real version of this woman, Betty Peddie, didn't much like Berryman. She felt he patronised her and boasted too much about his success, including his powers as a seducer. She read *Recovery* after his death, and delivered a report on it during a session of group therapy, which Haffenden reprinted in his book:

> When he tried to relate to other people he did make friends, but he couldn't ever be wholehearted about belonging with the rest of us; he was constantly retreating into his uniqueness, but he really thought it was all he had that made him worth anything. So he stayed shut out, and he couldn't make it alone.

This is one of the saddest statements I've ever read, and it says a great deal very simply about the corrosive effects of alcoholic grandiosity and pride. It's probably also a very accurate assessment of why Berryman killed himself. The key to recovery from alcoholism is faith: faith in one's fellows, faith in God, faith in the recovery process and those who've passed through it. The problem, of course, is that alcoholism is often related to a badly damaged sense of trust. For Berryman, the work of the Twelve Steps meant encountering a place inside himself that was utterly unconvinced of any sort of loving presence in the universe, any sort of meaning. (In 'Eleven Addresses to the Lord', written in 1970, he reported bleakly: 'my father's blow-it-all when I was twelve / blew out my most bright candle faith'.) For years, he'd been using drink to protect himself from this sense of abject terror and though it had never proved successful, without it he genuinely wasn't sure how it was possible to survive. As such, it's no coincidence that the only conclusion he could see for *Recovery* was Alan Severance's oncoming death.

Before the book foundered, Berryman sketched out where he wanted it to end: with a version of a walk he'd made with his own children, Paul included, up Pike's Peak in Colorado, where he'd had an intimation of death among the pines. He wrote down the last seven sentences on a notecard and they were printed in the appendix alongside some other scraps. 'He was perfectly ready. No regrets. He was happier than he had ever been in his life before. Lucky, and he didn't deserve it. He was very, very lucky. Bless everybody. He felt – fine.'

That's not recovery, though. That's flights of angels sing thee to thy rest, which is to say oblivion, escapism of the most conclusive kind. A sincere delusion, maybe, but the happiness is about as believable as it was in the Hartford poem that ends by screaming at Christ.

It was all so wasteful, so relentlessly destructive. I thought again of the dream he'd told Kate, about the decayed Russian aristocrat clipping holes in his Shakespeare notes. And then I remembered another dream he'd had, almost four decades before he died, when he was a young man in Cambridge, bewitched by language, half-drunk on the possibilities of what he might create. Up late one night in his rooms he went into a kind of trance, and saw when he closed his eyes a waking vision of Yeats, white-haired and tall, struggling to lift a great lump of coal. He raised it high above his head, then dashed it down on the polished floor, where it struck to pieces that rolled away, all silver. What a gap there was between the two scenes. That's what alcoholism does to a writer. You begin with alchemy, hard labour, and end by letting some grandiose degenerate, some awful aspect of yourself, take up residence at the hearth, the central fire, where they set to ripping out the heart of the work you've yet to finish.

8

HALF OF HIM

WHEN I WOKE THE NEXT morning we were travelling through a vast snowy valley full of pine trees. The sun had just come up, and the ridge was glittering. As I watched, a wave of light washed down the slope, turning the pines a dusty greenish-gold. I drank my coffee, thrilled. It's almost impossible, watching the sun restore the world, not to feel some sense of gladness, of a covenant being kept.

An alcoholic *can* stop drinking. I knew it from my own childhood, and I knew it from my reading. My mother's ex-partner got dry at a treatment centre she still describes as a hellhole, and came back into our lives sober. They remain good friends, and Diana hasn't had a drink in twenty-three years, an achievement I find astonishingly heroic.

John Cheever managed it too, though he experienced many of the same difficulties with the drying-out process as Berryman did. His last year of drinking was purgatorial, a dizzying ride through the switchback of late-stage alcoholism. After the year in Iowa with Raymond Carver, he took up a full professorship at Boston University in 1974. He moved into a furnished two-room fourth-floor walk-up and promptly set about drinking himself to death. The students seemed less bright than those at Iowa, and his isolation rapidly deepened. He was living, he claimed, off oranges and hamburgers; his apartment was full of empty bottles and in the mornings he could barely hold a glass, let alone piece a sentence together.

In such circumstances writing was impossible, and he resigned partway through the spring term, handing responsibility for his classes to his colleague John Updike. Luckily, his brother Fred came to his rescue then, or he may well have succeeded with the depressing little feints at suicide he'd been making all term. Fred drove over to the apartment, dressed his naked and incoherent brother and drove him home to Mary, in the course of which journey he drained a quart of Scotch and pissed in the empty bottle. Back in Ossining he was immediately hospitalised before being reluctantly transferred to Smithers Alcohol Treatment and Training Center in New York.

While staying at Smithers, he was often reprimanded for grandiosity. Like Berryman, his diction counted against him, as did his habit of shoring himself up by drawing attention to his prodigious achievements, both in bed and on the page. In fact, he read Berryman while he was there, and his counsellor explicitly compared the two men. 'But he was a brilliant poet and an estimable scholar, and I am neither,' Cheever said, faux-humbly, to which she replied: 'Yes, but he was also a phony and a drunk, and now he's *dead*; is that what you want?'

Later, she elaborated on her estimation in a progress report: 'He is a classic denier who moves in and out of focus. He dislikes seeing self negatively and seems to have internalized many rather imperious upper class Boston attitudes which he ridicules and embraces at the same time,' adding a tactical note: 'Press him to deal with his own humanity.'

By some miracle, he managed it. Over the course of his

twenty-eight-day incarceration he went from guarded and rigidly defended to tentatively open, even soft. Despite his snobbery and habit of making light of suffering (to which he responded, à la Tennessee Williams, with a disconcerting giggle), he took a genuine interest in other people, and managed at least occasionally the trick of recognising himself in them. 'I came out of prison 20 pounds lighter and howling with pleasure,' he wrote in a letter to a Russian friend on 2 June 1975, a month after his release, and though no cure had been found for his loneliness or sense of sexual confusion, he never drank again.

That howl of pleasure, of freedom and self-acceptance, reverberated into his new novel. For a long time, he'd been dickering helplessly over *Falconer*, the story of a man in prison for murdering his brother. He'd sold it to Robert Gottlieb at Knopf back in 1973 for an advance of $100,000 but had, despite his claims to the contrary, barely written a word before or since ('Sauced, I speculate on a homosexual romance in prison'). In his Smithers diary, however, he'd been writing almost as much about the book as he had about his recovery. Now, healthier and more energetic than he'd been for years, he rolled up his Brooks Brothers sleeves and set about it.

There is in all Cheever's long fiction a haltingness that would under normal circumstances be incompatible with the ambitions of a novel. His books resemble in their discontinuity dreams: dreams in which one passes by a succession of lighted rooms, each containing a tableau at once inexplicable and alluring. At intervals, control of the narrative slips unexpectedly into the hands of a stranger, a passer-by, and though it may eventually slot back on track, one is never quite certain after that of either the destination or the direction of travel. While this practice is not without its frustrations, it captures very precisely the realm most of us inhabit: a place of tailing off and interruption; irresolute, incomplete and infused with a melancholy and sometimes exultant beauty.

This hesitancy is still evident in *Falconer*, but here it gathers a new intensity. It's apparent that something imperative is being acted out on the page, although the urgency often seems incommensurate with the flimsiness of the players. The novel begins when a well-bred man named Farragut is brought into Falconer Correctional Faculty (the name Daybreak House hasn't caught on) and ends when he escapes from it. In the interim, he recovers from heroin addiction, survives a prison riot and falls in love with a fellow inmate, Jody, who effects his own escape by posing as a visiting bishop's aide. Unfree, confined, Farragut travels in his memories, which are for the most part Cheever's own. Farragut's father wanted him aborted; Farragut's father attempted to commit suicide on a rollercoaster at Nagasakit; Farragut suffers lapses in memory; Farragut's wife is very cold; and Farragut finds himself falling in love with a man, though he considers himself a paragon of the virtuous bourgeoisie.

His escape is not planned. A friend, Chicken Number Two, dies, and so on an impulse Farragut leaves Falconer by climbing into his body bag and being carried out as a corpse. 'How strange to be carried so late in life,' he thinks, 'and toward nothing that he truly knew, freed, it seemed, from his erotic crudeness, his facile scorn and his chagrined laugh – not a fact, but a chance, something like the afternoon light on high trees, quite useless and thrilling.'

The carriers talk casually about cars as they drop the body on the free side of the wall; about a man named Charlie and his problems with his distributor. Then they walk away and Farragut cuts himself out of the bag with a concealed razor, just as Cheever once cut himself out of a straitjacket during an attack of delirium tremens, back in the thickets of his own addiction. He hears piano music coming from the houses of the poor. There's blood in his boot. He peers in through the bright window of a laundromat, watching clothes tumble through the dryers. At a bus stop he meets a man who's been evicted from his lodgings; a man who takes a liking to Farragut's face and pays for his bus ticket, presenting him, unasked, with a winter coat. The book ends with Farragut getting off the bus at random. Stepping down into an unknown street, 'he saw that he had lost his fear of falling and all other fears of that nature. He held his head high, his back straight, and walked along nicely. Rejoice, he thought, rejoice.'

There's nothing ironic about this Lazarus-like return to life. I expect there are people who find it sentimental, even cloying. I didn't, though. It was earned, manifestly earned ('I wonder,' he'd written at Smithers, 'if I have the courage to leave confinement and seize my natural freedom'). Nor was it simply autobiographical, in the unidirectional way we tend to understand that word. Instead, the act of liberating Farragut seemed to ripple back into Cheever's own life, buoying him up even as he set it down. It was a confirmation and testament of his own liberation, but also a way of getting ahead of himself, of creating a fantasy he could then, in some magical way, be braced by; even inhabit. It wasn't so far from what Berryman had tried to do with *Recovery*, the difference being that Berryman had used Alan Severance, inadvertently or not, to evade his own duties to sobriety, while Cheever had made Farragut's escape from addiction and imprisonment a way of underscoring and fuelling his.

Among the many positive reviews was one by Joan Didion in the *New York Times*. Often prescient, always cool-headed, she observed that Farragut had undergone:

. . . a purification, a period of suffering in order to re-enter the ceremonies of innocence, and in this context the question of when he will be 'clean' has considerable poignancy. As a matter of fact it is this question that Cheever has been asking all along – *when will I be clean* was the question on every summer lawn – but he has never before asked it outright, and with such transcendent arrogance of style.

This is a very accurate assessment of Cheever's fiction, but what Didion couldn't possibly have known at the time was how deeply the question of cleanliness worked away at the man himself; how often in his journals he worried over the gulf in his life between immaculate outward setting and dirty, even deviant inward desires. Shaken by a day in which two strangers tried to pick him up, he once wrote in his diary: 'I mix myself a gin and vermouth. The polished icebucket, the white flowers on the piano, the music on the rack, are all part of some moral fortification that protects me from the two strangers' – though by *two strangers* what he really meant was the experience of seeing his own longing reflected back by them.

Unsurprisingly, this schism wasn't exactly resolved by getting sober, though taking the gin and vermouth out of the equation certainly helped both his outward behaviour and sense of self-esteem ('I am not better than the next man, but I am better than I was,' he wrote in 1976). Over time, he became far more at ease with the fact that his erotic urges included men, though in so doing he initiated a coercive relationship with a young heterosexual student, Max Zimmerman, who found it very hard – for a variety of reasons, none of them apparently related to sexual attraction – to say no to him. It seems probable, reading Cheever's diaries, that he would now be diagnosed with sex addiction. Certainly there's a distinct similarity between his desire to 'wallow, smear, engorge myself' with alcohol and his need for sexual contact, both of which (as he once acknowledged in a letter to his doctor) were 'brought on by my anxious and greedy urge to take more than my share of brute pleasure'.

Not perfect then. But sobriety doesn't necessarily mean a new character; rather a kind of slow sea change of spirit. Back a while, when I'd been digging through the papers at the Berg Collection in New York Public Library, I'd come across a few typed pages that seemed to be successive drafts of a speech about AA, which Cheever attended religiously in his remaining years.

To be confirmed in an enormous and splendid basilica, deafened by music and blinded by the fire of candles is much easier than it is to say in a smoke-filled Sunday school classroom that my name is John and I am an alcoholic although they are the same thing.

The difficulties of admitting to faith outside organized religion are much more than superficial. We have no history, we have no Dead Sea Scrolls, we have no past at all. In the earliest religious myths and legends, alcohol is one of the first gifts of the Gods. Dionysius is the son of Zeus. There is little if any censure of drunkenness in the Holy Bible. In the cardinal sins drunkenness might be included in sloth but there is nothing specific. The belief that to be drunk is to be blessed is very deep. To die of drink is sometimes thought a graceful and natural death – overlooking wet-brains, convulsions,

delirium tremens, hallucinations, hideous automobile accidents and botched suicides. Several friends said to me that
their affairs were in order, their children married, their money
soundly invested and they were going to leisurely drink
themselves to death. One of them choked to death on
whiskey. One of them jumped off a cliff. One of them set
fire to his house and incinerated himself and his children.
One of them is still in a strait jacket. For a while I somehow
thought this comprehensive, graceful, rather as the leaves fall
in the autumn. To drink oneself to death was not in any
way alarming, I thought, until I found that I was drinking
myself to death.

And so we have really no religious history at all. And yet
what we do believe is as old as the oldest faith. Religion is the
conviction that we can comprehend and conquer death and the
fear of death. We state for the first time in the history of religion,
that drunkenness is for some of us a guide of death, a mode of
suicide. For some of us it is terribly important to avoid the
crankiness of temperance societies and pledge unions. We recog-
nize drunkenness as a guide of obscene death and by helping
one another we can triumph over this.

And triumph he did. Even when he was dying of cancer, even when
all but one of his doctors said he might as well go back on the bottle,
he elected to stay dry. He wanted, he said, to keep his dignity, and
though poor Max might have had something to say about the mechanisms by which it was achieved, the fact remains that for the last
seven years of his life he was stone cold sober: still depressed, still

lonely, still at the mercy of his erections, but also in possession of his wit, and the old, magical capacity for being unsprung by joy.

★

I'd taken up a station in the viewing car. We were still running parallel to the Skykomish. The water was glass-green, ice-cold. It rushed beside the train, churning over boulders and tumbling down gorges, spray shooting up like foam from a bottle. Everything was moist, seeping, sodden; the trees lagged in luminous green moss.

I could have stayed up there forever, but by mid-morning we'd trundled back down to earth. In fact, we seemed to have arrived in the Home Counties. It all looked absurdly familiar – the grey skies, the tangles of brambles in the damp fields. Funny, to enter such an English landscape, when that afternoon I'd see my mother for the first time in months.

When it occurred to me that I might go to America, one of the first destinations I thought of was Port Angeles, the north-western town where Raymond Carver spent much of his final decade. Years ago, I'd taken *All of Us*, Carver's collected poems, on holiday to Greece. There were still petals of bougainvillea and olive leaves pressed between the pages. As for the poems, they'd sunk themselves into my mind. Many were set out here, or a little further west, in the Olympic Peninsula, a landscape hard-cut and intricately veined with creeks and trout streams: a magical counterpart to the richness of a life in which alcohol was no longer the dominating force.

I'd wanted to visit that place for a long time, and when I asked my mother if she'd like to join me in America I wasn't surprised that this was the section of the trip she chose. Her flight was getting in that afternoon, and after I'd dropped my bags and had a bath at the hotel I went to meet her at Sea-Tac airport, elated and a little nervous at the prospect of companionship.

The terminal was heaving with soldiers in desert uniform, most of them very young. I watched as one boy greeted his girlfriend. They clung together, oblivious to the crowd. Then, at the back of the queue, I saw my mother, pink-cheeked and bundled up in a quilted jacket, an Oxford Literary Festival bag slung across her shoulder. We hugged hard too. She was bubbling over with excitement, and that night in Seattle we drank little bottles of Coors and caught up on months of news.

We'd hired a white Ford, sturdy and unglamorous save for a set of Wyoming plates. After breakfast the next day we drove to Edmonds and caught the ferry across Puget Sound to Kingston. The Olympic Highway, the 101, ran right round the head of the peninsula. There were snow-capped mountains up ahead, looming a little threateningly. I looked at the map, tracing names. Hurricane Ridge, Mount Deception. Across the Juan de Fuca Strait we could see the blue shadows of islands, and beyond them the smudgy pencil line of Canada.

We reached Port Angeles mid-afternoon, weaving in past auto-repairs and building supply yards. The Red Lion was just off Main Street. From my bed I could see clean out to Victoria, across milky blue water that looked like churned ice. Raymond Carver used to fish out there, in his nutty, unsafe boats. He could only tie three kinds of knots, and used them willy-nilly, not caring whether they were appropriate or not. Once he ran out of gas and was too scared to call the coast-guard and tell them what he'd done. Instead he dragged west on the tide, slamming into a big red buoy and almost scuppering himself.

Luckily, some fishermen spotted the boat and towed him back to harbour. He'd got off lightly. The only harm done was a telling streak of colour below the fenders: yet another memento of a near-miss existence. He was always greedy for fish, gleeful to have them and glad, later, to give them away. This is Good Raymond, of course: the successful writer of the late 1970s and early 1980s, who'd managed to pull himself out of a self-made hell; a real pigsty of a life.

Unlike his friend John Cheever, Carver never tried to conceal the poverty of his origins. He was born on 25 May 1938 in Klatskanie, Oregon, the first of two brothers. His father was a mill worker who liked to fish and drink, though he lacked the knack for holding his liquor. Raymond Senior – C.R. – met his future wife on a sidewalk in Leola, Arkansas, as he was walking out of a tavern. 'He was drunk,' Carver recorded his mother as saying in an essay called 'My Father's Life'. 'I don't know why I let him talk to me. His eyes were glittery. I wish I'd had a crystal ball.' In the same essay he told tales on his parents' misdeeds, relating a night in which C.R. came home smashed and Ella locked him out of the house before whacking him between the eyes with a colander, which Ray figured later must have weighed the equivalent of a rolling pin. Other nights she'd water his whiskey, or pour it down the sink.

The Carvers settled in Yakima, Washington, a town famous for its apples and hops. Ray was a chubby, husky boy who didn't shine at school, though he loved passionately to read. Despite the drinking, they muddled along comfortably enough until 1955, when C.R. lost his job. He went alone to California and found another position in a mill in Chester. Somehow he got sick out there. He sent a letter home saying something about an infected saw cut, though an anonymous postcard in the same mail warned Ella that her husband was on death's door, adding ominously that he was drinking raw whiskey.

When they arrived in Chester, C.R. seemed gaunt and bewildered, and looked to have had the stuffing knocked clean out of him. Not long after that he had a breakdown and went back to Yakima, where he was treated with ECT on the fifth floor of Valley Memorial Hospital. By this time Ray had got his smart, stunning sixteen-year-old girlfriend pregnant. He married Maryann on 7 June 1957, a few days after she graduated high school. In 'My Father's Life', he wrote: 'My dad was still locked up when my wife went into this same hospital, just one floor down, to have our first baby. After she had delivered, I went upstairs to give my dad the news.'

In later life, Carver would come bitterly to regret taking on the burden of a family so young. When Christine was born he and Maryann could barely afford to eat a proper meal or heat two rooms – a situation that didn't improve when she discovered six weeks later that she was pregnant again. Though they were already sinking into a quicksand of debt, both remained determined to get an education and make something of their lives.

In her loving and sometimes shocking memoir, *What It Used To Be Like*, Maryann Burk Carver remembered an argument the couple had a few days after their wedding, in which her new husband announced that he regretted marrying and would always choose writing over her. Swallowing her own ambition, she decided that her duty was 'to preserve Ray's opportunity to be a writer . . . I would walk the tight-rope between Ray's writing life and our family. I'd walk it better than anyone ever had.' What this commitment meant in practice was hard labour: a run of punishing jobs that began with a summer stint in a warehouse packing cherries to buy Carver his first Father's Day present: an Underwood typewriter.

Maryann wasn't the only one working flat-out. It's almost impossible to overestimate the hardship of those years, in which Carver struggled to educate himself and get food on the table while stealing every spare minute in which to write. In such straitened circumstances, it's not difficult to understand why alcohol might have begun to seem like an ally, or else a key to a locked door. His father had drunk to escape the monotony of work and to ease the pressures of survival. For Ray, there was also bitterness to choke back; bitterness and self-reproach and a sense of spoiling time. These are the sort of things that can sour in your head if you're still working as a janitor at twenty-seven, swabbing corridors in Mercy Hospital. And these are the sort of things you might try to soothe in the Fireside Lounge on H Street, knocking back a boilermaker at the end of the night shift, readying up for another day with your own exhausting children.

There's no doubt that the odds were stacked against him; but nor is there much doubt that he became, six days out of seven, his own worst enemy. Reading Maryann's book reminded me of Brick's line about a drunk being two people, two men fighting one another for control of a bottle. The things Carver did seem so senselessly self-destructive. One Raymond – Good Raymond, I suppose – would get on to a Masters programme, or find a decent job, and the other Raymond, the perverse, malevolent one, would somehow conspire to mess it up. He published three volumes of poems during his drinking years, and wrote almost forty short stories, among them 'Will You Please Be Quiet, Please?', 'Tell the Women We're Going', 'Dummy' and 'So Much Water So Close to Home'. And at the same time he had affairs, and dragged his family back and forth across the country. He made his wife give up her best-paid and most emotionally satisfying job. He was unreliable, paranoid and violent, and as he approached the nadir of his drinking he could barely write at all. Years later, looking back at this period in an interview with the *Paris Review*, he said:

> I was in my late twenties or early thirties. We were still in a state of penury, we had one bankruptcy behind us, and years of hard work with nothing to show for it except an old car, a rented house, and new creditors on our backs. It was depressing, and I felt spiritually obliterated. Alcohol became a problem. I more or less gave up, threw in the towel, and took to full-time drinking as a serious pursuit . . . I suppose I began to drink heavily after I'd realized that the things I'd wanted most in life for myself and my writing, and my wife and children, were simply not going to happen. It's strange. You never start out in life with the intention of becoming a bankrupt or an alcoholic or a cheat and a thief. Or a liar.

Good Raymond emerged from the wreckage slowly, like a man struggling from a smashed car. Like Berryman, he spent a long time shuttling through recovery, getting dry and then going straight back out to drink. Early on, during the bad years in California, he had a seizure on the floor just as he was about to leave a treatment centre, smashing his forehead open. The doctor warned him that if he ever drank again he risked becoming a *wet-brain*, a graphic term for alcoholic brain damage. According to Maryann, he spent that evening 'sucking brandy from a bottle as if it were Pepsi, his stitches concealed under a bandage, indifferent to the doctor's warning'.

In 1976 his first volume of stories, *Will You Please Be Quiet, Please* was published. That same year he checked into Duffy's, a private treatment centre in Napa that was later the setting for the short story 'Where I'm Calling From'. The programme consisted of frequent AA meetings and controlled withdrawal by way of *hummers*, progressively weaker shots of rotgut bourbon in water, doled out every three hours for three days. Shortly after his release, he announced that he understood he could never drink hard liquor again, and would in future stick to Andre champagne.

Unsurprisingly, he was back again two months later, checking himself in on New Year's Eve. It was his last pass through formal treatment. That spring, around the time his old friend John Cheever published *Falconer*, he left his family and rented a house alone in McKinleyville, overlooking the Pacific. For the next few months he went to AA meetings and tried, not always successfully, to maintain his balance on the wagon. The turning point came on 29 May 1977, when he was offered an advance of $5,000 by McGraw-Hill for a novel. He was in the midst of a bender at the time, but four days later took his final drink in the Jambalaya bar in Arcata. 'June 2nd 1977,' he remembered in the *Paris Review*. 'If you want the truth, I'm prouder of that, that I've quit drinking, than I am of anything in my life. I'm a recovered alcoholic. I'll always be an alcoholic, but I'm no longer a practicing alcoholic.'

In those early months, he clung to AA, driving out to meetings once or twice a day. His marriage was breaking down and his children loathed him. For a long time he stayed on his toes, paranoid and leery of responsibility. The novelist Richard Ford met him around then, and later wrote down his memories of his friend in an essay for the *New Yorker*.

> In 1977 he was tall, skinny, and bony, hesitant, barely speaking above a clipped whisper. He seemed friendly but slightly spooked, though not in a way that spooked you; more in a way that suggested he'd recently been on the ropes and definitely didn't want to show up there again. His teeth needed work. His hair was dense and practically matted. He had rough hands, long fat sideburns, black horn-rimmed spectacles, a pair of mustard-colored trousers, an ugly brown-and-purple striped shirt from Penney's basement, and a taste in footwear that ran to Hush Puppies knockoffs. He looked as if he'd stepped down off a Greyhound bus from 1964, and from someplace where he'd done mostly custodial duties. And he was completely irresistible.

Slowly, over the next two years, this skinny, irresistible man backed away from his family, whose ongoing troubles he felt certain were capable of scuttling his recovery. For a while he barely wrote, and then the new stories started coming; stories infused with 'little human connections'; stories he'd 'come back from the grave' to write. In June 1980, he delivered a collection of these and a few older pieces to Gordon Lish, his beloved editor at Knopf, with the working title *So Much Water So Close to Home*.

Lish bought the book, which he retitled *What We Talk About When We Talk About Love*, but not without making changes. He brutally pruned each story, slashing by up to seventy per cent and excising any whiff of sentimentality or tenderness. He cut the last six pages of 'If It Please You', in which James Packer, knowing his wife's cancer has returned, prays for everyone he knows, the living and the dead. He cut the last eighteen pages of 'A Small, Good Thing', losing the entirety of its redemptive ending, in which a baker feeds a newly bereaved couple on cinnamon rolls and warm dark bread.

Carver was devastated by the cuts, the newly minimal landscape of silence and erasure. The expansiveness Lish objected to was intimately bound up with his own sense of recovery and renewed grace. 'I'm afraid, mortally afraid,' he told Lish in a long letter begun on 8 July at 8 a.m., 'that if the book were to be published as it is in its present edited form, I may never write another story, that's how closely, God Forbid, some of those stories are to my sense of regaining my health and mental well-being.'

He felt the changes, and the compromise they represented, were directly antagonistic to his sobriety, and that if the untruthful object the book had become was published in its current form, he was liable to stop writing and start drinking again. He referred to demons rising up and taking him over; to confusion and paranoia; to a sense that he might lose both his soul and his fragile sense of self-esteem. The letter rambles frantically on, begging for forgiveness, begging that publication be stopped. 'God almighty, Gordon,' he writes. 'Please forgive me . . . Please hear me . . . Please help me.'

Two days later, he wrote another, shorter letter, asking for a few specific changes. Four days after that he sent a third. This time, his mood had shifted: 'I'm thrilled about the book and its impending publication.' Once again he asked for a few reinsertions, to keep some semblance of the stories' original vision. No dice. Lish remained adamant that his own version was correct. *What We Talk About* was published in 1981, catapulting Carver to fame.

It's hard to know how to interpret those three letters, the volte-face they represent. In the first, Carver was evidently in the grips of what he sometimes called 'the willies', a sense of intolerable jitteriness common in newly recovered alcoholics. But whether the decision to accept Lish's edits came as a result of staring down his own anxiety or represented a capitulation born out of a weak will and an overdeveloped desire to please is difficult to gauge. He certainly valued Lish very highly. ('You're my mainstay,' he'd written in the spring of 1980. 'Man, I love you. I don't make that declaration lightly, either.') That said, he never let himself be edited so brutally again. By the time *Cathedral* came out in 1983, he was in full command, and Lish's changes were strictly cosmetic.

Carver's gathering self-confidence had a lot to do with a relationship begun in that same turbulent season of early sobriety. In the summer of 1978, he fell in love with the poet Tess Gallagher, the protector and companion of his second life. At the time, she'd just built a house in her home town of Port Angeles, and at the tail end of 1982 Ray moved in. It was in this period that he produced – though he might have preferred *caught* – clutch after clutch of poems, slippery and pristine as the dream salmon he sometimes encountered on his nights in town.

I'd read one of them so many times I'd almost worn a track in it. It's called 'Where Water Comes Together With Other Water'. 'I love creeks and the music they make,' the narrator begins, and then lists, exultantly, all the other waterways he knows, and the enlarging effects they have on his heart. 'I'm 45 years old today,' he announces.

Would anyone believe if I said
I was once 35?
My heart empty and sere at 35!
Five more years had to pass
before it began to flow again.

He elaborates on how it pleases him, loving rivers, and then ends with a characteristically heartfelt, sawn-off sentence, a kind of credo or manifesto: 'Loving everything that increases me.'

You could live like that all right, especially if you'd once felt, as he did, that every action you took was poisoning further the wellsprings of your life. It could be read, in fact, as a kind of boiled-down, idiosyncratic version of Step Three – *Made a decision to turn our will and our lives over to the care of God as we understood Him*. It has the same faith in enlargement, in the possibility of benediction from oblique and unexpected sources.

Somewhere along the line I'd found out that the title of the poem referred to a specific place. The Sky House, as Gallagher's new property was known, was situated not far from Morse Creek, an old steelhead run that gave out into the Juan de Fuca Strait. Carver walked and fished there often, and it was this confluence he was thinking of when he wrote the line about some places standing out in his mind as if they were holy. I knew what he meant. I share that susceptibility to water myself, and now we were in the town I was almost frantic to find the creek.

We went that afternoon, driving back along the 101 and leaving the car in a lot by the bridge. The river came down hard beneath it, bottle green, ploughing messily over waterworn rocks and boulders. There was a path that looked as if it might lead to the beach, though it skirted first around an estate of incongruously suburban houses. Many of the plants on the wayside were familiar. I counted nettles, cleavers, dandelion, even shepherd's purse. But I needed my *National Audubon Society Field Guide to the Pacific Northwest* to identify Scouler's willow and salmonberry, the pink flowers a cross between a clematis and a heraldic rose.

The beach was sandy and scattered with ninepins of driftwood. Some of the pieces were enormous: whole trees torn out by the roots, their bark worn down to a silky sandy grey that felt pleasantly animate to the touch. Sea grass grew up between stones big as ostrich eggs, in variegated shades of buff and gunmetal, marl and slate. Some were striped or stippled and a very few were pale pink. I kept picking up nubs of driftwood, little bone-white and ash-black twigs. All the time there was the sucking, rushing sound of water, sluicing and pulling in contrapuntal motion, each wave drowned out by the next. Up close, it was seal-grey and pitted with darker marks, like spots of rain on paving stones.

A few yards ahead the river joined the sea. Morse Creek cut out through a stretch of blackish sand, over stones that ranged in size from pebbles to boulders. It ran very fast now, maybe four feet deep, humping and shouldering, the surface breaking apart in pleats. I knelt and dipped my hand, wincing. It had come straight off the mountain: snowmelt, old ice, clear and astringent as gin. Two black and white birds came overhead then, driving hard against the wind. It had begun to rain. I leaned back on my heels and took it all in. A ferry was chugging out to sea and on the horizon I could just make out the thin ridge of Victoria, almost blotted out by cloud.

You could get back on your feet in a place like this, after a lifetime of messing up, of being torn apart by the overwhelming incompatibility of your needs. All those bad things you'd done, back in another life: they might rinse away out here, given time, given a landscape so explicitly devoted to the display of time's long reach. Watching water work through rock, you might come to a kind of accommodation with the fact that you'd once smashed your wife's head repeatedly against a sidewalk for looking at another man; that you'd hit her with a wine bottle, severing an artery and causing her to lose almost sixty per cent of her blood. Other things, too. Stupid, slippery things: drink-driving, bouncing cheques, running out on bills, committing fraud, letting people down, making up dumb and pointless lies. Hardly any wonder Carver's nickname was Running Dog, or that he said, a long time later, 'I made a wasteland out of everything I touched.'

On the way back to the car we passed a woman chewing gum, who stopped us and said, 'I don't know if you're interested in birds, but there are like five bald eagles up by the bridge.' We thanked her and hurried on. There were only two by the time we got there, in the tree between us and the 101. In flight they looked like a coat thrown into the air, ragged and enormous. The creek churned beneath them, goose green and full of bubbles. They were fishing, the woman had said. The nearest one roused, ruffling his feathers, wings ajar. He dipped forward to strop his beak on his chest, then looked up sharply as two ducks crossed well above the alders. Imagine a day of this. Imagine years: the increase, the effect it would have on your heart.

★

On the road to Elwha there was an Apostolic church with a sign outside announcing: *Satan subtracts and divides, God adds and multiplies.* Bright sky, a scum of cirrus. We were taking the Olympic Hot Springs Road into the mountains, stopping periodically to look down at the river, which shot grey-green through a rocky, moss-covered gorge. This is where the poem 'Lemonade' is set, the one that contains a hearsay story about a man whose son drowned on a fishing trip, and who watched his small body pulled from the water by a helicopter, using what looked like a set of kitchen tongs.

There were firs on the sheer banks and trees swagged in golden moss. We crawled by a herd of black-tailed deer. They looked up as we passed, faces soft and unguarded as sleepwalkers. The air above Elwha Bridge was full of swallows, darting their unfolding patterns into the mist. The river was nearly aquamarine and very deep now, rippling and fissuring like a pot of boiling water.

We drove on up towards the springs. The trees were glowing in the wet light. Spruce, hemlock, more firs than I could name. It began to rain, and then to rain hard. The road tacked up, higher and higher. The rain turned to sleet, then real snow, the fat flakes falling between the trees and making the air thick and soupy. We stopped to look down. The flakes fell past us, vanishing into the green bowl of water hundreds of feet below. At last my mother turned the car and we slithered round black switchbacks to the relative safety of the truckers' road.

We ate lunch that day at a roadside shack called Granny's Café. There was a man at the bar in a denim jacket and a baseball cap, with a lined, humorous face, well into his eighties. He came over to chat with us as we waited on our burgers. 'March had double the average rainfall,' he said. 'I got a big farm down from here. You go out into the hay and you sink on into it.' What do you raise, I asked him, and he said: 'I got a few beef cattle, hay,' then, deadpan, 'You gotta do something to keep you entertained.'

People always want to talk to my mother, to make her laugh, to have her attention. There's something about her that draws strangers; a kind of light. She was the best companion I could imagine that day. It's rare we spend time together, just the two of us, and we drove all over, screeching at one another to watch out for rocks and logging trucks. We drove up to Crescent Lake and took a stroll around it, marvelling at the colour of the water, which shifted as the sun passed in and out of clouds through different registers of indigo, ultramarine and then a deep saturated blue, like cornflowers in a field.

It was hard to express the effect the landscape was having on me. It was a place for settling, for setting down, for relinquishing the past. That evening my mother and I began to talk about Diana's recovery, about how miraculous her transformation had been, and how dear she was to us. During the course of this conversation I asked my mother what had happened over the last days at Tall Trees. I'd begun to doubt my own account, to suspect that there was something cobbled or misconstrued about it. I was right. The story my mother told me that night, in an Italian restaurant in Port Angeles, was one I'd never heard before, and that barely intersected with my fragmented version.

She said that my sister and I had spent the weekend at our father's house, as we did every month. At the time, Diana's work was very stressful, and for two days she sat in her study, drinking and brooding, the alcohol seeping like battery acid until it had contaminated all the regions of her life. On Sunday at six we came spilling back through the door, probably laden down with the presents my father almost always gave us. We rushed to my mother, chattering a mile a minute, and Diana felt, I suppose, poisonously excluded. She went up to our rooms and gathered everything she'd ever given us, armfuls of clothes and toys, and threw them over the balustrade.

My mother took us upstairs then, into the only bedroom in the house that had a lock. She shut the door and jammed the bed against it. Then she turned the radio up very high to drown out what Diana was screaming, down on her knees against the door. We stayed in there for hours, chatting and playing games, a piece of time that's been completely erased from my mind. Eventually my sister needed to go to the loo, and so my mother opened the door, pushed Diana backwards into her study, which had a captain's desk and oak chairs with green leather seats. She held the handle up and by the time she released it Diana had called the police and was shrieking down the phone that she was being held hostage in her own home.

They were there in minutes, and then I suppose my own memory kicks in with the scene on the stairs, the strongest element of which was my conviction that if only I were allowed to speak to her I could calm her down – a moment of absurdly unrealistic co-dependence that's had long-reaching consequences in the relationships of my adult life.

I lay in bed that night in my room at the Red Lion, tumbling the story over in my head. The Juan de Fuca Strait was moving blackly a few feet away. No matter how much I thought about it, I couldn't locate the place where I'd squirrelled away that afternoon. The only thing that seemed even remotely familiar was the sound of the radio, and the raging voice beneath it, though God knows there were no shortage of evenings in which someone screamed while I lay in bed, reading pony stories and listening to *The Phantom of the Opera* or *Thriller* on my yellow Walkman.

All of a sudden I felt very angry. I didn't like the thought of myself in that little room, and I hated the powerlessness of having lost whole episodes of my childhood. There was something almost ridiculously ironic about it, too. The thing I'd always found most frightening about alcoholism was the way it affected memory: the blackouts, the hiccups, the obliterations. It seemed directly erosive of a person's moral sense, since it's hardly possible to make amends for things you don't recall.

It struck me then that much of the work of the Twelve Step Programme is directed towards remembrance. How did it go? Step Four: 'Made a searching and fearless moral inventory of ourselves.' Step Five: 'Admitted to God, to ourselves, and to another human being the exact nature of our wrongs.' Step Eight: 'Made a list of all persons we had harmed, and became willing to make amends to them all.' Step Ten: 'Continued to take personal inventory, and when we were wrong, promptly admitted it.'

This line of thought reminded me of something else I didn't like: a snag I'd spotted in the fabric of Carver's recovery. 'I have a poor memory,' he admitted in a famous essay called 'Fires'.

By this I mean that much that has happened in my life I've forgotten – a blessing for sure – but I have these large periods of time I simply can't account for or bring back, towns and cities I've lived in, names of people, the people themselves. Large blanks . . . Perhaps this is why it's sometimes been said that my stories are unadorned, stripped down . . . None of my stories really *happened*, of course – I'm not writing autobiography – but most of them bear a resemblance, however faint, to certain life occurrences or situations. But when I try to recall the physical surroundings or furnishings bearing on a story situation (what kind of flowers, if any, were present? Did they give off any odor? etc.), I'm often at a total loss. So I have to make it up as I go along – what the people in the story say to each other, as well as what they do then, after thus, and so was said, and what happens to them next.

There's something missing in this account though – something, in fact, weirdly amnesiac about it. Elsewhere, Carver was explicit about the role of alcohol in the obliteration of his facility for recall. For example, in the *Paris Review* interview of 1983 he said: 'Toward the end of my drinking career I was completely out of control and in a very grave place. Blackouts, the whole business – points where you can't remember anything you say or do during a certain period of time. You might drive a car, give a reading, teach a class, set a broken leg, go to bed with someone, and not have any memory of it later. You're on some kind of automatic pilot.'

None of this is mentioned in 'Fires'. The essay is an attempt to answer the question of influence; to name the things that have driven and shaped Carver's writing. Apart from a poor memory, the main influence he can think of, the one he calls 'oppressive and often malevolent' and later 'heavy and often baleful', is the existence of his two children.

Bitterly, he describes a particular nadir: an afternoon in the mid-sixties, when he was at Iowa for the first time, as a grad student in the Writers Workshop. His wife was at work, his children were at a party, and he was spending Saturday afternoon in a laundromat, waiting with five or six loads of wet clothes for an empty dryer. Eventually one came free, but before he could grab it another customer pounced. In that moment of helpless failure, of drudgery and thwarted effort, he saw that he was never going to achieve the things he wanted. Soon afterwards, he said, the dreams went bust. No doubt at all whose fault this was.

The time came and went when everything my wife and I held sacred, or considered worthy of respect, every spiritual value, crumbled away. Something terrible had happened to us. It was something that we had never seen in any other family . . . It was erosion, and we couldn't stop it. Somehow, when we weren't looking, the children had got into the driver's seat. As crazy as it sounds now, they held the reins, and the whip.

He finishes up by accusing his children of eating him alive, adding that his life came 'to a dead stop off on a siding . . . If there'd once been a fire, it'd gone out.'

It's hard to express how disturbing I found this account, which was written at Yaddo in 1981, when Carver was five years dry. Despite his sobriety, it seemed to exemplify an alcoholic cast of mind: a tendency to blame external factors rather than fronting up to one's own role in kindling trouble. Psychologists call this having an external locus of control, and it's common among people with addictions. A person with an internal locus of control tends to think their own actions are responsible for their experience, while a person with an external locus of control tends to blame circumstances, to be superstitious, or to feel themselves at the mercy of forces outside themselves. In alcoholics, this sense of powerlessness tends to lead directly to drinking. (Cheever, on yet another psychiatrist: 'I think my problems enforce my drinking. He claims I invent my problems to justify my drinking.')

In 'Fires', Carver ducks responsibility for the consequences of his alcoholism entirely. Instead, he sidles the blame for the erosion of his writing and his family on to the two people who were most vulnerable and most damaged by it. It's a kind of moral blackout, a refusal to link cause and effect in any meaningful way – which isn't to say, of course, that poverty doesn't exact a cost or profoundly influence the destiny of a writer.

Recovery isn't a simple matter, a straightforward substitution of bad for good. Instead, it's a kind of evolution, slow and sometimes stuttering. Elsewhere, Carver fronted up to his behaviour more honestly. In the 1982 poem 'Alcohol', he wrote with deliberate hesitation:

> and then . . . something: alcohol –
> what you've really done
> and to someone else, the one
> you meant to love from the start.

This poem also ends with a memory lapse: 'But you don't remember. / You honestly don't remember.' This time, though, there seems to be a suggestion, contained in the gentle irony of that *honestly*, that the narrator realises his excuses and ellipses might not be enough any more, never mind the seeming helplessness with which they're being proffered.

I turned over on the big bed. The curtains weren't quite closed. I could see two darknesses outside, one still, the other shifting on itself. There's a saying in AA that addiction isn't your fault, but recovery is your responsibility. It sounds simple enough, but making that step away from blame is, as Berryman discovered, about as easy as standing up and dancing on a sheet of black ice.

I clicked the light back on and got *All of Us* from my bedside table. I'd marked 'Wenas Ridge' a long time back. It opens with the narrator remembering a boyhood afternoon spent grouse hunting with two friends. He'd just got a girl pregnant, as Carver had in the spring of 1957. The boys – bozos, he calls them – shoot six grouse and then, on the ridge above the river, they stumble upon a rattlesnake: fat and dark, thick as a boy's wrist. It rears up, singing its sinister song. They back away and scramble down, climbing over fallen trees and crawling through deer paths, seeing snakes in every shadow.

During his descent the boy prays to Jesus, but in some other quarter of his mind a rival prayer starts up, a prayer to the singing snake itself. 'Keep believing in me,' it says, and in response the boy makes 'an obscure, criminal pact'. The final stanza returns him to adulthood. 'I got out, didn't I?' he asks, shruggingly, and then answers himself: not quite. He remembers the troubles that followed on that day: that he poisoned his beloved wife's life; that lies 'began to coil in my heart and call it home'. He weighs up the two powers, the fearful rattlesnake against the uncertain, doubted presence of Jesus. The poem ends with another ambivalent statement, a pivot of a line:

> But someone, something's responsible for this.
> Now, as then.

You could go two ways from there. You could keep on marinating in blame, in helpless submission to your circumstance. Or you could stop, just clean stop, and take up the liberating burden of responsibility for yourself.

★

The next day was my thirty-fourth birthday. I hadn't made any plans. We went to the Cornerhouse for eggs Benedict and coffee. My mother could barely sit still, and eventually she told me, bursting with pride, that she'd found somewhere where I could shoot a gun. She'd driven out of town the day before to find a range, and seen two longhaired men shambling up the highway. She pulled over on a hunch and they shifted from foot to foot and sucked their teeth, and eventually remembered Matt Dryke's place on the road to Sequim. Then one of them asked for five bucks, and she gave it to him, entirely satisfied by the exchange.

The shooting thing had started in New Hampshire, plinking wine bottles with a Crossman air pistol. I liked it; liked the steadiness, the concentration. Later, I'd graduated to my friend John's CZ rifle. We'd drive up to a deserted sandpit in his truck and set up a coyote target on the pitted wooden stand. All afternoon we'd trudge back and forth to check our shots, a turkey vulture wheeling overhead. I loved loading the cartridges and hunkering down over the hood, pressing the stock into my cheekbone, bending my left knee and peering in through the enlarging circle of the sights. Not much I've ever done has been as satisfying as sighting in that rifle and clipping the target in the clean pink circle of its heart.

It was a different business at Sunnydell. 'Turn left at the yellow rocking chair,' the woman in the office had told my mother on the phone. 'If you get to Kitchen Dick's you've gone too far.' There was a duck pond, a shooting range and an old tennis court planted with a sagging ping-pong table. We rang the bell and after a long while Matt came loping up the yard. 'You ladies the ones that want to shoot pistols?' he asked. 'You got everything you need? You got ear defenders? You got pistols?' My mum looked a little startled. 'No,' she said. 'The woman in the office said you had pistols.' 'No, we don't got any pistols,' he said laconically. 'I got shotguns. I can get you set up with shotguns.' He got two guns out of a locked cabinet, a .410 and a big, ugly thing, its butt lagged with padding and masking tape. We went up to the platform together. 'I've never shot skeet,' I said, and he grinned and handed over the first gun. 'Tuck it close into your shoulder,' he said. 'Lean your cheek into it and don't be afraid of it, then it won't kick up. Watch the target, not the sights.' I kept missing and then, after a long time, my eye slotted in. 'Pull,' I said and the green disc flicked up into the sky, and I tracked and squeezed and it shattered and splashed down into the water. It seemed almost magical, the knack of swinging upwards. My heart was running hard and the air smelled harshly of spent shells. 'Follow him up,' Matt said. 'Follow him up. You're a bit over. Now you're getting him. Don't let him suffer.'

When we'd shot through the box we went back to the office to settle up. There were medals on the wall and I took a look. 'Jesus, Matt,' I said. 'You were an Olympic Gold.' He grinned, that same swift grin. 'Yep. I grew up out here. Been shooting all my life.'

As we drove away, I could still feel my hands shaking from the reverberations of the big shotgun. Funny, I used to hate guns. Somehow the old air rifle at Tall Trees had become a symbol of everything I loathed about those years. My mother used to shoot squirrels with it, out of her bedroom window. My job was to take the bins out, and often I'd find their little frozen corpses curled amid the rubbish. When the gun itself was taken by the police, it somehow lodged in my head as a way of encoding all the disorder and potential danger of alcoholism itself. It was the only thing about that night that had stayed clear to me: the policeman walking out of the front door, carrying our rifle.

At some point, you have to set down the past. At some point, you have to accept that everyone was doing their best. At some point, you have to gather yourself up, and go onward into your life. That evening I went for a walk on the beach on my own, and got to thinking about the Carver story I most love. It was called 'Nobody Said Anything' and he wrote it in 1970, slam in the middle of the Bad Raymond period. He might have been in his study, or he might have scribbled it in his car, as he sometimes did back then, hunched up with a legal pad, trying to sidestep for an hour or two the unseating demands of his domestic life.

It's written in the first person, from the perspective of a boy called R, who wakes to hear his parents in the kitchen, knee-deep in a row. He nudges his younger brother awake, but George misunderstands the shove and thinks he's picking a fight. 'Stop gouging me, you bastard,' he says. 'I'm going to tell!' R decides he doesn't want to go to school, and persuades his mother he's unwell. He watches her get ready for work, rattling off instructions and prohibitions. Don't turn the burners on. There's tuna fish in the icebox. Take your medicine. Before she leaves he switches the TV on, sound down, but she doesn't say anything about that.

After she's gone, he takes possession of the house. He prowls around his parents' bedroom, looking for some evidence of their sex lives. He can't find any rubbers, but he gets a quick thrill from inspecting a jar of Vaseline. Something dirty about that, for sure. He opens a few drawers, checks around for money and then decides to walk to Birch Creek and see if he can catch a trout. It's fall, and the season is open for a week or two more.

As he's walking down Sixteenth Avenue, a red car passes and pulls over. A skinny woman with spots around her mouth offers him a ride. He listens to her talk and fantasises about going home with her, though it's evident from the halting scenario he builds that he isn't entirely sure what two people do in bed. Down by the river, he jerks off and ejaculates into the creek. He casts a few times, meandering through different spots. The water's low, and in some places there are drifting yellow leaves.

Up by the airport he tries again, putting salmon eggs on the line and casting into a deeper pool. Just as he starts thinking about French-kissing the pimply woman, the tip of his fly rod jiggles. He's hooked a trout, a green trout that lies on its side and doesn't fight the line. There's something not quite right about it. 'He was the colour of moss, that colour green. It was as if he had been wrapped up in moss for a long time, and the colour had come off all over him.'

He carries the trout back to the bridge. A smaller boy is down there now. He's skinny and unkempt, about George's size, with big buck teeth. He's very excited about a fish he's seen, and when R looks his heart jumps too. The fish is a giant, as long as his arm. They decide to try and corral him. The first attempt goes wrong, and the little boy ends up sopping, drenched to his collar. They scream at one another and then they find the fish again. This time R makes the boy drive it down towards him. He grabs it in his hands and hurls it to the bank. It's huge, the biggest fish he's ever caught, but there's something wrong with it too. 'His sides were scarred, whitish welts as big as quarters and kind of puffy. There were nicks out of his head around his eyes and on his snout where I guess he had banged into the rocks and been in fights. But he was so skinny, too skinny for how long he was, and you could hardly see the pink stripe down his sides, and his belly was grey and slack instead of white and solid like it should have been. But I thought he was something.'

R kills it by yanking its head back until its spine crunches. Then they put a stick through it and carry it back to the road together. There's some tension over whose fish it is, and eventually they decide to cut it in half with R's pocket knife. An aeroplane takes off above their heads. The day is getting colder, and the small boy looks freezing.

Both want the head end, but R manages to convince him to take the tail by making a bribe of the green trout.

When he gets home his parents are arguing again and the kitchen is full of smoke. It's another one of those corrosive domestic scenes, a more violent version of the tensions simmering in Hemingway's Nick Adams stories. R's mother throws the burning contents of the pan against the wall. R opens the door then, just as his father is wiping up the mess. 'You won't believe what I caught at Birch Creek,' he says. He shows his mother the creel and she looks inside and starts to scream. 'Oh, oh my God! What is it? A snake! What is it? Please, please take it out before I throw up.' Instead he shows it to his dad, his gigantic summer steelhead. His dad screams too. 'Take that goddamn thing out of here! What in the hell is the matter with you? Take it the hell out of the kitchen and throw it in the goddamn garbage!'

R goes back outside. He has the creel in his hands. He looks into it. Under the porch light its contents have turned silver. They fill the creel. 'I lifted him out,' he says. 'I held him. I held that half of him.'

★

I was still thinking about that story the next morning. It was our last day in Port Angeles and I got up just before dawn. In the afternoon we were taking the car back to Seattle, and the next day I'd catch a plane from Sea-Tac airport. It was hard to get my head around. I'd been away from England too long. I needed to get home, to sleep in my own bed. All the same, there was one last thing I wanted to do before I left America.

I got dressed and slipped outside. It was very cold. The mountains looked as if they'd been dusted in icing sugar overnight. Mist was pouring off them and drifting through the valleys. I started the car, scraping ice off the windshield with a credit card. I got lost twice, once by the Nippon paper factory and again by the airfield, but eventually I found my way to Ocean View Cemetery and parked the car under a dripping tree.

There were pines at the edge of the field, and beyond them the land dropped away, falling 400 feet or so to the water beneath. I could hear the waves moving very softly, a lush, lulling, impossibly rich sound. In September 1987, Carver was out there on his boat with a friend when they looked up and saw a group of people on the bluff. 'I think they're planting somebody up there,' he said, and turned his attention back to the sea. He'd been coughing all month, but wouldn't know for another few weeks that there were malignant tumours in his lungs.

The sky was glazed with cloud like curds and whey. I saw his headstone immediately. I recognised it from photographs: black marble, with the poem 'Late Fragment' carved on it. I hadn't realised it was a double grave, though. The other headstone was for Tess Gallagher. Both had the same legend: *Poet, Short Story Writer, Essayist*, though the rest of hers was blank. Between them was a hoop of slightly bedraggled artificial flowers and another slab engraved with the text of 'Gravy', with Carver's signature beneath both poems.

Under a bench I found the black metal box I'd heard about. I opened it and pulled out a Ziploc bag. Inside was a spiral-bound notebook. I squatted down on the grass and started reading. The sun was streaming through the trees in dusty shafts, stirrable as honey. It was a visitors' book, each entry written in a different hand. Gallagher used it the most, but there were also many letters from strangers and old friends. Some wanted to say how much Carver's writing meant to them, and others talked about addiction in tones that sounded as if they were speaking to a priest or an AA sponsor, someone non-judgemental and sympathetic.

'Spending is an escape just like alcohole,' one read. 'We are all trying to fill that empty hole.' Another: 'I started drinking . . . hard. If I can keep my head above water hopefully I won't drown. I turned 23 yesterday.' Tess had scribbled a reply to that one. 'Ray would say, have faith, grasp at straws and *go to AA.*'

I was crying by then. Faith. In the end, recovery depends on faith, of one kind or another. Carver once said that he didn't believe in God, 'but I have to believe in miracles and the possibility of resurrection. No question about that. Every day that I wake up, I'm glad to wake up.' It's this faith that became explicit in his late stories – 'Cathedral', 'Errand', 'Intimacy' – though there are traces of it in things he wrote much earlier too.

It struck me then that by driving out to a writer's grave, all these anonymous, suffering strangers were putting their faith in stories, in the capacity of literature to somehow salve a sense of soreness, to make one feel less flinchingly alone. I thought of myself as a child, of how I became a reader because tracts of my life were unendurable. In 1969, six years before he got sober, John Cheever was asked by the *Paris Review* if he felt godlike at the typewriter. Perhaps you could read his answer as a delusion – the word Berryman scratched all through the proofs of his own interview. Perhaps it wasn't, though. Perhaps it could be taken at face value.

No, I've never felt godlike. No, the sense is of one's total usefulness. We all have a power of control, it's part of our lives: we have it in love, in work that we love doing. It's a sense of ecstasy, as simple as that. The sense is that 'this is my usefulness, and I can do it all the way through.' It always leaves you feeling great. In short, you've made sense of your life.

I thought of them all then. I thought of Fitzgerald as a boy, standing very upright in his white duck pants, singing 'Far Away in Colon Town' and thinking he might die of shame. I thought of Berryman driving to Tampa for his father's funeral ('how did I *act* in the car'), and Cheever dressed in a blue serge suit too small for him, stuck in 'the galling loneliness of my adolescence'. I thought of Williams when he was still called Tom, walking full-tilt through the streets of St. Louis to try and calm his racing heart. I thought of Hemingway at the age of nine, writing to his father, in his earliest surviving letter: 'I got six clams in the river and some weat six feet tall.'

I thought of the things they'd written; the sense they'd made of their mangled lives. And sitting there in the grass at the top of the cliff, I realised why I loved the story about R and the severed fish. We're all of us like that boy sometimes. I mean we all carry something inside us that can be rejected; that can look silver in the light. You can deny it, or try and throw it in the garbage, by all means. You can despise it so much you drink yourself halfway to death. At the end of the day, though, the only thing to do is to take a hold of yourself, to gather up the broken parts. That's when recovery begins. That's when the second life – the good one – starts.

AUTHORS' DATES

F. Scott Fitzgerald   24 September 1896 – 21 December 1940

Ernest Hemingway   21 July 1899 – 2 July 1961

Tennessee Williams   26 March 1911 – 25 February 1983

John Cheever   27 May 1912 – 18 June 1982

John Berryman   25 October 1914 – 7 January 1972

Raymond Carver   25 May 1938 – 2 August 1988

THE TWELVE STEPS OF
ALCOHOLICS ANONYMOUS

1. We admitted we were powerless over alcohol – that our lives had become unmanageable.

2. Came to believe that a Power greater than ourselves could restore us to sanity.

3. Made a decision to turn our will and our lives over to the care of God as we understood Him.

4. Made a searching and fearless moral inventory of ourselves.

5. Admitted to God, to ourselves, and to another human being the exact nature of our wrongs.

6. Were entirely ready to have God remove all these defects of character.

7. Humbly asked Him to remove our shortcomings.

8. Made a list of all persons we had harmed, and became willing to make amends to them all.

9. Made direct amends to such people wherever possible, except when to do so would injure them or others.

10. Continued to take personal inventory and when we were wrong promptly admitted it.

11. Sought through prayer and meditation to improve our conscious contact with God, as we understood Him, praying only for knowledge of His will for us and the power to carry that out.

12. Having had a spiritual awakening as the result of these Steps, we tried to carry this message to alcoholics, and to practice these principles in all our affairs.

NOTES

To write a book of this kind is to depend inevitably on the research of generations of scholars. Each of the six writers I've discussed in *The Trip to Echo Spring* has been the subject of at least one biography, and often many more. While all these works helped to direct and shape my thinking, I owe a particular debt of gratitude to John Haffenden, Carol Sklenicka and Blake Bailey, the biographers, respectively, of John Berryman, Raymond Carver and John Cheever.

In the case of Fitzgerald, Hemingway and Williams, much of what one might consider private material (letters, journals and other ephemera) has been published. For Berryman, Carver and to some extent Cheever, much of this material is not yet in print (Cheever's published journal and letters represent only the tip of a very large iceberg). As such, I'm indebted to Haffenden, Sklenicka and Bailey, not only for their remarkable and insightful biographies, but for making what were often vital letters and diary entries available when visits to far-flung American archives were impossible.

Hemingway, Fitzgerald and Cheever were notably poor spellers. I have preserved their idiosyncrasies in quotations, though I may as well admit that I struggled with the spelling of 'idiosyncrasies' myself.

EPIGRAPHS

vii   *'When alcoholics do drink . . .'*: David P. Moore and James W. Jefferson, eds., *Handbook of Medical Psychiatry* (Elsevier, 2004), p. 85.

vii   *'Easy, easy, Mr. Bones . . .'*: John Berryman, 'Dream Song 36', *The Dream Songs* (Faber, 1969), p. 40.

CHAPTER 1: ECHO SPRING

1   *'By the time I got inside the store . . .'*: Raymond Carver, 'The Art of Fiction No. 76', *Paris Review*.

3   *'It was one of those midsummer . . .'*: John Cheever, 'The Swimmer', *The Stories of John Cheever* (Cape, 1979), pp. 603–11.

7   *'Four of the six Americans . . .'*: Lewis Hyde, *Alcohol and poetry: John Berryman and the booze talking* (Dallas Institute, 1986), p. 1.

7   *'impaired control over drinking . . .'*: Robert M. Morse, Daniel K. Flavin, 'The Definition of Alcoholism', *The Journal of the American Medical Association*, Vol. 268, No. 8, August 1992, pp. 1012–14.

8   *'The cause of alcoholism is unknown . . .'*: Robert Berkow, ed., *The Merck Manual of Diagnosis and Therapy, Sixteenth Edition* (Merck Reseach Laboratories, 1992), p. 1552.

8   *'However, such generalizations should not obscure . . .'*: Robert S. Porter, ed., *The Merck Manual of Diagnosis and Therapy* (Wiley-Blackwell, 2011), online.

8   *'Inspiration contained a death threat . . .'*: Saul Bellow, introduction to John Berryman's *Recovery* (Faber, 1973), p. xii.

10   *'There have been thousands of sexually . . .'*: Jay McInerney, introduction to *The Letters of John Cheever*, ed. Benjamin Cheever (Cape, 1989), p. xiii.

13   '*I love them* ...': Raymond Carver, 'Where Water Comes Together With Other Water', *All of Us: The Collected Poems* (Harvill Press, 2003), p. 64.

14   '*These stories seem* ...': John Cheever, preface to *The Stories of John Cheever*, p. vii.

CHAPTER 2: THE COFFIN TRICK

16   '*the most important American* ...': *New York Times*, 26 February 1983.

17   '*No growth, no change* ...': Walter Kerr, *New York Times*, 27 March 1980.

17   '*We are still receiving his messages* ...': *Life*, 13 June 1965.

17   '*Gallant is the word* ...': Elia Kazan, in Donald Spoto, *The Kindness of Strangers: The Life of Tennessee Williams* (The Bodley Head, 1985), p. 358.

18   '*O'Neill had a terrible* ...': Tennessee Williams, 'The Art of Theater No. 5', *Paris Review*.

19   '*It rained last night* ...': Tennessee Williams, *Memoirs* (Penguin, 2007), p. 127.

21   '*We have just concluded* ...': Tennessee Williams, *The Selected Letters of Tennessee Williams, Volume I, 1920–1945* (New Directions, 2000), pp. 11–16.

22   '*a hairsbreadth of going quite mad* ...': Tennessee Williams, *Memoirs,* p. 20.

23   '*Life at home was terrible, just terrible* ...': Dakin Williams, in Donald Spoto, *The Kindness of Strangers*, p. 18.

23   '*was a terrifying man*': Tennessee Williams, 'The Art of Theater No. 5', *Paris Review*.

24   '*I was in those days an excellent dancer* ...': Tennessee Williams, *Memoirs,* pp. 20–22.

26   '*The house is palatial and not at all shabby* ...': *The Letters of John Cheever*, p. 311.

27   '*The click ... This click that I get* ...': Tennessee Williams, *Cat on a Hot Tin Roof and Other Plays* (Penguin, 1976), p. 66.

27   '*The next engagement* ...': John Cheever, in Blake Bailey, *Cheever: A Life* (Picador, 2009), p. 51.

27   '*you felt as if* ...': Tennessee Williams, *Memoirs*, p. 142.

28   '*A maladaptive* ...': American Psychiatric Association, *Diagnostic and Statistical Manual of Mental Disorders, Fourth Edition (DSM-IV-TR)* (American Psychiatric Publishing, 2000), p. 197.

29   *'the striking and inescapable . . .'*: *American Journal of Psychiatry* 92, 1935, pp. 89–108.

30   *'It is well established . . .'*: Mary Ann Enoch, 'The role of early life stress as a predictor for alcohol and drug dependence', *Psychopharmacology*, Vol. 214, 2011, pp. 17–31.

35   *'Together, we can do what none of us could . . .'*: AA World Services.

40   *'New York is terrifying . . .'*: Tennessee Williams, *Letters, Volume I,* p. 22.

41   *'constant suspense . . .'*: Tennessee Williams, ibid., p. 270.

41   *'I was still very shy . . .'*: Tennessee Williams, *Memoirs*, p. 52.

41   *'I have started off . . .'*: Tennessee Williams, *Letters, Volume I,* p. 265.

43   *'a structure whose name . . .'*: Tennessee Williams, *The Glass Menagerie*, in *A Streetcar Named Desire and Other Plays* (Penguin, 1962), p. 233.

43   *'I knew it was whisky . . .'*: ibid., p. 255.

44   *'I went much further . . .'*: ibid., p. 313.

45   *'Before the success of Menagerie . . .'*: Tennessee Williams, 'The Art of Theater No. 5', *Paris Review.*

46   *'Frankie and I kept looking at one another . . .'*: Tennessee Williams, *Memoirs*, pp. 155–6.

48   *'Guess what the bill is?'*: John Cheever, in Leslie Aldridge, 'Having a Drink with Cheever', *New York Magazine*, 28 April 1969.

48   *'Oh Lord, no . . .'*: Mary Cheever, interviewed by Blake Bailey, *Cheever: A Life*, p. 162.

48   *'as decadent, I think . . .'*: John Cheever, *The Journals* (Cape, 1990), pp. 12–13.

50   *'I was offered two kinds of drinks . . .'*: John Cheever, in Malcolm Cowley, 'The Novelist's Life as Drama', *Sewanee Review*, Vol. 91, No. 1, 1983.

52   *'The darkness would come into the soft air . . .'*: 'The Day the Pig Fell into the Well', *The Stories of John Cheever*, pp. 224–34.

52   *'The sea . . .'*: John Cheever, 'Goodbye, My Brother', ibid., p. 9.

52   *'There were a hundred clouds in the west . . .'*: 'The Summer Farmer', ibid., p. 85.

54   *'They sat together with their children . . .'*: 'The Pot of Gold', ibid., p. 107.

54   '*The rent is not paid . . .*': John Cheever, *Journals*, p. 14.

55   '*It is a tonic to my self-respect . . .*': ibid., p. 21.

55   '*It was my decision, early in life, to insinuate myself . . .*': ibid., p. 16.

55   '*every comely man, every bank clerk . . .*': ibid., p. 219.

56   '*I found myself driving . . .*': John Cheever, in Blake Bailey, *Cheever: A Life*, p. 113.

57   '*Mary was waiting . . .*': ibid., p. 122.

59   '*holding in his generous mouth . . .*': John Cheever, 'The Country Husband', *Stories*, p. 346.

CHAPTER 3: FISHING IN THE DARK

62   '*Here surely is the place . . .*': Tennessee Williams, *Notebooks*, ed. Margaret Bradham Thornton (Yale University Press, 2006), p. 131.

63   '*sleep problems . . .*': Kirk Brower, 'Alcohol's Effects on Sleep in Alcoholics', *Alcohol Research and Health*, Vol. 25, No. 2, 2001, pp. 110–25.

63   '*Zelda painting, me drinking*': F. Scott Fitzgerald, *F. Scott Fitzgerald's Ledger: A Facsimile* (NCR/Microcard Editions, 1972), p. 179.

65   '*We had a great trip together . . .*' Ernest Hemingway, *Selected Letters*, ed. Carlos Baker (Granada, 1981), pp. 162–3.

65   '*sneers, superiorities . . .*': F. Scott Fitzgerald, *A Life in Letters* (Touchstone, 1995), pp. 142–3.

66   '*Our life is all gone to hell . . .*': Ernest Hemingway, *Selected Letters*, p. 217.

67   '*I myself did not want to sleep . . .*': Ernest Hemingway, 'Now I Lay Me', *The Complete Short Stories* (Scribner, 1987), pp. 276–80.

70   '*THE FIRE . . .*': F. Scott Fitzgerald's Ledger, p. 187.

72   '*Last of real self-confidence . . .*': ibid., Appendix I.

72   '*I have drunk too much . . .*': F. Scott Fitzgerald, *The Letters of F. Scott Fitzgerald* (The Bodley Head, 1963), p. 254.

73   '*I'm on the wagon . . .*': F. Scott Fitzgerald, in Tony Buttita, *After the Good Gay Times* (Viking, 1974), p. 4.

77   '*get stinking drunk and do every possible . . .*': Ernest Hemingway, *Selected Letters*, p. 425.

78   'Non sleeping is a hell of a damned thing too . . .': ibid., pp. 428–9.

79   'When some years ago . . .': F. Scott Fitzgerald, 'Sleeping and Waking', *On Booze* (New Directions, 2011 [1934]) pp. 55–62.

80   'had a great deal of malicious humor . . .': Tennessee Williams, 'The Art of Theater No. 5', *Paris Review*.

80   'Denial is ubiquitous in alcoholism . . .': David P. Moore and James W. Jefferson, eds., *Handbook of Medical Psychiatry*, p. 85.

81   'Instead of willingly . . .': Sigmund Freud, in Janet Malcolm, *Psychoanalysis: The Impossible Profession* (Vintage, 1982), p. 20.

82   'by arising at the dinner . . .': H.L. Mencken, *The Diary of H.L. Mencken* (Vintage, 1991), p. 63.

84   'of cavalry officers . . .': Andrew Turnbull, *Scott Fitzgerald* (The Bodley Head, 1963), p. 231.

85   'Drink heightens feeling . . .': ibid., p. 233.

85   'Drink is an escape . . .': ibid., p. 238.

86   'Also alcohol, that we use as the Giant Killer . . .': Ernest Hemingway, *Selected Letters*, p. 690.

88   'I have drunk since I was fifteen . . .': ibid., p. 420.

89   'natural distilled liqueurs . . .': Ernest Hemingway, *A Moveable Feast* (Cape, 1964), p. 133.

90   'a light, pleasant white wine . . .': ibid., p. 151.

91   'It was hard to accept him as a drunkard . . .': ibid., p. 145.

91   'Anything he drank seemed to stimulate . . .': ibid., p. 151.

92   'drink hells any amount of whiskey . . .': Ernest Hemingway, *Selected Letters*, p. 169.

92   'There is evidence of genetic or biochemical . . .': Robert S. Porter, ed., *The Merck Manual of Diagnosis and Therapy*.

92   'I can drink Yevtushenke . . .': John Cheever, John Cheever Collection of Papers, 1942–1982, Henry W. and Albert A. Berg Collection of English and American Literature, New York Public Library (hereafter Berg Collection).

93   'two small, fabric-covered, rectangular boxes . . .': Mary Hemingway, 'The Making of the Book: A Chronicle and a Memoir', *New York Times* 1 May 1964.

93   '*was filled with a ragtag collection ...*': A.E. Hotchner, 'Don't Touch A Moveable Feast', *New York Times*, 19 July 2009.

94   '*It is not unnatural ...*': Ernest Hemingway, in Jacqueline Tavernier-Courbin, 'The Mystery of the Ritz-Hotel Papers', *College Literature*, Vol. 7, No. 3, Fall 1980, pp. 289–303.

95   '*On the corporal front ...*': Ernest Hemingway, *Selected Letters*, p. 877.

96   '*The maladaptive pattern of drinking ...*': Robert S. Porter, ed., *Merck Manual of Diagnosis and Therapy*.

97   '*and then, just as it was about to eat him ...*': Gregory Hemingway, *Papa: A Personal Memoir* (Houghton Mifflin, 1976), pp. 62–3.

98   '*When a person who is dependent on alcohol ...*': ADAM, 'Alcoholism and Alcohol Abuse', *New York Times*, 13 January 2011.

101 '*If I can be said to have a home ...*': Tennessee Williams, in Donald Spoto, *The Kindness of Strangers*, p. 121.

101 '*New Orleans isn't like other cities*': Tennessee Williams, *A Streetcar Named Desire and Other Plays*, p. 121.

CHAPTER 4: A HOUSE ON FIRE

103 '*Those cathedral bells ...*': Tennessee Williams, *A Streetcar Named Desire and Other Plays*, p. 219.

104 '*You know, New Orleans is ...*': Tennessee Williams, *Memoirs*, p. 109.

104 '*the remains of a fallen southern family ...*': Tennessee Williams, *Letters, Volume 1*, p. 557.

105 '*a peculiarly tender blue ...*': Tennessee Williams, *A Streetcar Named Desire and Other Plays*, p. 115.

106 '*Open your pretty mouth ...*': ibid., p. 120.

106 '*The music is in her mind ...*': ibid., p. 200.

107 '*Well, honey, a shot never ...*': ibid., p. 170.

107 '*Why, it's a liqueur, I believe*': ibid., p. 202.

107 '*You ought to lay off his liquor ...*': ibid., pp. 202–3.

110 '*Holocaust in Germany ...*': Tennessee Williams, *Notebooks*, p. 195.

111 'So I turn to my journals . . .': ibid., p. 457.

112 'twenty-eight thousand acres . . .': Tennessee Williams, *Cat on a Hot Tin Roof and Other Plays*, p. 73.

112 'it's spread all through him . . .': ibid., p. 97.

112 'fallen in love with Echo Spring . . .': ibid., p. 40.

113 'The thing they're discussing . . .': ibid., p. 75.

113 'charm of that cool air . . .': ibid., p. 19.

114 'Got a 5 page letter from Gadg . . .': Tennessee Williams, *Notebooks*, p. 663.

114 'I "buy" a lot . . .': Tennessee Williams, *The Selected Letters of Tennessee Williams, Volume 2* (New Directions, 2004), pp. 555–8.

115 'Of course it is a pity . . .': Tennessee Williams, *Cat on a Hot Tin Roof and Other Plays*, p. 7.

118 'Looked through the new play script . . .': Tennessee Williams, *Notebooks*, p. 595.

119 'When he came back out . . .': Tennessee Williams, 'Three Players of a Summer Game', *Collected Stories* (Secker & Warburg, 1986), p. 311.

120 'the play that threw me . . .': Tennessee Williams, *Letters, Volume 2*, p. 525.

120 'The sun shines over the straits . . .': Tennessee Williams, *Notebooks*, p. 599.

121 'All hell is descended on me . . .': ibid., pp. 611–13.

121 'fierce geranium that shattered . . .': Tennessee Williams, 'Three Players of a Summer Game', *Collected Stories*, p. 307.

122 'induced partly by liquor . . .': Tennessee Williams, *Notebooks*, p. 631.

122 'Here's the dilemma . . .': ibid., p. 647.

123 'someday, I fear, one of these panics will kill me . . .': ibid., p. 657.

124 'A double neurosis . . .': ibid., pp. 657–61.

125 'A man that drinks . . .': Tennessee Williams, 'Three Players of a Summer Game', *Collected Stories*, p. 310.

126 'the startling co-existence of good and evil . . .': Tennessee Williams, *Letters, Volume 2*, p. 552.

128 'One of those no-neck monsters . . .': Tennessee Williams, *Cat on a Hot Tin Roof and Other Plays*, p. 17.

128 'I wish you would lose your looks . . .': ibid., p. 25.

128 'You look so cool, so cool . . .': ibid., p. 26.

130 ‘*The subject was everywhere . . .*’: Evelyn Waugh, *Brideshead Revisited* (Penguin, 1964) p. 158.

131 ‘*Been drinking whisky up here . . .*’: ibid., p. 127.

CHAPTER 5: THE BLOODY PAPERS

136 ‘*One does not travel so much as . . .*’: John Cheever, ‘The Bloody Papers’, Berg Collection.

137 ‘*I am not in this world . . .*’: John Cheever, *Journals*, p. 357.

137 ‘*With a hangover and a light fever . . .*’: John Cheever, in Blake Bailey, *Cheever: A Life*, p. 462.

137 ‘*clearer and clearer . . .*’: Susan Cheever, *Home Before Dark* (Houghton Mifflin, 1984), p. 161.

137 ‘*In the morning I am deeply depressed . . .*’: John Cheever, *Journals*, p. 103.

138 ‘*I cannot remember my meanness . . .*’: ibid., p. 218.

140 ‘*psychiatrists would call . . .*’: John Cheever, in Blake Bailey, *Cheever: A Life,* p. 620.

140 ‘*Might the seasons change . . .*’: John Cheever, *Journals*, p. 187.

140 ‘*When he finds it's dark and cold . . .*’: John Cheever, ‘The Art of Fiction No. 62’, *Paris Review*.

141 ‘*My memory is full of holes . . .*’: John Cheever, *Journals*, p. 186.

141 ‘*In church, on my knees . . .*’: ibid., p. 188.

142 ‘*and so deeply involved . . .*’: ibid., p. 215.

142 ‘*When I told him I liked swimming . . .*’: John Cheever, *Letters*, p. 261.

143 ‘*When I think back to my parents . . .*’: John Cheever, ‘The Bloody Papers’, Berg Collection.

146 ‘*I am, he was . . .*’: John Cheever, *Journals*, p. 212.

146 ‘*considered himself to be . . .*’: John Cheever on F. Scott Fitzgerald, *Brief Lives: A Biographical Companion to the Arts* (Allen Lane, 1972), pp. 275–6.

146 ‘*Straight 1850 potato-famine Irish . . .*’: F. Scott Fitzgerald, in Arthur Mizener, *The Far Side of Paradise* (Houghton Mifflin, 1951), p. 2.

148 ‘*A neurotic, half insane . . .*’: ibid., p. 202.

148 ‘*He remembers the day . . .*’: F. Scott Fitzgerald's *Ledger*, p. 162.

148 'He came home that evening . . .': Andrew Turnbull, *Scott Fitzgerald*, p. 22.

149 'he kept his samples of rice . . .': ibid., p. 24.

149 'It's everything I've forgotten . . .': F. Scott Fitzgerald, 'Author's House', *Afternoon of an Author*, ed. Arthur Mizener (The Bodley Head, 1958), pp. 232–9.

151 'The tonic or curative force. . .': John Cheever, Berg Collection.

151 'to give some fitness and shape. . .': John Cheever, in Blake Bailey, *Cheever: A Life*, p. 44.

152 'The writer cultivates, extends . . .': John Cheever, *Journals*, p. 213.

152 'I must convince myself . . .': ibid., p. 255.

153 'Why is you an addict . . .': John Cheever, *Falconer* (Cape, 1977), p. 726.

154 'Only lets hurry and get to Havana . . .': Ernest Hemingway, *Selected Letters*, p. 275.

154 I am indebted to Michael Reynolds for his reconstruction of the Hemingway family's various movements over this period in *Hemingway: The American Homecoming* (Blackwell, 1992).

155 'Like a dream to think . . .': Unpublished letter from Clarence Hemingway to Ernest Hemingway, 11 April 1928, The Ernest Hemingway Collection, John F. Kennedy Presidential Library.

155 'Oh Ernest, how could you . . .': Clarence Hemingway to Ernest Hemingway, in Michael Reynolds, *Hemingway*, p. 137.

155 'Daddy wiped a tear from his eye . . .': Marcelline Hemingway, *At the Hemingways: A Family Memoir* (Putnam, 1963), p. 227.

157 'The big frame, the quick movements . . .': Ernest Hemingway, 'Fathers and Sons', *The Complete Short Stories*, p. 370.

157 'I'm so glad you liked the Doctor story . . .': Ernest Hemingway, *Selected Letters*, p. 153.

157 'The reason most of the book . . .': ibid., p. 327.

158 'Dear, I don't think . . .': Ernest Hemingway, 'The Doctor and the Doctor's Wife', *The Complete Short Stories*, pp. 75–6.

159 'many things that were not to be moved . . .': Ernest Hemingway, 'Now I Lay Me', ibid., p. 278.

162 *'Isn't that old River Forest woman terrible . . .'*: Ernest Hemingway, *Selected Letters*, p. 591.

163 *'I can't seem to think of a way . . .'*: Unpublished letter from Clarence Hemingway to Ernest Hemingway, 23 October 1928, The Ernest Hemingway Collection, John F. Kennedy Presidential Library.

164 *'You were damned good . . .'*: Ernest Hemingway, *Selected Letters*, p. 291.

164 *'Various worthless land . . .'*: ibid., p. 292.

165 *'Tears Henry shed . . .'*: John Berryman, 'Dream Song 235', *The Dream Songs*, p. 254.

166 *'The most brilliant . . .'*: Philip Levine, 'Mine Own John Berryman', in Richard J. Kelly and Alan K. Lathrop, eds., *Recovering Berryman: Essays on a Poet* (University of Michigan Press, 1993), pp. 40–41.

167 *'everything went like snow . . .'*: Martha Berryman, *We Dream of Honour: John Berryman's letters to his mother*, ed. Richard Kelly (W.W. Norton, 1988), p. 378.

168 *'That mad drive . . .'*: John Berryman, 'Dream Song 143', *The Dream Songs*, p. 160.

169 *'Hunger was constitutional . . .'*: John Berryman, 'Dream Song 311', ibid., p. 333.

171 *'Perhaps most novels are . . .'*: Edmund White, 'In Love with Duras', *The New York Review of Books*, 26 June 2008.

171 *'Then after your father had shot himself . . .'*: Ernest Hemingway, *For Whom the Bell Tolls* (Penguin, 1966 [1941]), pp. 318–19.

CHAPTER 6: GOING SOUTH

178 *'I'm still in bed most of the time . . .'*: Ernest Hemingway, *Selected Letters*, p. 337.

178 *'This is really going . . .'*: ibid., p. 340.

180 *'By January 11 . . .'*: Michael Reynolds, *Hemingway: The 1930s* (W.W. Norton, 1997), p. 162.

181 *'It said in Black's . . .'*: Ernest Hemingway, 'Snows of Kilimanjaro', *The Complete Short Stories*, pp. 40–56.

181 'If I could have made this ...': Ernest Hemingway, *Death in the Afternoon* (Penguin, 1966 [1932]), p. 255.

182 'I put all the true stuff in ...': Ernest Hemingway, 'The Art of Fiction No. 21', *Paris Review*.

183 'pooped': Ernest Hemingway, *Selected Letters*, p. 436.

183 'I saw that for a long time ...': F. Scott Fitzgerald, 'The Crack-up', *The Crack-Up, with other pieces and stories* (Penguin, 1965), p. 48.

184 'Scott is gone the first week ...': Ernest Hemingway, *Selected Letters*, p. 440.

185 'Please lay off me ...': F. Scott Fitzgerald, *The Letters of F. Scott Fitzgerald*, p. 311.

185 'Never had the real old melancholia ...': Ernest Hemingway, *Selected Letters*, p. 436.

186 'I wish he would pull out ...': ibid., p. 444.

187 'He shot himself ...': Ernest Hemingway, *For Whom the Bell Tolls*, p. 66.

187 'the other one ...': ibid., pp. 321–2.

188 'the giant killer ...': ibid., p. 441.

188 'That is what kills the worm ...': ibid., p. 198.

188 'the drunkard stinks ...': ibid., p. 201.

188 'a deadly wheel ...': ibid., p. 218.

189 'The poor son-of-a-bitch ...': John Berryman, in John Haffenden, *The Life of John Berryman* (Routledge & Kegan Paul, 1982), p. 297.

189 'He put down an immense vision ...': John Cheever, *Journals*, p. 268.

189 'the most fantastic place ...': Tennessee Williams, *Letters, Volume 1*, p. 304.

190 'although he might be decadent ...': Elaine Dundy, 'Our men in Havana', *Guardian*, 9 June 2001.

190 'Is he the commodore of something ...': George Plimpton, *Shadow Box: An Amateur in the Ring* (Andre Deutsch, 1978), pp. 142–3.

190 'He was exactly the opposite ...': Tennessee Williams, *Memoirs*, p. 67.

191 'furtively away ...': Andrew Turnbull, 'Perkins's Three Generals', *New York Times*, 16 July 1967.

192 'He approaches Scott ...': Tennessee Williams, *Clothes for a Summer Hotel: A Ghost Play* (New Directions, 1983), pp. 64–8.

193 *'But my guess is . . .'*: Ernest Hemingway, *For Whom the Bell Tolls*, p. 161.

194 *'It would be all right to do it now . . .'*: ibid., p. 443.

194 *'I chose Key West . . .'*: Tennessee Williams, *Memoirs*, pp. 63–4.

194 *'Sponge and deep sea fishing . . .'*: Tennessee Williams, *Letters, Volume 1*, p. 304.

195 *'like ladies running barefooted . . .'*: Tennessee Williams, *Five O'Clock Angel: Letters of Tennessee Williams to Maria St Just* (Andre Deutsch, 1991), p. 75.

195 *'Oh how I long . . .'*: Tennessee Williams, *Notebooks*, p. 619.

196 *'I am going . . . to rest . . .'*: Tennessee Williams, *Tennessee Williams: Letters to Donald Windham* (Penguin, 1980) p. 294.

196 *'He was just plain good . . .'*: Christopher Isherwood, in Donald Spoto, *The Kindness of Strangers*, p. 153.

196 *'I love F. . . .'*: Tennessee Williams, *Notebooks*, p. 501.

197 *'plush-lined loony-bin . . .'*: Tennessee Williams, *Five O'Clock Angel*, p. 148.

197 *'drinking a bit more than my quota . . .'*: Tennessee Williams, *Notebooks*, p. 707.

197 *'and has succeeded in destroying . . .'*: Tennessee Williams, *Five O'Clock Angel*, p. 150.

197 *'I miss the horse & dog . . .'*: Tennessee Williams, *Notebooks*, p. 719.

198 *'There is probably not an episode . . .'*: Donald Windham, in *Tennessee Williams: Letters to Donald Windham*, p. x.

198 *'like a jungle cat . . .'*: Tennessee Williams, *Memoirs*, pp. 185–6.

199 *'The Horse has done . . .'*: Tennessee Williams, *Five O'Clock Angel*, p. 175.

199 *'Frank, I want to get my goodness back . . .'* Tennessee Williams, *Memoirs*, p. 188.

200 *'like the skeleton of a sparrow . . .'* ibid., p. 193.

200 *'As long as Frank was well . . .'*: ibid., p. 194.

200 *'next to my work . . .'*: Tennessee Williams, in *Tennessee Williams: Letters to Donald Windham*, p. 315.

202 *'sewn up in a clean white sack . . .'*: ibid., p. 117.

203 *'I shall eat an unwashed grape . . .'*: Tennessee Williams, *A Streetcar Named Desire and Other Plays*, p. 220.

204 *'I showed him . . .'*: Tennessee Williams, *The Night of the Iguana*, in *Cat on a Hot Tin Roof and Other Plays*, p. 309.

204   'Nothing human disgusts me . . .': ibid., p. 318.

204   'to be dropped in the sea . . .': ibid., p. 259.

205   'I wish a Greek Orthodox service . . .': Tennessee Williams, *Notebooks*, p. 753.

207   'Liquor and swimming . . .': Tennessee Williams, in Donald Spoto, *The Kindness of Strangers*, p. 246.

209   'When difficulties became insurmountable . . .': F. Scott Fitzgerald, 'The Swimmers', *Saturday Evening Post*, 19 October 1929.

209   'To be embraced . . .': John Cheever, 'The Swimmer', *The Stories of John Cheever*, p. 604.

210   'that one night . . .': John Berryman, 'Henry's Understanding', *Collected Poems 1937–1971* (Farrar, Straus & Giroux, 1987), p. 256.

211   'All good writing . . .': F. Scott Fitzgerald, *Letters to His Daughter* (Scribner, 1963), p. 165.

213   'Dakin . . . just threw me into Barnes Hospital . . .': Tennessee Williams, 'The Art of Theater No. 5', *Paris Review*.

214   'The rest is not blank . . .': Tennessee Williams, *Notebooks*, p. 733.

214   'Did I die by my own hand . . .': ibid., p. 739.

215   'dog shit all over the place . . .': Truman Capote, *Answered Prayers* (Hamish Hamilton, 1986), pp. 59–64.

216   'You have been as brave as anybody . . .': Marlon Brando to Tennessee Williams, republished on *Letters of Note* (*www.lettersofnote.com*), 26 March 2010.

217   'Why not?': Tennessee Williams, *Notebooks*, p. 739.

217   'Structurally wasteful . . .': Walter Kerr, *New York Times*, 27 March 1980.

217   Michiko Kakutani's essay 'Williams, Quintero and the Aftermath of a Failure' (*New York Times*, 22 June 1980) was invaluable in reconstructing the last days of *Clothes for a Summer Hotel*.

CHAPTER 7: THE CONFESSIONS OF MR. BONES

All otherwise unacknowledged John Berryman quotations in this chapter are drawn from the magnificently detailed *The Life of John Berryman* by John Haffenden (Routledge & Kegan Paul, 1982). This material itself derives from the John Berryman Papers at the University of Minnesota.

222 *'thin and gratingly intense . . .'*: Dorothy Rockwell, interviewed by John Haffenden, *The Life of John Berryman*, p. 65.

222 *'affected'*: Lionel Trilling, interviewed by Haffenden, ibid., p. 73.

222 *'unwilling monkhood . . .'*: John Berryman, 'Monkhood', *Collected Poems 1937–1971*, p. 195.

223 *'he is to my certain knowledge . . .'*: Mark Van Doren, in Haffenden, *The Life of John Berryman*, p. 110.

224 *'alternately hysterical and depressed . . .'*: Eileen Simpson, *Poets in their Youth* (Faber, 1982), p. 157.

225 *'Both of our worlds unhanded us . . .'*: John Berryman, 'Homage to Mistress Bradstreet', *Collected Poems 1937–1971*, p. 133.

226 *'He entered the room . . .'*: Philip Levine, 'Mine Own John Berryman', in Richard J. Kelly and Alan K. Lathrop, eds., *Recovering Berryman*, p. 38.

230 *'losing altitude . . .'*: John Berryman, *The Dream Songs*, p. 61.

230 *'out of everything . . .'*: ibid., p. 371.

230 *'At first the brain aches . . .'*: Robert Lowell, 'The Poetry of John Berryman', *New York Review of Books*, 28 May 1964.

230 *'creepy and scorching . . .'*: Adrienne Rich, 'Mr. Bones, He Lives', *The Nation*, Vol. 198, Issue 22, 25 May 1964.

230 *'I've been in & out of hospitals . . .'*: John Berryman to William Meredith, 16 September 1965, William Meredith Collection of Papers, 1941–1973, Berg Collection.

231 *'Berryman is the only poet . . .'*: John Montague, in Haffenden, *The Life of John Berryman*, p. 340.

231 *'all but dead . . .'*: Isabella Gardner, in ibid., p. 346.

231 *'He was all regret …':* John Berryman, 'Dream Song 310', *The Dream Songs*, p. 332.

232 *'Pt. admits that he is an alcoholic …':* Hazelden notes, in Haffenden, *The Life of John Berryman*, p. 340.

232 *'I am having the best winter …':* John Berryman to William Meredith, 1 February 1970, Berg Collection.

234 *'I'm just out of 6 wks in hospital …':* John Berryman to William Meredith, 18 June 1970, ibid.

235 *'twice-invited guest …':* John Berryman, *Recovery*, p. 7.

236 *'This is the last drink you will ever take …':* ibid., p. 3.

237 *'sick old lion …':* ibid., p. 127.

238 *'This was hard, very hard …':* ibid., p. 167.

238 *'Maybe it's easier to be a monster …':* ibid., p. 188.

238 *'Alcoholics are rigid …':* ibid., p. 138.

239 *'That's my Middle West …':* F. Scott Fitzgerald, *The Great Gatsby* (Penguin, 1966 [1926]), p. 183.

240 *'But in the morning …':* Saul Bellow, introduction to John Berryman, *Recovery*, p. xii–xiv.

241 *'nearly crucified …':* John Berryman, 'The Art of Poetry No. 16', *Paris Review*.

241 *'Let me be clear about this …':* John Berryman, 'The Facts & Issues', *Collected Poems 1937–1971*, p. 263.

242 *'Of course I am determined …':* John Berryman in Eileen Simpson, *Poets in their Youth*, p. 250.

242 *'I admit I am putting myself …':* John Berryman to Mark Van Doren (undated, 1970–71?), Berg Collection.

244 *'no real warmth shown us …':* Ralph Ross, in Paul Mariani, *Dream Song: The Life of John Berryman* (University of Massachusetts Press, 1996), p. 495.

248 *'1. Did I hear Daddy …':* John Berryman to Jill Berryman, *We Dream of Honour: John Berryman's letters to his mother*, p. 376–7.

249 *'the blue father':* 'Dream Song 70', John Berryman, *The Dream Songs*, p. 77.

249 *'this dreadful banker':* 'Dream Song 384', ibid., p. 406.

250 *'New problem …':* John Berryman, *Recovery*, p. 192.

251   '*uncharacteristic* . . .': ibid., pp. 139–40.

251   '*Missing someone* . . .': Sigmund Freud, in John Bowlby, *Separation: Anxiety and Anger* (Basic Books, 1973), p. 27.

252   '*In our detailed study* . . .': Vincent Felitti, 'The Origins of Addiction: Evidence from the Adverse Childhood Experience Study', *Program*, 2004, pp. 547–59.

254   '*Under the table, no* . . .': John Berryman, 'Dream Song 96', *The Dream Songs*, p. 113.

255   '*And it's only 18 days* . . .': John Berryman, *We Dream of Honour: John Berryman's letters to his mother*, p. 19.

256   '*They were alone* . . .': ibid., p. 4.

258   '*great friend of his* . . .': John Berryman, *Recovery*, p. 238.

259   '*When he tried to relate* . . .': Betty Peddie, interviewed by Haffenden, *The Life of John Berryman*, p. 374.

259   '*my father's blow-it-all* . . .': John Berryman, 'Eleven Addresses to the Lord', *Collected Poems 1937–1971*, p. 219.

260   '*He was perfectly ready* . . .': John Berryman, *Recovery*, p. 242.

CHAPTER 8: HALF OF HIM

262   '*But he was a brilliant poet* . . .': John Cheever, in Blake Bailey, *Cheever: A Life*, p. 513.

262   '*Yes, but he was also a phony* . . .' Carole Kitman, interviewed by Blake Bailey, in ibid., p. 513.

263   '*I came out of prison 20 pounds lighter* . . .': John Cheever, *Letters*, p. 317.

263   '*Sauced, I speculate* . . .': John Cheever, *Journals*, p. 285.

264   '*How strange to be carried* . . .': John Cheever, *Falconer*, p. 822.

265   '*he saw that he had lost his fear of falling*': ibid., p. 827.

265   '*I wonder if I have the courage* . . .': John Cheever, *Journals*, p. 300.

266   '*a purification, a period of suffering* . . .': Joan Didion, 'Falconer', *New York Times*, 6 March 1977.

266   '*I mix myself a gin and vermouth* . . .': John Cheever, Berg Collection.

266   '*I am not better than the next man* . . .': John Cheever, *Journals*, p. 321.

267 *'wallow, smear, engorge myself . . .'*: John Cheever, in Blake Bailey, *Cheever: A Life*, p. 472.

267 *'brought on by my anxious and greedy . . .'*: John Cheever to Ray Mutter, in ibid., p. 403.

267 *'To be confirmed . . .'*: John Cheever, Berg Collection.

271 *'He was drunk . . .'*: Raymond Carver, 'My Father's Life', *Fires: Essays, Poems, Stories* (Vintage 1983), pp. 14–18.

272 *'to preserve Ray's opportunity . . .'*: Maryann Burk Carver, *What It Used To Be Like: A Portrait of My Marriage to Raymond Carver* (St Martin's Griffin, 2006), p. 65.

274 *'I was in my late twenties . . .'*: Raymond Carver, 'The Art of Fiction No. 76', *Paris Review*.

274 *'sucking brandy from a bottle . . .'*: Maryann Burk Carver, *What It Used to Be Like*, pp. 286–7.

276 *'In 1977 he was tall . . .'*: Richard Ford, 'Good Raymond', *New Yorker*, 5 October 1998.

277 All three letters from Raymond Carver to Gordon Lish quoted here were published as 'Letters to an Editor', *New Yorker*, 24 December 2007.

278 *'I'm 45 years old today . . .'*: Raymond Carver, 'Where Water Comes Together with Other Water', *All of Us*, p. 63.

285 *'I have a poor . . .'*: Raymond Carver, 'Fires', *Fires: Essays, Poems, Stories*, pp. 29–39.

287 *'I think my problems enforce my drinking'*: John Cheever, *Journals*, p. 297.

288 *'and then . . . something: alcohol . . .'*: Raymond Carver, 'Alcohol', *All of Us*, p. 10.

289 *'Keep believing in me . . .'*: Raymond Carver, 'Wenas Ridge', ibid., p. 75.

292 *'Stop gouging me, you bastard . . .'*: Raymond Carver, 'Nobody Said Anything', *The Stories of Raymond Carver* (Picador, 1985), pp. 42–54.

297 *'No, I've never felt godlike . . .'*: John Cheever, 'The Art of Fiction No. 62', *Paris Review*.

297 *'the galling loneliness . . .'*: John Cheever, *Journals*, p. 77.

297 *'I got six clams in the river . . .'*: Ernest Hemingway, *Selected Letters*, p. xiii.

BIBLIOGRAPHY

Aldridge, Leslie, 'Having a Drink with Cheever', *New York Magazine*, 28 April 1969

American Psychiatric Association, *Diagnostic and Statistical Manual of Mental Disorders, Fourth Edition (DSM-IV-TR)* (Amer Psychiatric Pub, 2000)

Anderson, Daniel J., *Perspectives on Treatment* (Hazelden Foundation, 1981)

Atlas, James, 'Speaking Ill of the Dead', *New York Times Magazine*, 6 November 1988

Baker, Carlos, *Ernest Hemingway: A Life Story* (Collins, 1969)

Bailey, Blake, *Cheever: A Life* (Picador, 2009)

Barton, Anne, 'John Berryman's Flying Horse', *New York Review of Books*, 23 September 1999

Bellow, Saul, 'On John Cheever', *New York Review of Books*, 17 February 1983

Benson, Jackson J., *Hemingway: The Writer's Art of Self-Defense* (University of Minnesota Press, 1969)

Robert Berkow, ed., *The Merck Manual of Diagnosis and Therapy, Sixteenth Edition* (Merck Research Laboratories, 1992)

Berkson, Bill, *Sudden Address: Selected Lectures 1981–2006* (Cuneiform Press, 2007)

—— and Joe LeSueur, eds., *Homage to Frank O'Hara* (Big Sky, 1988)

Berryman, John, *Berryman's Shakespeare: Essays, Letters and Other Writings by John Berryman*, ed. John Haffenden (Tauris Parke Paperbacks, 2001)

—— *Collected Poems 1937–1971* (Farrar, Straus & Giroux, 1987)

——*The Dream Songs* (Faber, 1969)

—— *The Freedom of the Poet* (Farrar, Straus & Giroux, 1976)

—— *Recovery* (Faber, 1973)

—— *We Dream of Honour: John Berryman's letters to his mother*, ed. Richard Kelly (W.W. Norton, 1988)

Blackmur, R.P., *Selected Essays of R.P. Blackmur*, ed. Denis Donoghue (The Ecco Press, 1985)

Bloom, Harold, ed., *Bloom's BioCritiques: Tennessee Williams* (Chelsea House Publishers, 2003)

—— *Modern Critical Views: John Berryman* (Chelsea House Publishers, 1989)

Bowlby, John, *Separation: Anxiety and Anger* (Basic Books, 1973)

Bollas, Christopher, *The Shadow of the Object: Psychoanalysis of the Unknown Known* (Free Association Books, 1987)

Brenner, Gerry, 'Are We Going To Hemingway's Feast?', *American Literature*, Vol. 5, No. 4, pp. 528–44, December 1982

Brower, Kirk J., 'Alcohol's Effects on Sleep in Alcoholics', *Alcohol Research and Health*, Vol. 25, No. 2, pp. 110–25, 2001

Brower, Kirk J., et al, 'Insomnia, Self-Medication and Relapse to Alcoholism', *American Journal of Psychiatry*, Vol. 158, pp. 399–404, 2001

Bruccoli, Matthew, *Some Sort of Epic Grandeur* (Harcourt Brace Jovanovich, 1981)

—— and Margaret Duggan, eds., *Correspondence of F. Scott Fitzgerald* (Random House, 1980)

Burgess, Anthony, *Ernest Hemingway* (Thames & Hudson, 1986)

Canterbury, E. Ray, and Birch, Thomas D., *F. Scott Fitzgerald: Under the Influence* (Paragon House, 2006)

Buttitta, Tony, *After the Good Gay Times* (Viking, 1974)

Calabi, Silvio, and Helsley, Steve, *Hemingway's Guns: The Sporting Arms of Ernest Hemingway* (Shooting Sportsman Books, 2011)

Capote, Truman, *Answered Prayers* (Hamish Hamilton, 1986)

—— *Too Brief a Treat: The Letters of Truman Capote*, ed. Gerald Clarke (Random House, 2004)

Carver, Maryann Burk, *What It Used To Be Like: A Portrait of My Marriage to Raymond Carver* (St Martin's Griffin, 2006)

Carver, Raymond, *All of Us: The Collected Poems* (Harvill Press, 2003)

—— *Beginners* (Vintage, 2010)

—— *Carver Country: The World of Raymond Carver* (Macmillan, 1990)

—— *Elephant and other stories* (Vintage, 2003)

—— *Fires: Essays, Poems, Stories* (Vintage 1989 [1983])

—— *No Heroics, Please: Uncollected Writings*, ed. William L. Stull (Harvill Press, 1991)

—— *Where I'm Calling From: The Selected Stories* (Harvill Press, 1995)

—— *The Stories of Raymond Carver* (Picador, 1985)

—— 'Coming of Age, Going to Pieces', *New York Times*, 17 November 1985

—— 'Letters to an Editor', *New Yorker*, 24 December 2007

Cheever, John, *Complete Novels* (Library of America, 2009)

—— *Falconer* (Cape, 1977)

—— *The Journals* (Cape, 1990)

—— *The Letters of John Cheever*, ed. Benjamin Cheever (Cape, 1989)

—— *The Stories of John Cheever* (Cape, 1979)

Cheever, Susan, *Home Before Dark* (Houghton Mifflin, 1984)

—— *Note Found in a Bottle* (Washington Square Press, 1999)

Coale, Samuel, *John Cheever* (Frederick Unger, 1977)

Cowley, Malcolm, 'The Novelist's Life as Drama', *Sewanee Review* 91, No. 1, 1983

Crandell, George W., ed., *The Critical Response to Tennessee Williams* (Greenwood Press, 1996)

Crane, Hart, *The Complete Poems and Selected Letters and Prose of Hart Crane*, ed. Brom Weber (Oxford University Press, 1968)

Dardis, Tom, *The Thirsty Muse: Alcohol and the American Writer* (Tichnor & Fields, 1989)

Davies, Martin, 'The role of GABAA receptors in mediating the effects of alcohol in the central nervous system', *Journal of Psychiatry and Neuroscience*, Vol. 28, No. 4, pp. 263–274, July 2003

Descombey, Jean-Paul, 'Alcoholism', in *International Dictionary of Psychoanalysis* (Macmillan, 2004)

Devlin, Albert J., *Conversations with Tennessee Williams* (University Press of Mississippi, 1986)

Didion, Joan, 'Falconer', *New York Times*, 6 March 1977

Donaldson, Scott, *Hemingway Vs. Fitzgerald* (John Murray, 2000)

—— *John Cheever: A Biography* (Random House, 1988)

Downing, Cynthia, *Triad: The Evolution of Treatment for Chemical Dependency* (Herald House/Independence Press, 1989)

Dundy, Elaine, 'Our men in Havana', *Guardian,* 9 June 2001

Elledge, Jim, ed., *Frank O'Hara: To Be True to a City* (University of Michigan Press, 1990)

Enoch, Mary-Anne, 'The role of early life stress as a predictor for alcohol and drug dependence', *Psychopharmacology*, Vol. 214, pp. 17–31, 2011

—— with Colin A. Hodkinson, Quiaoping Yuan, Pei-Hong Shen, David Goldman, and Alec Roy, 'The Influence of *GABRA2*, Childhood Trauma, and Their Interaction on Alcohol, Heroin and Cocaine Dependence', *Biological Psychiatry*, Vol. 67, pp. 20–27, 2010

Felitti, Vincent J., 'The Origins of Addiction: Evidence from the Adverse Childhood Experience Study', *Program*, pp. 547–59, 2004

Fitzgerald, F. Scott, *Afternoon of an Author*, ed. Arthur Mizener (The Bodley Head, 1958)

—— *The Beautiful and the Damned* (Penguin, 1966 [1922])

—— *The Crack-Up, with other pieces and stories* (Penguin, 1965)

—— *The Diamond as Big as the Ritz and Other Stories* (Penguin, 1962)

—— *The Great Gatsby* (Penguin, 1966 [1926])

—— *The Last Tycoon* (Penguin, 1968 [1941])

—— *F. Scott Fitzgerald's Ledger: A Facsimile* (NCR/Microcard Editions, 1972)

—— *The Letters of F. Scott Fitzgerald*, ed. Andrew Turnbull (The Bodley Head, 1963)

—— *Letters to His Daughter*, ed. Andrew Turnbull (Scribner, 1963)

—— *A Life in Letters*, ed. Matthew J. Bruccoli (Touchstone, 1995)

—— *The Lost Decade and Other Stories* (Penguin, 1968)

—— *The Notebooks of F. Scott Fitzgerald*, ed. Matthew J. Bruccoli (Harcourt Brace Jovanovich, 1978)

—— *On Booze* (New Directions, 2011 [1931–1945])

—— *The Pat Hobby Stories* (Penguin, 1962)

—— *Tender is the Night* (Penguin, 1966 [1939])

Ford, Richard, 'Good Raymond', *New Yorker*, 5 October 1998

Forseth, Roger, 'Alcohol and the Writer: some biographical and critical issues', *Contemporary Drug Problems*, Vol. 361, 1986

—— 'Ambivalent Sensibilities: Alcohol in History and Literature', *American Quarterly*, Vol. 12, No. 1, March 1990

Garcia-Valdecasas-Campelo, Elena, et al., 'Brain Atrophy in Alcoholics: Relationship with Alcohol Intake; Liver Disease; Nutritional Status, and Inflammation', *Alcohol and Alcoholism*, Vol. 42, No. 6, pp. 553–8, 2007

Gilmore, Thomas B., *Equivocal Spirits: Alcoholism and Drinking in Twentieth-Century Literature* (University of North Carolina Press, 1987)

Gooch, Brad, *City Poet: The Life and Times of Frank O'Hara* (Alfred A. Knopf, 1993)

Grant, M., 'Drinking and Creativity: A Review of the Alcoholism Literature', *Alcohol and Alcoholism*, Vol. 16, No. 2, pp. 88–93, 1981

Haffenden, John, *The Life of John Berryman* (Routledge & Kegan Paul, 1982)

Hamill, Peter, *A Drinking Life: A Memoir* (Little, Brown, 1994)

Hanneman, Audre, *Ernest Hemingway: A Comprehensive Bibliography* (Princeton University Press, 1967)

Harvey, Giles, 'The Two Raymond Carvers', *New York Review of Books*, 27 May 2010

Hemingway, Ernest, *Across the River and into the Trees* (Penguin, 1950)

—— *The Complete Short Stories* (Scribner, 1987)

—— *Death in the Afternoon* (Penguin, 1966 [1932])

—— *A Farewell to Arms* (Penguin, 1964 [1929])

—— *For Whom the Bell Tolls* (Penguin, 1966 [1941])

—— *A Moveable Feast* (Cape, 1964)

—— *Men Without Women* (Arrow, 2004 [1927])

—— *Selected Letters*, ed. Carlos Baker (Granada, 1981)

—— *The Snows of Kilimanjaro* (Penguin, 1967)

—— *To Have and Have Not* (Penguin,1969 [1937])

—— *Torrents of Spring* (Arrow, 2006 [1926])

Hemingway, Gregory H., *Papa: A Personal Memoir* (Houghton Mifflin, 1976)

Hemingway, Leicester, *My Brother, Ernest Hemingway* (Weidenfeld & Nicolson, 1962)

Hemingway Sandford, Marcelline, *At the Hemingways: A Family Memoir* (Putnam, 1963)

Hemingway, Mary, *How It Was* (Weidenfeld & Nicolson, 1977)

—— 'The Making of the Book: A Chronicle and a Memoir', *New York Times*, 1 May 1964

Henderson, Mary C., *Mielziner: Master of Modern Stage Design* (Back Stage Books, 2001)

Hoffman, Peter (as told to Anita Shreve and Fred Waitzkin), 'The Last Days of Tennessee Williams', *New York Magazine*, 25 July 1983

Hotchner, A.E., *Papa Hemingway: A Personal Memoir* (Weidenfeld & Nicolson, 1955)

—— 'Don't Touch A Moveable Feast', *New York Times*, 19 July 2009

Hyde, L., *Alcohol and poetry: John Berryman and the booze talking* (Dallas Institute, 1986)

Jackson, Esther Merle, *The Broken World of Tennessee Williams* (University of Wisconsin Press, 1965)

Jeste, Neelum D., Palmer, Barton W., and Jeste, Dilip V., 'Historical Case Conference: Tennessee Williams', *American Journal of Geriatric Psychiatry*, Vol. 12, pp. 370–75, 2004

Jia F., Pignataro, L., Harrison, N.L., 'GABAA receptors in the thalamus: alpha4 subunit expression and alcohol sensitivity', *Alcohol*, Vol. 41, No. 3, pp. 177–85, May 2007

Kakutani, Michiko, 'Williams, Quintero and the Aftermath of a Failure', *New York Times*, 22 June 1980

Kazin, Alfred, 'The Giant Killer: drink and the American writer', *Commentary*, Vol. 61, pp. 44–50, March 1976

—— 'Hemingway as His Own Fable', *Atlantic*, Vol. 213, No. 6, pp. 54–7, June 1954

Kerr, Walter, 'Clothes for a Summer Hotel', *New York Times*, 27 March 1980

Kert, Bernice, *The Hemingway Women* (W.W. Norton, 1983)

Kronenberg, Louis, ed., *Brief Lives: A Biographical Guide to the Arts* (Allen Lane, 1972)

Kuehl, John, and Bryer, Jackson R., eds., *Dear Scott/Dear Max: The Fitzgerald–Perkins Correspondence* (Cassell, 1971)

Lania, Leo, *Hemingway: A Pictorial Biography* (Thames & Hudson, 1961)

Leavitt, Richard F., *The World of Tennessee Williams* (W.H. Allen, 1978)

Leonard, Elmore, 'Quitting', in *The Courage to Change*, ed. Dennis Wholey (Houghton Mifflin, 1986)

LeSueur, Joe, *Digression on Some Poems by Frank O'Hara* (Farrar, Straus & Giroux, 2003)

Leverich, Lyle, *Tom: The Unknown Tennessee Williams* (Crown, 1995)

Levine, Philip, 'Mine Own John Berryman', in Richard J. Kelly and Alan K. Lathrop, eds., *Recovering Berryman: Essays on a Poet* (University of Michigan Press, 1993)

Lilienfeld, Jane, *Reading Alcoholisms: Theorizing Character and Narrative in Selected Novels of Thomas Hardy, James Joyce, and Virginia Woolf* (Macmillan, 1999)

—— and Jeffrey Oxford, eds., *The Language of Addiction* (Macmillan, 1999)

London, Jack, *John Barleycorn* (Mills & Boon, 1914)

Lowell, Robert, *Life Studies* (Faber, 1959)

—— 'For John Berryman', *New York Review of Books*, 6 April 1972

—— 'The Poetry of John Berryman', *New York Review of Books*, 28 May 1964

Ludwig, Arnold M., *Understanding the Alcoholic's Mind* (Oxford University Press, 1988)

Lukas, J. Anthony, 'One Too Many for the Muse', *New York Times Book Review*, 1 December 1985

Lynn, Kenneth J., *Hemingway* (Simon & Schuster, 1987)

Kopelman, Michael D., Thomson, Allan D., Guerriniand, Irene, and Marshall, Jane, 'The Korsakoff Syndrome: Clinical Aspects, Psychology and Treatment', *Alcohol & Alcoholism*, Vol. 44, No. 2, pp. 148–54, 2009

Malcolm, Janet, *Psychoanalysis: The Impossible Profession* (Vintage, 1982)

—— *Reading Chekhov: A Critical Journey* (Granta, 2003)

Mariani, Paul, *Dream Song: The Life of John Berryman* (University of Massachusetts Press, 1996)

Martz, William J., *University of Minnesota Pamphlets on American Writers No. 85: John Berryman* (University of Minnesota Press, 1969)

Max, D.T., 'The Carver Chronicles', *New York Times*, 9 August 1998

Mazzocco, Robert, 'Harlequin in Hell', *New York Review of Books*, 29 July 1967

Mellow, James R., *Invented Lives: F. Scott and Zelda Fitzgerald* (Souvenir Press, 1985)

Meyers, Jeffrey, *Disease and the Novel: 1880–1960* (St Martins Press, 1985)

—— *Scott Fitzgerald: A Biography* (Macmillan, 1994)

—— *Hemingway: The Critical Heritage* (Routledge & Kegan Paul, 1982)

Milford, Nancy, *Zelda* (Harper & Row, 1970)

Mizener, Arthur, *The Far Side of Paradise* (Houghton Mifflin, 1951)

—— *Scott Fitzgerald* (Thames & Hudson, 1999 [1972])

Mollon, Phil, *Shame and Jealousy: The Hidden Turmoils* (Karnac, 2002)

Moore, David P., and Jefferson, James W., eds., *Handbook of Medical Psychiatry* (Elsevier, 2004)

Morse, Robert M., and Flavin, Daniel K., 'The Definition of Alcoholism', *Journal of the American Medical Association*, Vol. 268, No. 8, August 1992

Moss, Howard, 'Good Poems, Sad Lives', *New York Review of Books*, 15 July 1982

Nabokov, Vladimir, *Lectures on Russian Literature* (Weidenfeld, 1982)

National Institute on Alcohol Abuse and Alcoholism, 'Alcohol and Sleep', *Alcohol Alert*, No. 41, 1998

—— 'The Genetics of Alcoholism', *Alcohol Alert,* No. 60, July 2003

—— 'Neuroscience: Pathways to Alcohol Dependence', *Alcohol Alert,* No.77, April 2009

Oates, Joyce Carol, 'Adventures in Abandonment', *New York Times Book Review*, 28 August 1988

O'Hara, Frank, *The Collected Poems of Frank O'Hara*, ed. Donald Allen (University of California Press, 1995)

—— *Early Writings* (Grey Fox Press, 1977)

—— *Lunch Poems* (City Lights Books, 1964)

—— *Standing Still and Walking in New York* (Grey Fox Press, 1975)

Plimpton, George, *Shadow Box: An Amateur in the Ring* (Andre Deutsch, 1978)

Robert S. Porter, ed., *The Merck Manual of Diagnosis and Therapy* (Merck Research Laboratories, 2006)

Prizogy, Ruth, *Illustrated Lives: F. Scott Fitzgerald* (Penguin, 2001)

Purdon, James, 'Skin and Bones: Dissecting John Berryman's *Dream Songs*' (unpublished essay)

Rasky, Harry, *Tennessee Williams: A Portrait in Laughter and Lamentation* (Dodd, Mead & Company, 1986)

Reynolds, Michael, *The Young Hemingway* (Blackwell, 1987)

—— *Hemingway: The Paris Years* (Blackwell, 1989)

—— *Hemingway: The American Homecoming* (Blackwell, 1992)

—— *Hemingway: The Thirties* (W.W. Norton, 1997)

—— *Hemingway: The Final Years* (W.W. Norton, 1999)

Rich, Adrienne, 'Mr. Bones, He Lives', *The Nation*, Vol. 198, Issue 22, 25 May 1964

Roberts, Amanda J., and Koob, George F., 'The Neurobiology of Alcohol', *Alcohol Health and Research World*, Vol. 21, No. 2, pp. 101–6, 1997

Roudane, Matthew C., ed., *The Cambridge Companion to Tennessee Williams* (Cambridge University Press, 1997)

Schiff, Jonathan, *Ashes to Ashes: Mourning and Social Difference in F. Scott Fitzgerald's Fiction* (Susquehanna University Press, 2001)

Simpson, Eileen, *Poets in their Youth* (Faber, 1982)

Sklenicka, Carol, *Raymond Carver: A Writer's Life* (Scribner, 2009)

Smith, Paul, 'The Bloody Typewriter and the Burning Snakes', *Hemingway: Essays of Reassessment*, ed. Frank Scafella (Oxford University Press, 1991)

Spoto, Donald, *The Kindness of Strangers: The Life of Tennessee Williams* (The Bodley Head, 1985)

Stephen, David N., and Duka, Theodora, 'Cognitive and emotional consequences of binge drinking: role of amygdala and pre-frontal cortex', *Philosophical Transactions of the Royal Society*, Vol. 363, No. 1507, October 2008

Stern, Milton R., *The Golden Moment: The Novels of F. Scott Fitzgerald* (University of Illinois Press, 1971)

Stull, William L., 'Raymond Carver', in *Dictionary of Literary Biography, Volume 130* (Gale, 1993)

Tavernier-Courbin, Jacqueline, 'The Mystery of the Ritz-Hotel Papers', *College Literature*, Vol. 7, No. 3, pp. 289–303, Fall 1980

Taylor, Kendall, *Sometimes Madness is Wisdom: Zelda and Scott Fitzgerald, A Marriage* (Robson Books, 2002)

Thistlewaite, Harriet, 'The Replacement Child as Writer', *Sibling Relationships*, ed. Prophecy Coles (Karnac Books, 2006)

Turnbull, Andrew, *Scott Fitzgerald* (The Bodley Head, 1963)

—— 'Perkins's Three Generals', *New York Times*, 16 July 1967

Walcott, Derek, 'On Robert Lowell', *New York Review of Books*, 1 March 1984

Waugh, Evelyn, *Brideshead Revisited* (Penguin, 1964 [1945])

Weatherill, Rob, ed., *The Death Drive: New Life for a Dead Subject* (Karnac Books, 1999)

White, Aaron M., 'What Happened? Alcohol, Memory Blackouts and the Brain', *Alcoholic Research and Health*, Vol. 27, No. 2, 2003

Williams, Edwina Dakin, *Remember Me to Tom* (Cassell, 1964)

Williams, Tennessee, *Cat on a Hot Tin Roof and Other Plays* (Penguin, 1976)

—— *Collected Stories* (Secker & Warburg, 1986)

—— *Clothes for a Summer Hotel: A Ghost Play* (New Directions, 1983)

—— *Five O'Clock Angel: Letters of Tennessee Williams to Maria St Just* (Andre Deutsch, 1991)

—— *Memoirs* (Penguin, 2007)

—— *Notebooks*, ed. Margaret Bradham Thornton (Yale University Press, 2006)

—— *Plays 1957–1980* (The Library of America, 2000)

—— *The Selected Letters of Tennessee Williams, Volume 1, 1920–1945* (New Directions, 2000)

—— *The Selected Letters of Tennessee Williams, Volume 2, 1945–1957* (New Directions, 2004)

—— *A Streetcar Named Desire and Other Plays* (Penguin, 1962)

—— *Where I Live: Selected Essays*, ed. Christine R. Day and Bob Wood (New Directions, 1978)

Wilson, Andrew, *Beautiful Shadow: A Life of Patricia Highsmith* (Bloomsbury, 2004)

Windham, Donald, *Tennessee Williams: Letters to Donald Windham* (Penguin, 1980)

Gaby Wood, 'Raymond Carver: The Kindest Cut', *Observer*, 27 September 2009

Wood, Michael, 'No Success Like Failure', *New York Review of Books*, 7 May 1987

World Health Organisation, *Lexicon of drug and alcohol terms* (WHO, 1994)

—— *Neuroscience of psychoactive substance use and dependence* (WHO, 2004)

Young, Thomas Daniel, ed., *Conversations with Malcolm Cowley* (University Press of Mississippi, 1986)

ACKNOWLEDGMENTS

MY THANKS GO FIRST TO those who made this book possible. Nick Davies at Canongate, who understood what I intended in a paragraph, and who has been a meticulous, inspired editor and ally. Jessica Woollard and the staff at the Marsh Agency, for their stalwart work and support. This project was supported using public funding by the National Lottery through Arts Council England and by the Authors' Foundation, who together funded the original trip to Echo Spring. The MacDowell Colony, for the best place to work imaginable. Mr. and Mrs. David F. Puttnam and Rose and Sigmund Strochlitz, for travel grants. The wonderful Claire Conrad and PJ Mark, and all at Janklow & Nesbit.

I've spent much of the past two years in libraries. I'd like to thank Anne Garner and the staff at the Berg Collection of New York Public Library, who performed feats of research magic and gave me a beautiful place to work in the city. I'm also very grateful to Melissa Waterworth-Batt and all at the Thomas J. Dodd Research Center at the University of Connecticut. Thanks too to Stephen Plotkin at the John F. Kennedy Presidential Library, the staff at Butler Library at the University of Columbia, Fales Library at NYU, Sussex University Library, Brighton Library and the British Library. Andi Gustavson at the Harry Ransom Center also helped with electronic enquiries.

For interviews and logistical assistance, I'm grateful to the following: Dr. Petros Levounis, Director at the Addiction Institute. Kathy Kalaijin, SENY Public Information Chair at Alcoholics Anonymous. Professor Dai Stephens at the University of Sussex, who not only increased my understanding of the neurobiology of alcoholism but also went well beyond the call of duty in reading and commenting on an early draft. Blake Bailey, who alerted me to the whereabouts of Cheever's Bloody Papers. Ellen Johnson at the Tennessee Williams Literary Festival. Ellen Borakove at the Office of the Chief Medical Examiner in New York City.

My trio of angels at Canongate: Norah Perkins, managing editor; Annie Lee, copy editor; and Anna Frame, publicist par excellence. Thanks too to the new guard: Jenny Lord, Vicki Rutherford and Jaz Lacey-Campbell.

Particular thanks are due to three early readers: Helen Macdonald, without whose wise counsel and exceptional support this book wouldn't exist; James Purdon, a magnificent sounding board and editor, who introduced me to John Berryman besides; and Elizabeth Day, dear and brilliant in all ways. I'm also very grateful to my father (a demonically talented copy editor) for looking the manuscript over pre-publication.

Then there are the friends and colleagues who've discussed, encouraged, aided and housed me. In the UK: Jean Edelstein (who wangled my room at the Elysée), Lili Stevens, Clare Davies, Robert Macfarlane, Tony Gammidge, Anna Fewster, Jordan Savage, Sarah Wood, John Gallagher, Kristen Treen, Stuart Croll, Robin McKie, Bob Dickinson and Tom de Grunwald. In the USA: John Pittman (who provided me with a bed, hunted down all kinds of Hemingway ephemera, let me shoot his guns between writing sessions, and told me what *punk* means to a woodsman), Liz Tinsley (bestower of library cards), Dan Levenson and his airbed, Matt Wolf, David Adjmi, Liz Adams, Alex Halberstadt, Joseph Keckler, Francesca Segal (whose spreadsheet kept me sane), Alastair Reid and Michael Reid Hunter. I'm also grateful to my editors: Jonathan Derbyshire at the *New Statesman* and William Skidelsky at the *Observer*. Errors and infelicities are of course my own.

Finally, my deepest thanks and gratitude go to my family: Peter Laing, Kitty Laing and Denise Laing, whose story this is too.

PERMISSIONS ACKNOWLEDGMENTS

Every effort has been made to trace copyright holders and obtain their permission for the use of copyright material. The publisher apologises for any errors or omissions and would be grateful if notified of any corrections that should be incorporated in future reprints or editions of this book.

Grateful thanks to Kate Donahue and to The Henry W. and Albert Berg Collection of English and American Literature at the New York Public Library Astor, Lenox and Tilden Foundations for permission to use John Berryman's work.

'Dream Song 36', 'Dream Song 96', 'Dream Song 143', 'Dream Song 235', 'Dream Song 310' and 'Dream Song 311' taken from *The Dream Songs* by John Berryman. Reprinted by permission of Faber & Faber.

'Eleven Addresses to the Lord,' 'The Facts & Issues,' 'Henry's Understanding,' and 'Homage to Mistress Bradstreet' from *Collected Poems: 1937-1971* by John Berryman. Copyright © 1989 by Kate Donahue Berryman. Reprinted by permission of Farrar, Straus and Giroux, LLC.

'Where Water Comes Together With Other Water', 'Alcohol' and 'Wenas Ridge' taken from *All of Us: The Collected Poems* by Raymond Carver, published by Harvill Press. Reprinted by kind permission of The Random House Group Ltd/The Wylie Agency, LLC.

'Nobody Said Anything' taken from *Will You Please Be Quiet, Please?* by Raymond Carver, published by Vintage. Reprinted by kind permission of The Random House Group Ltd/The Wylie Agency, LLC.

Raymond Carver, 'The Art of Fiction No. 76' originally printed in the *Paris Review*. Copyright © 1983, used by permission of The Wylie Agency, LLC.

'Fires' by Raymond Carver. Copyright © 1983, 1984, used by permission of The Wylie Agency, LLC.

Grateful thanks to The Wylie Agency and The Henry W. and Albert Berg Collection of English and American Literature at the New York Public Library Astor, Lenox and Tilden Foundations for permission to use John Cheever's unpublished work.

'Preface', 'The Swimmer', 'The Country Husband' and 'The Day the Pig Fell Into the Well' taken from *The Stories of John Cheever*, published by Cape. Reprinted by kind permission of The Random House Group Ltd./The Wylie Agency, LLC

All previously unpublished material by Ernest Hemingway reprinted by kind permission of The Ernest Hemingway Foundation and Society.

Extracts from *Ernest Hemingway: Selected Letters 1917-1961* Reprinted with the permission of Scribner, a Division of Simon & Schuster, Inc. from *Ernest Hemingway: Selected Letters 1917-1961* by Ernest Hemingway, by Carlos Baker, editor. Copyright © 1981 by Carlos Baker and The Ernest Hemingway Foundation, Inc. All rights reserved.

Extracts from 'The Doctor and the Doctor's Wife' by Ernest Hemingway. Reprinted with the permission of Scribner, a Division of Simon and Schuster, Inc. from *The Short Stories of Ernest Hemingway* by Ernest Hemingway. Copyright © 1925 Charles Scribner's Sons; Copyright © 1953 by Ernest Hemingway. All rights reserved.

'The Doctor and the Doctor's Wife' taken from *The Essential Hemingway* by Ernest Hemingway, published by Vintage Books. Reprinted by permission of The Random House Group Ltd.

Extracts from 'Now I Lay Me' by Ernest Hemingway. Reprinted with the permission of Scribner, a Division of Simon and Schuster, Inc. from *The Short Stories of Ernest Hemingway* by Ernest Hemingway. Copyright © 1927 Charles Scribner's Sons; Copyright © 1955 by Ernest Hemingway. All rights reserved.

'Now I Lay Me' taken from *Men Without Women* by Ernest Hemingway, published by Jonathan Cape. Reprinted by permission of The Random House Group Ltd.

Extracts from 'Fathers and Sons' by Ernest Hemingway. Reprinted with the permission of Scribner, a Division of Simon and Schuster, Inc. from *The Short Stories of Ernest Hemingway* by Ernest Hemingway. Copyright © 1933 Charles Scribner's Sons; Copyright © 1961 by Mary Hemingway. All rights reserved.

'Fathers and Sons' taken from *Winner Take Nothing* by Ernest Hemingway, published by Jonathan Cape. Reprinted by permission of The Random House Group Ltd.

Extracts from 'Snows of Kilimanjaro' Reprinted with the permission of Scribner, a

LIST OF ILLUSTRATIONS

CHAPTER 1
John Cheever riding a bicycle. Copyright © Nancy Crampton.

CHAPTER 2
Tennessee Williams as a young man. Courtesy of the Harry Ransom Humanities Research Center, the University of Texas at Austin.

CHAPTER 3
Scott and Zelda Fitzgerald at La Paix, surrounded by their furniture, the morning after the fire, June 1933. Courtesy of the Arthur Mizener Papers on F. Scott Fitzgerald at Princeton University, New Jersey.

CHAPTER 4
Hotel Monteleone, New Orleans. Copyright © Olivia Laing.

CHAPTER 5
Clarence and Ernest Hemingway in Key West, Florida, 10 April 1928. Copyright © Unknown. Courtesy of the Ernest Hemingway Collection, John F. Kennedy Presidential Library.

CHAPTER 6
Tennesse Williams. Copyright © W. Eugene Smith Magnum Photos.

CHAPTER 7
John Berryman. Courtesy of the University of Minnesota Archives.

CHAPTER 8
Raymond Carver as a boy (James Carver and the William Charvat Collection of American Fiction, Rare Books and Manuscripts Library at the Ohio State University Libraries)